£18.95

SHEFFIELD HALLAM
UNIVERSITY LIBRARY
PSALTER LANE
SHEFFIELD S11 8UZ

101 589 782 7

D0537204

FOUR HUNDRED YEARS OF FASHION

SHEFFIELD HALLAM UNIVERSITY
LEARNING CENTRE
WITHDRAWN FROM STOCK

FOUR HUNDRED YEARS OF
FASHION

Editor: Natalie Rothstein

Text by
Madeleine Ginsburg
Avril Hart
Valerie D. Mendes
and with other members
of the Department of Textiles & Dress

Photography by Philip Barnard

Victoria & Albert Museum

Published by the Victoria & Albert Museum,
reprinted 1992, 1995, 1996

British Library Cataloguing in Publication Data

Four hundred years of fashion.
1. Costume – England – History
391'.00942 GT733
First published in 1984
© Crown Copyright 1984

ISBN 185177 116 6

Set in Monophoto Plantin by
Ace Filmsetting Ltd, Frome, Somerset
Made and printed in Italy by
Grafiche Milani

Cover photography by Daniel McGrath

Front Cover:
Dress Coat and Waistcoat, probably Italian, 1760s. Sprigged red silk velvet, probably French, 1760s. Embroidered in silver gilt thread, purl and sequins.
T.28 & A-1952

Back Cover:
Evening Dress. Vivienne Westwood, 1990. Cotton voile.
T.187-1991

Frontispiece:
Afternoon dress and jacket, printed crepe de Chine by Mainbocher, Paris about 1935.
The pliant fabric is cut on the cross so that it softly moulds to the body and the garments are trimmed with rows of minute petals in matching crepe.
T.239&A-1984

CONTENTS

Press photograph of preparations for the
first temporary display in Gallery 40
- *The Little Black Dress*. June 1983.
Courtesy of the *Evening Standard*

INTRODUCTION

The V&A's Dress Collection was redisplayed in 1984 and immediately became one of the most popular galleries in the Museum. The display has retained its attraction for the enormous and ever-growing audience for dress though it now requires a rethink which must take into account current museological developments. The appeal of the display is broad based and it supplies scholarly information as well as enjoyment to a wide range of visitors including families, school parties, students, academics and a wide spectrum of professional designers. Although dress studies have long been an accepted part of Art History and, more recently, Cultural Studies, dress collections and displays have too often been regarded as mere entertainment for a largely female audience. Since the 1980s, however, there has been a major international reappraisal of the place of dress in museums. In various ways, especially exhibitions, long established, together with recently formed collections, have raised the standing of the art. The V&A has played an important role in the emergence of this awareness.

The fact that everyone wears clothes ensures the universal appeal of the subject. Visitors are at ease with the exhibits, quickly relating them to their own bodies and they are uninhibited about expressing opinions about clothes of the past as well as recent times. This instant familiarity generates curiosity and often precludes the need for a specialist interpreter. Questions are usually practical - "What has she or he got on underneath that?" and "When would you wear it and how could you sit down in it?" Extended labels in the display aim to answer most of these queries.

The new display of 1984 with its revised approach to presentation, provoked many reactions. Some critics detested the ghostly appearance of the mannequins, others preferred headless display figures, while some wanted the clothes placed in pseudo-period interiors. Such criticism is healthy and will be considered when the display is redone. Low light levels are essential to avoid the irreversible fading and destruction of vulnerable fabrics, though this sometimes upsets visitors. Another endemic curatorial problem is labelling. Whatever position and size of printed labels they never satisfy everyone and perhaps in the future they will be replaced by modern audio technology. A static display is an inevitability and the frequently expressed desire to see original historical dress in movement cannot be satisfied. The well-being of the collection is paramount and it is policy that once clothes enter the V&A, they are never worn again. Dressing modern beings in clothes of even the recent past would strain and soil the garments and drastically shorten their already precarious existence. Although they have their obvious drawbacks, replicas offer the safest way to experience the nature of period dress and film gives an accurate record of modern dress in motion. Exhibiting almost two hundred ensembles prompted much new information which led to redating objects and the assigning of designer names to previously anonymous works. The revelation of the collection's range after a long closure prompted welcome gifts of fashionable clothes and accessories.

Since 1984, the collection has expanded considerably and while many significant historical objects have been acquired, dress dating from the Twenties to the present is the fastest growing area. Historical dress has not survived in enormous quantities. Clothes, other than those for special occasions, tended to get worn out and were thrown away or were remodelled by thrifty owners. But, in keeping with the Museum's collecting policy, Textiles and Dress has been active in the acquisition of important historical objects to ensure the maintenance of a high quality reference collection upon which the public displays draw. Some notable 18th century garments have been acquired but the main area of acquisition has been in women's day and evening wear of the 19th century. Men have always been less profligate with their wardrobes than women and require their clothes to be extremely long lasting. Women's clothes with their excesses of style and colour have always been instantly attractive but from the early 19th century the immediate decorative appeal of men's dress was replaced by subtleties of cut and detail. Now, as in the past, men often wear their clothes until they are threadbare when they are thrown away and thus the survival rate of men's dress is not high. Nevertheless the Museum has acquired some outstanding menswear. A fine three piece suit of the 1750s was purchased in 1985 to show the type of high quality, plain wool suit an English gentleman would select for day wear. In 1991, a French, 1790s dress coat, once worn by an elegant young man, joined the collection. Its excellent condition, fashionable cut and luxurious fabric - a flecked grey wool impressed with vertical stripes - make it an object of scholarly worth.

The 1980s witnessed a spate of international exhibitions and publications concerning 18th century dress with an inevitable effect on collecting. However, generous donors ensured that the V&A's collection remained buoyant. In 1985 a rare 1730s mantua (a trained woman's robe) was generously given to the Museum by Mrs Gladys Windsor Fry. Miss Crawley's kind gift of an unpicked 1750s court dress in white silk with silver patterning will teach us much about the construction of such imposing attire. In 1990 a superb figured yellow silk sack back robe and petticoat of the 1750s was purchased. It is remarkable in that it is completely unaltered and the bright yellow silk is fresh and unfaded. Other rare 18th century survivals are two elegant riding jackets dating from the 1760s and 1770s. As is often the case, their matching skirts have not endured. Because they contained many yards of fabric they were probably remade into later styles.

Three piece suit of burgundy woollen bouclé and navy woollen jersey by Chanel, 1960s. Given by Sir Anthony Nutting in memory of his wife 'Annie', the top fashion model Anne Gunning.
T.123-B.1990

One of the most remarkable and important objects, acquired in 1991, is a humble undergarment - a hoop petticoat of 1740-50. In an unpretentious striped linen the exceptionally wide petticoat has its original cane hoops but had obviously lain without a covering in an attic and was so grimy and frail that it resembled an archeological find. However, the undergarment has been cleaned and repaired and now resembles its original state. Accurate replicas of the hoop will be made to go under robes and mantuas on display in the Dress Collection to give them the authentic shape of the period.

A group of garments dating from the 1850s and 1860s improved the 19th century women's dress collection and includes a two piece, black and white cotton pique, an 1860s day dress of the type favoured for playing croquet, and a smart brown linen duster coat of the 1870s. The Hon. Mrs Tyser gave an important gift of 1880s fashionable attire in memory of her mother the Dowager Lady Remnant. The clothes were once worn by Lady Remnant's ancestress, May Primrose who died tragically in a riding accident in 1885, just a year after her marriage to Major Littledale. The collection includes her wedding dress and a magnificent silk and lace ball

gown. The latter has been filmed during its conservation as part of a BBC series (Autumn 1992) investigating the world of clothing and textiles.

From the sale of the wardrobe of Mary Goelet, the daughter of a New York banker who married the 8th Duke of Roxburghe in 1903, the Museum acquired a magnificent 1890s *sortie de bal* by Worth and an elaborate tea gown of the same date by Rouff. In toffee pink silk with ornate trimming in matching silk chiffon the *sortie de bal* is in such pristine state that it may have never been worn.

In the eight years since this book was first published the collecting policy for later 20th century dress has broadened in recognition of the pluralistic nature of fashion during this period. This shift in approach recognises 'streetstyle' together with sport and leisure wear as leading forces, especially in British fashion. The emphasis is still upon design that leads and the majority of acquisitions are high quality designer label garments from the world's great fashion centres. However, the collection now embraces influential high street styles such as a studded leather jacket (identical to one worn by Madonna) bought in the Kings Road in 1991. A pair of chunky soled Doc Marten lace up shoes represent a continuing trend among the young while Red or Dead's watch shoes are footwear with an amusing twist. The V&A has acknowledged certain youthful fashion constants by accepting into the collection a pair of Levi 501 denim jeans and pairs of the ubiquitous trainers by Reebok and by Nike

The majority of new acquisitions have been by generous donation. Among the most exciting of these is a collection of Chanel clothing worn by the top fashion model, Anne Gunning and given in her memory by her husband, Sir Anthony Nutting. A more recent and extensive donation was a bequest from Rupert Michael Nolan, who was a passionate fan of the London designer Vivienne Westwood. Some seventy garments represent a cross section of this influential designer's work from the early 1980s to 1991. Dolan was young, fashion conscious and adventurous in his dress. The collection ranges from an Edwardian style Norfolk suit, a blue synthetic lace shirt, a football parody leotard, sweatshirts with screen prints by the American pop artist Keith Haring to more conventional suits, shirts and jackets. This donation is a curator's dream being well documented by receipts and press cuttings.

In recent years the collection of fashion accessories has multiplied in a controlled manner. Mr Beck, a retired button manufacturer, has given fascinating buttons and has shared his unique and first hand knowledge of the industry unstintingly. The hat collection has grown considerably in the 1980s and 90s with acquisitions ranging from a toque by the gifted feltmaker Annie Sherburne to an eyecatching black and white wedge shaped straw hat by the milliner David Shilling. Fine examples of handbags, gloves, stockings, belts, fans, shawls, shoes, umbrellas, watches and contemporary personalia such as a Mont Blanc pen, a Filofax diary and a Sony Walkman have joined the collection.

A small purchase vote is reserved for garments of outstanding interest which are not already represented in the collection or which will complement existing pieces. The escalation of interest in dress has been reflected in the development of specialist markets and competition for top rate objects is fierce. Given our modest resources, the V&A is sometimes

'Carnival' Long dress and bolero, printed cotton seersucker by Sally Tuffin for Foale and Tuffin, London 1972. This ensemble reveals the designer's skill in mixing vibrant coloured printed fabrics.
T.228&A-1984

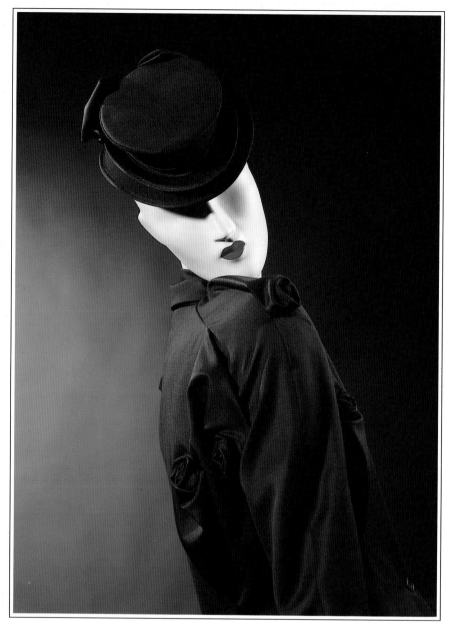

Dress, jacket, hat and T-shirt
woollen gaberdine by John Galliano,
Autumn/Winter 1987. The jacket is
decorated with rosettes which are not
separate attachments but are integral parts
of the skilfully cut jacket.
Given by John Galliano
T.21-B-1988

Opposite:
Printed wool 'Beasts of England'
dress by English Eccentrics, 1988.
English Eccentrics became famous for
their individual and highly creative
printed fabrics.
T.304-1988

unable to compete in this forum. Occasionally, however, we are fortunate
and significant buys include a sweeping figured silk cloak made in Paris in
about 1910, a collection of Yves Saint Laurent, *Rive Gauche* ready to wear
from the 1970s and a rose pink, silk velvet robe by Gallenga of about
1912.

The museum's dedication to dress is reflected in its active programme
of temporary fashion exhibitions. These fall into two categories - large
scale exhibitions which are presented in the V&A's major temporary
exhibition galleries and smaller scale displays which are mounted within
the temporary display cases in Gallery 40, the Dress collection. Ideas for
exhibitions and displays come from inside and outside the Museum and
curators are receptive to all proposals.

Recently we have been accused of commercial endorsement. In fact
the Museum operates a rigorous vetting process and the the criteria for
acceptance are strict. Above all, with contemporary commercial

production, it is a prerequisite that V&A exhibitions encompass stylish objects that represent the cutting edge of fashion. Of course it would be safer to avoid the contemporary and possibly controversial but this would be to ignore the challenge of the new and the museum would be shirking its responsibilities to current design.

A list of fashion displays and exhibitions held in the V&A since 1984 illustrate the diversity of areas covered - they range from the thematic to the work of individual designers. Displays included *The Little Black Dress, Certain Shawls 1839-49, Louis Vuitton: Travelling with Style, Knit one Purl One, Gianni Versace, Fashion Tracks: Designer Clothes for the Pirelli Calendar, The Collection Grows: New Acquisitions, The Burberry Story, Top British Designers for the Sock Shop, Plastics in Fashion, The Work of Caroline Charles* and *Four Italian Couturiers*. Most recently, four ensembles were shown to commemorate Vivienne Westwood's winning of the coveted British Designer of the Year award for the second year running (1991 and 1992). This ran concurrently with a display of dramatic and sculptural special occasion evening and day wear by Anouska Hempel. Not all displays focus upon high fashion by established designers. In 1991, the annual *Lloyds Bank Fashion Challenge*, which is open to young people, required entrants to design for a celebrity of their choice two outfits - one to wear at an interview with their bank manager and another to wear at a gala evening event. Winning entries were made up and after being filmed for BBC 1's *The Clothes Show* went on show in the Dress Collection.

In Spring 1992, a temporary display opened to celebrate the extraordinary versatility of the work of the London based fashion designer, Yuki. This was followed by a selection of garments designed by BAFTA award winner Joan Wadge and worn in the highly acclaimed BBC costume drama *The House of Eliott* The display explored the relationship between costumes conceived and made for television drama and their sources, including fashionable dress in the V&A.

Exhibitions in the V&A's main temporary exhibition galleries arranged by Textiles and Dress in the past eight years have included *John French Fashion Photographer, Designer Denim for Blitz, Ascher: Fabric, Art, Fashion, Salvatore Ferragamo: The Art of the Shoe, Fashion and Surrealism, Australian Fashion - The Contemporary Art, Flowered Silks: A Noble Manufacture of the 18th Century* and *Pierre Cardin: Past, Present, Future*. All these exhibitions have been accompanied by catalogues. Dress and accessories have also featured in cross media V&A exhibitions such as *Collecting for the Future, The Art of Death* and they are part of the new permanent installation, *The Gallery of Ornament*.

In the past fifteen years or so dress and its history has attracted a wider audience partly through increased coverage in the media and partly through pre-occupation with personal style. Inevitably this movement has links with consumerism and the fashion year which attempts to impose biannual shifts in the latest look. The museum world has been part of the change and, in addition to an increasing number of exhibitions devoted to dress, has seen increased membership of professional groups such as the International Council of Museums Costume Committee. Most museums and galleries with dress collections acknowledge them as major assets and, like the V&A, give them due prominence alongside other arts. Significant thrusts are being

View of an applique evening cloak by Yuki and a sequinned evening dress by Caroline Charles, part of the temporary display Fashion Tracks: Designer Clothes for the 1985 Pirelli Calendar which opened in November 1986.
T.16-1986 Given by Lady Rothermere
T.488-1985 Given by Miss Diana Stevens

Platform sandal, gold kid and suede covered cork by Salvatore Ferragamo, Florence, Italy 1938. Probably created for use in the cinema or theatre this lavish sandal was part of the Salvatore Ferragamo donation which marked the retrospective exhibition held in the V&A in 1987.
Given by Mrs Wanda Ferragamo
T.84-1988

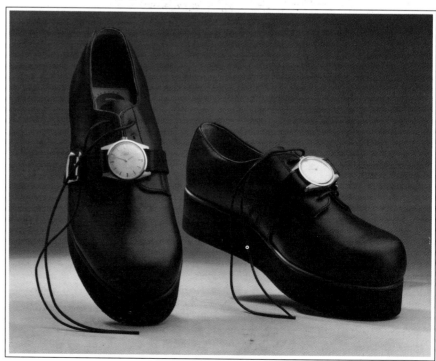

'Watch Shoes', leather with moulded rubber soles and wrist watch fastenings designed by Red or Dead, London Spring/Summer 1988. Wayne Hemingway's shop Red or Dead opened in 1987 specialising in this type of off-beat, amusing footwear.
Given by Red or Dead
T.115&A-1989

'Instructor Mid-Ers' aerobic shoes, by Reebok UK, 1991. Sportswear has exerted a great influence upon contemporary fashion and shoes like these are as likely to be worn in the high street as in the sports arena. These shoes are displayed in the Ornament Gallery.
T.92-1991

made to make vulnerable collections of dress accessible through computerised cataloguing and imaging. Internationally, great strides have been made by the Smithsonian Museum in Washington and the Musée de la Mode in Paris (with its exemplary fashion video-discs), while the V&A is currently investigating the potential of such new technology. In formal education from primary school to post-graduate level, there is a growing recognition of the validity of dress studies and new courses are emerging. With its active programme in the field of fashionable dress the V&A acknowledges and supports this development.

It is eight years since Four Hundred Years of Fashion was first published, and this introduction brings our activities up to date. That this standard guide to the V&A's Dress Collection has long been the Museum's best seller reflects the popularity and importance of dress within the decorative arts.

Valerie D. Mendes, Curator
Avril Hart, Assistant Curator (Dress pre-1900)
Amy de la Haye, (Dress post-1900)
Textiles and Dress Collection
1992

Women's Dress before 1900

MADELEINE GINSBURG

The Museum began to collect costume and textiles in 1844. Later the purpose was defined: 'artisans, designers and workers' in all textile fields might 'gather a lesson for their respective crafts' from its collections of work of a high artistic quality.[1] In 1864 the Museum received its first major gift of costume from the Rev. R. Brooke, and this was described in the Rev. Daniel Rock's catalogue, *Textile Fabrics in the South Kensington Museums*, 1870. Rock explained that the collection of textile fabrics aimed 'to take a peep at the private female life in ages gone by . . . (and to) learn how women high born and lowly, spent or rather ennobled many a day of life in needlework, not merely graceful but artistic.'

During the latter part of the century the retrospective classes of exhibits in the International Exhibitions helped to foster a wider popular interest in dress. The History of Dress section of the International Health Exhibition of 1884, with dummies designed by Madame Tussaud's, was one of the most popular. Madame Tussaud's also showed costume of the past and fashions of the present among their own exhibits; while, for those who preferred their historical costume new, there were always Messrs Liberty's gowns. By 1883 a Costume Society had been founded in London, although it does not appear to have lasted very long.

The Museum's dress collection was useful to artists and designers—for historical accuracy was a quality much in demand in the late nineteenth century. In 1899, Seymour Lucas, R.A., an artist of repute, a notable collector and a long-standing friend of the Museum, justified his attempt to obtain the Isham Collection of sixteenth and seventeenth-century dress for the nation by stating that: 'Historical painters have generally to go abroad for materials and information relating to costume.'[2] The Isham Collection, which is described more fully in the next essay and which is still the most important series of pre-1900 material in the Museum's dress collection, was the product of an antiquarian interest in costume for its own sake. Ralph Thoresby's collection of clothing, included in the curiosities which he listed in the *Ducatus Leodensis* of 1715, was small by comparison.

In the early seventeenth century women all over western Europe wore flowing, floor-length overgarments like this one from the Isham Collection. It is made in brocaded Italian silk, with a standing lace-edged collar which is held in position by a supportasse.

189-1900   [1]

Despite its early start, the dress collection at the Victoria and Albert Museum grew fairly slowly and sporadically; and unfortunately the past policy of the Civil Service to 'weed' files has led to the removal of much information on the background of these early acquisitions and the reasons for their acceptance. The one exception to this seems to have been wedding and trousseau dress, which tend to have kept their associations.[3] In 1913, the Museum was given the single largest collection of dress that it had received so far—the Harrods Gift. One hundred and fifty costumes and a large quantity of accessories had been purchased from the artist Talbot Hughes by Messrs Harrods, and then given to the Museum (see next essay). A catalogue of the Harrods Gift was published in 1913 and issued in a revised edition as the *Guide to the Collection of Costume* in 1924.

During the 1930s, Mr J. L. Nevinson, then Assistant Keeper in the Department of Textiles, began to publish his fine series of articles and catalogues on the sixteenth and seventeenth centuries.[4] This was the first serious attempt to rescue lost provenances, and though this work still continues the prospects of success diminish with the passage of time. Today, information about the origin of a costume is considered to be of paramount importance, but it is often difficult to trace original owners when items coming into the Museum have passed through several hands. A project of which Talbot Hughes would have approved is the publication of scale drawings of dresses in the collection. His contribution to the *Artistic Crafts Series of Technical Handbooks, Dress Design*, 1913, put the collection into context and included sketch patterns. More recently, museum objects have been published by Norah Waugh in *The Cut of Women's Clothes*, 1968, and by Janet Arnold in *Patterns of Fashion*, 1964 and 1966. Meticulously recorded information of this kind is the grammar of the study of dress.

Despite the differing aims of past curators, and the varied opportunities they have had, there is a logic of events which suggests that the survival of a particular object is more than mere accident. There are many collections of costume in Great Britain and most of them include the same kind of artifacts from much the same dates. (There is a useful list of collections in Janet Arnold's *A Handbook of Costume*, 1973.) What is obvious in any collection of dress is that the clothes will be those of the affluent and that, on the whole, they will be their 'best' clothes, made from expensive materials, too good to cut up and too distinctive to give away or to be sold second hand. There was always a thriving second-hand clothes market and a demand for linen and, in the nineteenth century, for wool for recycling. It was this as much as moths or other domestic pests which destroyed much of the clothing of the past.[5] Less obvious is the reason why there are disproportionate numbers of surviving garments from some periods rather than others. For example, many informal dresses from the 1740s survive, although most have been altered to suit later styles up to the 1760s. Similarly, there are many surviving formal dresses from between the 1770s and 1790s, others from around 1810, 1820, the late 1830s, the 1860s and the 1890s. The probable explanation lies in the fact that each of these dates marks the end of a period of typological development; alteration was either no longer possible or, where it could have been achieved, unacceptable

BODICE, silk with a cut (pinked) surface pattern
English, 1630–35
This was probably worn with a stomacher, matching skirt and deep, lace-trimmed collar. Dresses of the 1630s were characterized by their high waists and full, elbow-length sleeves.
172-1900

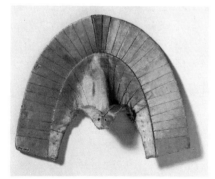

SUPPORTASSE, silk, satin mounted on paper
English, 1610–20
Back view. The supportasse was worn as a support for a ruff or band; it was attached by several ties at the back and at the throat. The fluted surround is a series of satin strips wrapped round card or parchment. The effect is continued into the centre with lines of stitching.
192-1900

because the material would have been wrong in design or weight for the new style.

The Museum has hardly any items of women's dress from before 1600. Almost nothing remains either in this collection or any other of the richness and variety which is satirized by Thomas Tomkiss in *Lingua, or The Conflict of Tongues*, 1607, when he complains that 'A ship is sooner rigged by far than a gentlewoman made ready', listing the 'cascanets, dressings, purls, falls, squares, busks, bodies, scarfs . . . carcanets, rebatoes, borders, tires, fans, palisadoes, puffs, ruffs, cuffs, muffs, pulses, fusles, partlets . . . fardingales, kirtles, busk-points, shoe ties' necessary for the operation.

Although a few items (mainly accessories) made from or trimmed with lace and embroidery have survived and were collected by the V & A because of its commitment to fine textiles, very few complete women's garments exist in any other country from this period. It is only from early seventeenth-century portraits that we can appreciate the appearance of the lady of the period, with her long pointed bodice, her skirt held out at the hips with a farthingale and her neck surrounded by a multiplicity of collars.

The earliest major women's garments in the Museum are three incomplete early seventeenth-century gowns from the Isham Collection. Portraits and European cutting books indicate that these flowing, floor-length over-garments were worn throughout western Europe. Fynes Moryson in his *Itinerary*, 1607–15, observed that Englishwomen wore 'gownes hanging loose at the backe with a kirtle and close upper body of silke or light stuffe'. It is tempting to consider that two of the gowns, which are unusual in having no hanging sleeves, have lost them because they were awaiting alteration: Fynes Moryson noted 'the ladies have lately left off the French sleeves borne out with whalebone'.[6] The most incomplete of the gowns (178&A-1900; not displayed) is also the best in basic condition and quality. It is made from red figured velvet and is lined with pinked matching silk.[7] The second, on the other hand, [1; see p. 12]* is very similar in cut but much less well made. It looks fresh and fashionable, but close examination reveals that the material had already been used for some other purpose, since some rather random pieces of silver and sequined braid appear on the inner seams. This gown is shown with a standing, lace-edged collar that is held in position by a replica of the supportasse, or collar support, shown here. The original supportasse, of silk-covered card, is also from the Isham Collection. When the replica was laced into position through the matching holes in the collar of the gown, it fitted exactly.

It was fortunate that the Isham family kept these gowns; they were in common use but they marked the end of an era. Versions of the loose over-gown had been in use almost constantly since the fifteenth century but after 1630 they were hardly ever worn. Similarly, the slashed decoration of [1; see p. 12] is a survival of another sixteenth-century fashion which was little used after the mid-1630s.[8]

* Figures in square brackets refer to the catalogue which describes all items on display in the Dress Collection, beginning on page 121.

EMBROIDERED BODICE, linen
embroidered with silver and silver-gilt
thread and silks in detached buttonhole, stem, chain, plaited braid,
knotted and speckling stitch, trimmed
with silver and silver-gilt bobbin lace
and spangles
English, about 1620
The bodice was worn by Margaret
Laton when she sat for the portrait
painted by Marcus Gheeraerts.
Lent anonymously

WOMAN'S JACKET, hand-knitted with
silk and silver-gilt thread, mainly in
stocking stitch. The neck and front
edges bound with silk; worked buttonholes and buttons of silver-gilt thread
*Possibly Italian, second quarter 17th
century*
Jackets of this type seem to have been
produced via the centre of the knitting
industry. Most are knitted as a series of
simple rectangles (sleeves, two front and
two back panels) and appear to have
been put together domestically.
473-1893

The Isham Collection also includes an embroidered linen jacket
(T.4-1935; not displayed), one of a number which have survived from
this period. They seem to have been peculiar to England and to have
been worn between about 1600 and the 1630s. Immensely attractive,
with their finely embroidered decoration, usually of flowers and birds
enclosed by scrolling stems, they must have been prized possessions in
their time. Many ladies were painted wearing them, including Margaret
Laton. Her jacket, shown here, close fitting and with long sleeves,
dates from a period when waists were comparatively long, perhaps
about 1620. In an accompanying portrait a high-waisted effect, such as
was fashionable about 1615, is achieved by wearing an apron above the
natural waist level. Nearly all the surviving jackets are made in the same
way: basically straight-cut but with gores at the hips to provide fullness,
they have curved fronts and under-arm seams.[9] The cut of the sleeves
differs: the later examples from the 1630s have wider sleeves and are
decorated with larger, more varied motifs. One very fine example in the
Museum's collection (T.324-1935; not displayed) is made from fine
white linen decorated with pulled and drawn-thread work, lace and
spangles.[10] It is possible that it resembles those fashionable in 1631,
when Dorothy Randolph, in reporting on London fashions to Lady
Jane Bacon, noted: 'They wear whit sattine wascots plane rased printed
and some embroidered with lase more than any one thing.'[11] Easy-
fitting and unstructured, these jackets were an attractive alternative to
the stiff, long bodices of the early seventeenth century and they continued to be worn when the fashionable bodice became shorter, in the
1630s.

Another type of jacket, which was not peculiar to England, is shown
here. It is knitted with pale blue silk and silver-gilt thread, mainly
in simple stocking stitch. The large, upright floral sprigs with which it
is decorated are reminiscent of silk designs of the 1630s. A number of
these jackets survive in museum collections throughout Europe and the
variety of designs with which they are patterned suggests that they had
a very long period of popularity. One of the last English references
appears in a London newspaper of 1712, where the theft was reported
of 'a green silk knit waistcoat with gold and silver flowers all over it'. In
nearly all cases, the surviving jackets are made up from simple rectangles, and any shaping at the neck or under the arms is achieved by
turning under pieces of the fabric. This suggests that they were mass-
produced in some common centre, perhaps being sold as kits to be made
up at home.[12] In the portraits of the ladies of the reign of Charles I by
Van Dyck and his contemporaries, the dress of the 1630s looks easy-
fitting; but a firm structure is concealed under the soft flow of the
gleaming satin so popular at the time. A series of Isham bodices illustrates the change of line from the 1630s to the 1660s [see pp. 17 and 18].
The first is made from pearl-white satin decorated with slashing, and has
a short, boned, canvas lining which laces in front. It has large, full
sleeves pleated into the armhole, which is set deeply into the narrow
back. Its basque, like those of the embroidered linen jackets, is gored
for extra fullness. Another bodice (171-1900; not shown), made from
black velvet, is fully boned and fastens at the front. It has the longer
waist and the straight sleeves with deep epaulettes which were fashion-

BODICE, silk trimmed with parchment lace
English, 1660s
The lining is heavily boned. Probably worn with matching skirt and a lace collar.
429-1889

Previous page :
This fine quality brocaded silk mantua of the 1720s is the earliest dress in the V & A collection. The train is stitched so that it lies face outwards only if it is folded sides to middle and turned up to hip-level.
T.88-1978   [2]

Opposite :
This mantua made from Spitalfields silk dates from the 1730s. It was a formal dress and the material is of very high quality.
T.9&A-1971   [4]

able in the 1640s and early 1650s. A formal bodice in greenish white satin, shown here, is typical of the early 1660s. This is boned like a corset and laces at the back. The waist is very long and the full sleeves are set in very low beneath the shoulder. A trimming of matching parchment lace enhances its sweeping, low line. The neckline is plain, for it would have been covered with a deep lace border. None of these bodices has a skirt. As far as is known, only one matching bodice and skirt set of the period exists: it is in the collection of the Museum of Costume at Bath. [13] The skirts would have been made from straight breadths, of material tightly gathered at the waist; they could easily be cut up, re-used and eventually destroyed.

There are no late-seventeenth-century dresses in the V & A's collection. Fortunately, Randle Holme's *The Academy of Armory and Blazon*, 1688, also contains the *Instruments used in all Trades and Sciences, together with their terms of Art.* Many of the terms used were not to change until the nineteenth century, so this extract from the section on *Terms used by Taylors* has a value far beyond its own period:

> In a WOMAN'S GOWN there are . . . the STAYES, which is the body of the Gown before the sleeves are put too, or covered with the outward stuff . . . the FORE PART or FORE BODY: which is the Breast part which hath two peeces in it; as . . . The TWO SIDE PARTS, which are peeces under both Arms on the sides . . . The SHOULDER HEADS, or SHOULDER STRAPS; are two peeces that come over the Sholders and are fastned to the Forebody; through which the Arms are put . . . CORDY ROBE SKIRTS . . . are such Stayes as are cut into Labells at the bottom, like long slender skirts . . . the STOMACHER is that peece as lieth under the lacing or binding on of the Body of the Gown . . . A BUSK, it is a strong peece of Wood or Whalebone thrust down the middle of the Stomacher to keep it streight . . . that the Breast nor Belly shall not swell too much out . . . the WINGS are WELTS or PEECES set over the place on the top of the Shoulders . . . OPEN SKIRTS, is open before, that thereby rich and costly Peti-coat may be fully seen. TURNED UP SKIRTS, are such as have a draught on the Ground a yard and more long; these in great Personages are called Trains . . . BEARERS, ROWLS, FARDINGALES . . . to put under the Skirts . . . at their setting, on at the Bodies; which raise up the skirt at that place . . . SKIRTS about the WAIST, are either whole in one entire peece with Goares, or else cut into little laps or cordy robe skirts; Gowns with these skirts are called Waistcoat Gowns.

In addition, he mentions two types of outfit which will have relevance in the next period to be described:

> A MANTUA, is a kind of loose Coat without any stays in it, the Body part and sleeves are of as many fashions as I have mentioned in the Gown Body. . . . THE RIDING SUIT for Women [which besides hood, cap, mantle and safeguard includes] The RIDING COAT, it is a long Coat buttoned down before like a Man's Jacket with Pocket-holes; and the Sleeves turned up, and buttons.

All these were the work of the tailor. The seamster dealt with what we would term lingerie—the light washable accessories and underwear.

Randle Holme was describing dress at a point of change. Dresses

with 'stiff bodies', that is boned bodices, were relegated in the last quarter of the seventeenth century to formal wear and then, in the eighteenth century, to Court use; they were to become obsolete and their cut was to fossilise. The future lay with the 'mantua', the loose gown. But, in the late seventeenth century, it was still informal and close to its origins, a T-shaped dressing gown-like garment, adapted from the gowns imported from the East.[14] Straight, voluminous and with minimal shaping, these were easily re-used and lost their identity. There are none in the Museum's collection.

But fortunately the Museum does own two very valuable documents of this fashion: two dolls of the mid-1690s, 'Lord and Lady Clapham' (T.846-Y and T.847-Y-1974), which were purchased by public subscription in 1974. 'Lady Clapham' is completely dressed, from the wire '*Monte la Haut*' which supports her cap frill, to her tiny high-fronted, high-heeled shoes. She wears a formal dress, open at the front over a decorative corset, with the bodice pleated and held inside at the back with a band of lining. The fronts of the skirt are held back with loops and buttons. Her petticoat matches her gown and is trimmed with a frill at the level of the hips. She also has an informal gown which is very close in shape to the T-shaped gowns of the East, a version of which is worn by 'Lord Clapham'. The only difference is that in 'Lady Clapham's' gown, the fullness at the shoulders is hitched towards the centre, forming pleats which are held by turning down the neckband. With this, she has a matching petticoat.

Here, in origin, are the ways in which the loose 'mantua' described by Randle Holme was to develop in the eighteenth century. One type of gown would have pleats held to the torso and, if it retained the train, would continue as the 'mantua', worn for formal occasions until the middle of the century. If it lacked the train, it would be the conventional English gown worn for most ordinary occasions. The other style, with pleats flowing loose from neck to hem, would become the 'sack', as it was known in England. In France it was the *robe ordinaire* and, according to M. Roland de La Platière in the *Encyclopédie Méthodique*, 1785, the *robe à la Française*.

The development of fashion between the 1680s and the early 1700s cannot easily be studied in portraits because so many ladies preferred to be painted in loose robes without accessories or trimmings. But, even though English fashions were never quite the same as those of France, the general development was similar, for French fashion was an important export. Fortunately, it is just at this period that the main series of French fashion plates began to be published.[15] These indicate a lengthening of the line; the waistline became longer and the sleeves, puffed in the early 1680s, became narrower and lengthened to the elbow from the mid-1680s onwards. The line was echoed in the hair, which was dressed increasingly high from the mid-1680s. In England the most evocative sources are literary. To be fashionable was to be more or less French; and in *The Ladies Dictionary* by John Dunton, 1683, and in *Mundus Muliebris or The Ladies Dressing-Room Unlock'd*, 1690,[16] there are many interpretations of the 'franglais' terms for types of garment and hairdressing. The line continued to lengthen until after 1700, and it was not until July 1711 that Addison and Steele's

The most magnificent dress in the collection, this mantua is made from ribbed silk and embroidered to shape with silver thread in a design showing a tree bearing fantastic fruit and flowers. Dating from the 1740s, when skirts were at their widest, it would have been worn at the Court of George II; but its original owner is unknown.
T.227&A-1970 [6]

Spectator, which commented on every aspect of fashionable life, noted a sudden and dramatic change:

The fair sex are run into great extravagancies. Their petticoats . . . are now blown up into a most enormous concave. . . . the Superfluity of Ornaments . . . seems only to have fallen from their Heads upon their lower parts. What they have lost in Height they have made up in Breadth and contrary to all Rules of Architecture widen

[6]

their foundations at the same time as they shorten the Super-structure.'

For the greater part of the eighteenth century, it was to be width, not height, that was all-important.

The dress which illustrates what happened to the mantua between the late seventeenth century and 1720 is at Shrewsbury.[17] It is T-shaped, has the sleeves set in well below the shoulders, and the train trails. The earliest complete dress in the Museum collection is a mantua of the 1720s [2; see p. 16] in a fine quality blue and silver brocaded silk. By this date there had already been considerable modifications in the cut. The gown is not T-shaped and the sleeves are set in at shoulder level. The train does not trail; instead it is stitched so that it lies face outwards only if it is folded sides to middle and has the end turned up. [4; see p. 19] is similar in cut, although from the design of the material it must date from the 1730s. There are many similar dresses in other museums which can be dated as late as the 1740s.

Mantuas, as formal dresses, were usually made in the finest silks or embroidered—an expensive but a sure way of obtaining an exclusive dress. The most magnificent dresses in the V & A collection are two embroidered mantuas of the 1740s, when skirts were at their widest. Such dresses were worn at the Courts of George I and George II. Considerable splendour was expected of and expenditure incurred by those attending such formal gatherings as the Royal birthdays and weddings.[18] Mary Granville, Mrs Delany, described several rich dresses.[19] As an amateur embroidress she had an eye for such things. In 1740, for example:

The Duchess of Bedford's petticoat was green paduasoy, embroidered very richly with gold and silver and a few colours; the patterns were festoons of shells, coral, corn, corn-flowers, and sea-weeds; everything in different works of gold and silver except the flowers and coral, the body of the gown white satin, with a mosaic pattern of gold facings, robings and train the same (as) the petticoat.

For sheer gleaming splendour the red and silver mantua [6; see p. 21] outshines any dress in this or indeed any other museum. Even the betrothal dress of the future Empress Catherine, now in the Hermitage Museum, Leningrad, also red embroidered with silver, is smaller and less densely worked. A comparable piece in a British collection is that in the National Museum of Wales, St Fagans, which to judge from the pattern of the silk was probably worn by Rachel, Lady Morgan, in about 1718–24.[20] Being earlier it is also smaller, lacking the magnificent spread of skirt.

According to A. W. Esq's *The Enormous Abomination of the Hoop Petticoat*, 1745, this form was introduced in 1743. It is very sad that the red and silver mantua has lost its eighteenth-century provenance, but a fortunate chance has preserved the name of the embroiderers of the dress. Written under the stitches on the underside of the train is 'Rec's of Mme Leconte by me Mag^d Giles', probably a receipt for work which has been subcontracted. Even though it has not so far been possible to identify which members of the Leconte and Gil(l)es families worked on the dress, it is certain that they were Hugenots, members of the French Protestant community who had emigrated to England in the early eighteenth century and who were responsible for so much fine craftsmanship at this time. Thomas Leconte was noted in the records of the Huguenot community as an embroiderer,[21] and was connected by kinship to Mme Garneron, who embroidered clothes for the royal family. Another embroideress with a royal appointment in 1746–7 was Elizabeth Johnson, formerly Leconte.[22] The quantity of silver in the dress, about ten pounds in weight, may have prompted the inscription. Legal records do carry instances of the theft of material by subcontractors.

The workmanship of the embroidery on the dress is very fine indeed, though the design, a Tree of Life pattern, looks back to the embroidered crewel work hangings of the earlier eighteenth century and does not reflect the decorative trends of the 1740s. There was a change of mind during the work, for some of the embroidery on the petticoat has been worked over coloured silks.

The white mantua [7] may have been worn at the wedding of Isabella Courtenay, fifth daughter of Sir William Courtenay, 2nd Baronet and *de jure* 5th Earl of Devon, in 1744. It is embroidered with silver and

[7]

A sack with a train was conventional formal wear in the 1750s. This one in yellow ribbed silk, dating from about 1760, is trimmed with flounces with pinked edges, fly braid, and matching silk tassels.
T.77 to B.1959   [10]

coloured silks in a rococo design. The pattern is effective but the workmanship less consistent: the embroidery at the top of the petticoat is much less good than that at the bottom. The organization of an embroiderer's workshop is described in *L'Art du Brodeur*, 1771, in the *Dictionnaire des Sciences* by M. de St Aubin. This description may suggest an explanation: the person who dealt with one half of the petticoat was less competent than the other. A very tentative alternative conjecture is that the bride or her sisters may have been involved. Professional embroiderers made most fashionable dresses and accessories but Mrs Delany, at least, embroidered accessories for herself and her friends. Samuel Richardson, describing his ideal of girlhood, Clarissa Harlow, in 1746, comments on the high quality of her needlework.[23]

Wide side-hoops continued to be worn for formal occasions until the 1780s. During the late 1740s and early 1750s, however, the mantua with a draped-up train seems to have gone out of fashion and to have been replaced by a dress which retained the draped and buttoned basques but which had only a vestigial train, a pleated flap from waist to hem [8]. This style is not uncommon and there are similar dresses in the V & A collection and other British museums. The only other European country in which these dresses seem to have been fashionable is the Netherlands.

The 'long robe' with a train which trailed was a variation upon the mantua. A doll in the collection wears a dress of this kind and is labelled in an eighteenth-century hand: 'long robe coat dress for a lady of 16/1758' (W.183-1919). Unfortunately, none of the full-sized dresses in the Museum collection, dating from the 1750s to the 1770s, is in its original condition. There is an unaltered dress of this type at the Museum of Costume, Bath, which can be dated to 1761.[24] Such dresses were not conventional Court dresses, if one can accept Sophie von la Roche's comment made in 1786 that at the English Court only royalty was permitted to have a train which trailed.[25] This was a rule which did not necessarily apply at the Courts of other countries, each of which had its own regulations.

There was also a type of dress with a skirt made with a closed front, which appeared on both formal and informal occasions. The Museum possesses only one unaltered formal version (T.87-1920; not displayed).

The shape of the basic informal dress, the robe with a stitched and pleated back, made it very vulnerable to alteration. Indeed, there do not seem to be any in the Museum collection which have not been changed in some way, either within their own period or for fancy dress in the nineteenth century. The form of the dress was relatively simple. It was coat-like, with an open front. The back of the bodice was pleated and seamed to the shape of the torso. The centre panels at the back either run straight into the skirt [14] or have a joining seam at low hip level [5]. The skirt is pleated to the bodice and attached at the sides of the waist. There is a facing band at the back of the square neck. The robings, which are the folded fronts to the bodice and skirt opening, are either continuous with it or seamed on. With this kind of dress changes in fashion were more concerned with proportion than with basic cut. The design of the sleeves and cuffs are the only features which alter radically.

The fashionable line of the 1720s was long-waisted with a narrow front opening. The waist was shortened in the 1730s but lengthened again in the 1740s, when a broad front opening also became fashionable. This was retained through the 1750s. The sleeves were long and wide with deep cuffs in the 1720s [2; see p. 16], rather short and tight with a narrow cuff in the 1730s [4; see p. 19], longer and wider in the 1740s [5 and 7; see pp. 25 and 23] but becoming narrower towards the end of the decade when a wide, stiff, wing-like cuff was introduced. The frilled cuff seems to have been introduced in England in the mid-1750s [10 and 8; see p. 24 and catalogue]. The changes of shape to the skirt from being round in the 1730s to wide in the 1740s hardly affected informal dress.

With robings to absorb the change of shape in the bodice, plenty of seams at the back of the bodice and a facing at the neck to cover adjustments, much could be tactfully rearranged. The bodice has seldom been completely severed from the skirt at the centre of the back. Sleeves could be altered if a larger shape was adapted to a smaller one. Otherwise, material for new sleeves and cuffs would have to be found, which may explain why so few of these dresses have matching petticoats and why there are hardly any early gowns with closed fronts. The extra panels would have been extremely useful. The kerchiefs and aprons usually worn with informal dress would have covered worn spots. Quilted petticoats were, in any case, acceptable for dresses of this kind.

There is a very good series of dresses made from dated brocaded silks from the 1720s to the 1750s.[26] It is a pity that because they were so attractive this group has been especially vulnerable to alteration. Very few eighteenth-century ladies were as frank as Mrs Papendiek. She had a puce satin gown which was much altered between 1782 and 1788.[27] 'Fashion', she noted, 'was not then *exigeant* in the matter of continual change. A silk gown would go on for years a little fashioned up with new trimming.' The Museum does have a number of sources for the dating of new patterns of dress materials. The album of Barbara Johnson contains samples of dress materials from 1746 to 1823 together with notes of the name of the fabric, its price, width, who gave it to her, and for what purpose it was used (T.219-1973).[28] There is also a large collection of fashionable dress silks, pattern books of samples of dress silks, and dated designs for woven silks—in effect the seasonal changes in fashion can here be followed from 1706 to the end of the century. The collection of eighteenth-century dolls offers another way of checking the variety of forms of dress, for many are in their original condition and have their appropriate accessories.[29]

The Museum has a fine collection of lace, whitework and embroidery used for fashionable sleeve-ruffles, neckerchiefs, cap trimmings and aprons. There are also a large number of the quilted petticoats which were worn with informal dress and intended to show in the front opening or used as an additional support for the skirt instead of the hoop. It is difficult to explain the extreme scarcity of eighteenth-century hoops in this and other British collections. They were worn throughout the century and were both sturdy and fairly expensive. One [74] can be dated by its bill to 1778. Corsets are fairly common: most of those in the collection have the characteristically low scooped neckline of the 1770s and 1780s. A few shifts have survived with their original pleating on the

[74]

A sack of cream satin embroidered to shape with chenille chain stitch and silk ribbon in an all-over floral sprig design. Dating from the late 1770s, it is probably French, and may be typical of dress pieces which were sold in Lyon embroidered and ready to make up.
T.180&A-1965   [19]

[12]

[17]

The *polonaise* was a favourite *habit de fantaisie* of the 1770s in both France and England. The dress was made shorter than its petticoat, and the skirt caught up and draped in puffs at the back.

T.30-1910   [13]

sleeves still in place. (The collection of underwear is described on page 143.)

Most of the dresses from the second half of the eighteenth century in the Museum's collection are 'sacks'—a type of gown which was worn for formal or full dress occasions between the 1750s and the late 1780s. They are similar to the *robe à la française* in cut, and instructions for making them are given in F. D'Alembert's *Le Tailleur* in the *Dictionnaire des Sciences* in 1771. They were made with two widths of silk in the back arranged in a double pleat and with one width for each front. The facing at the neck held the pleats in place and extended into the robings. Gores were inserted from the hips to the hem if greater fullness was required. The petticoat was pleated from the centre to the sides and contained five or seven widths of material according to the size of the hoop. Silks were generally from nineteen to twenty-two inches wide. The petticoat was bound around the top and fastened with tapes tied at the hips. After fitting, the dress was mounted on a bodice lining. In France this was adjusted with a lacing at the centre of the back; but lacing was unusual in England except in the most elaborate gowns.

It is easy to underestimate the very high level of skill which went into the making of an eighteenth-century dress. As we have seen few are unaltered; secondly, the recommended size of stitch, eight to an inch, is quite coarse by modern standards and the thread is often quite thick.[30] Pinking was much used, a technique which not only stopped fraying but gave a light, broken line with the minimum bulk. Both in France and in England pinking seems to have been carried out by a specialist worker. The eighteenth-century dressmaker was judged by the skill with which she fitted her customer, something which can no longer be assessed, by the way she cut without waste and by the way she matched patterns for, even if the fabrics were narrow, patterns could extend in length to forty or forty-four inches. Sometimes an extra join was necessary, but dressmakers were so skilled that seams of this kind may only be apparent on the reverse.

Trimmings were very varied. The most expensive dresses (such as [9]) might make use of metal lace and artificial flowers. After the middle of the century such vivid contrasts of colour lost their appeal and matching decorations of a three-dimensional character were preferred. Pleating, padding and pinking were combined in a number of simple, yet ingenious, ways [10, 12 and 17; see p. 24 and left]. The fashion plates in the *Ladies' Pocket Books* and other fashion journals provided models to follow (and Barbara Johnson certainly collected them).

Pastel colours—pale pink, green, blue, beige and cream—were the typical colours of the 1770s. Silks with woven patterns diminished in importance after 1775, while embroidered decoration was increasingly emphasized. As materials grew plainer their trimmings grew more elaborate. The total effect of chenille, beads, flowers, feathers, lace and gauze is of a *collage*. In the *Encyclopédie méthodique*, 1785, M. Roland de la Platière noted a development which had taken place between 1770 and 1778: six thousand embroiderers were working with the weavers of Lyon: '*ils marient avec beaucoup d'intelligence les chefs d'oeuvre de la navette à ceux de l'aiguille.*'[31] Much of what they produced was exported, despite restrictions and high tariffs. All-over floral patterns on silk

dresses virtually disappeared in the 1780s when the characteristic pattern was a stripe of even width, often contrasting a very dark stripe with a lighter one. These stripes continued in fashion well into the 1790s, sometimes embellished by embroidered flounces. The richest embroidery, however, is found on plain materials, when it rivals that found on men's waistcoats of the time. Printed cotton dresses were also high fashion, particularly cottons with very dark grounds and lively floral patterns. The V & A collection lacks any striped dresses like the one worn by Mrs Siddons in the portrait painted by Gainsborough in 1785 (now in the National Gallery), but has several good printed cotton dresses [21, 26 and 28; see p. 33 and catalogue] from the late eighteenth and early nineteenth centuries.

The proportions of the dresses and the posture of the wearers altered radically in the last quarter of the eighteenth century. The change can first be detected in the increasing size of the *coiffure* in the later 1760s. Hairstyles grew steadily higher through the 1770s and then began to broaden, before diminishing in the late 1780s. The edifice was sometimes so copiously trimmed with flowers, feathers and ribbons on formal occasions that it became a popular target for satirists.[32] Caps were usually worn informally, their design becoming an important part of the milliner's art. Such fragile confections hardly ever survive; but the Museum has one of about 1770, worn by the 'beautiful Duchess of Argyle [sic]'—a delightful combination of cherry ribbons, bobbin lace and embroidered net [14; see p. 25]. The Duchess was drawn in a similar one in a pastel portrait by Katherine Read, now in the collection of Invarary Castle.[33]

[20]

A higher heel was introduced in the 1770s, altering women's stance. Extra fullness at bust and hips made dresses look higher-waisted than they actually were. A wide range of new styles can be found in French fashion magazines such as *La Gallerie des Modes*, 1776–1787, and *Le Cabinet des Modes*, 1785–1792, and in the English *Ladies Magazine*. Rose Bertin, the best known of French milliners, was an influential figure of the time. She was so closely linked with Marie Antoinette that she was known to her critics as *La Ministre des Modes*.

To the authors of the *Encyclopédie méthodique* one of the most significant informal *habits de fantasie* was the *polonaise* [13; see previous page]. This was a dress made shorter than its petticoat, with the skirt caught up on each side of the front and in three swags at the back. The drapes were looped up with braids and buttons. Introduced in the mid-1770s, it was as popular in England as in France. Another novelty was the *levette*, a simple loose gown with a sash, which was introduced in the early 1770s. This was primarily a French style and there are no examples in the V & A collection. Later it was tightly seamed and merged with the *robe en chemise*, anticipating the one-piece dress which was the basic form in the nineteenth century.

It is the *robe à l'anglaise* [20, 21 and 22] which predominated in the 1780s. This was essentially a dress with a fitted bodice, a refined version of the English informal gown of the first half of the eighteenth century, which has already been described. A dress defining the figure was a revelation to the French, who were accustomed to the loose pleats of the *robe à la française*, or sack. M. de la Platière, who was influenced by

[22]

anglomanie, the fashionable admiration for all things English, considered this dress to be '*uni, elegant et noble*'.[34] But if it was English in inspiration it was French in interpretation. The distinguishing feature is the cut of the bodice: it was made rather like a corset, with three back seams each reinforced with whalebone, the two outer seams curving towards the centre at the waist. In [20] each side of the front of the bodice is cut in one piece, but most of the dresses have a separate shoulder piece, which saves material. Not much of the neckline could be seen in any case under the bouffant kerchiefs which were then fashionable. The skirts were cut separately and gathered onto the bodice; and in the finest examples, such as [20] and [22], the fan of pleats inside the back of the waist provides additional fullness.

Little has been said so far about outdoor dress, of which there is far less in the collection. Among the rarest pieces is a 'domino' of about 1760–80 (T.195-1968; not displayed),[35] a loose full-length coat worn as fashionable disguise at a masquerade. During the 1780s the 'redingote' became increasingly popular for everyday wear. As in the days of Randle Holme, a century before, it was a man-tailored coat with a collar and long sleeves. [15] may actually have been a riding habit. It is made from fine woollen cloth, unaltered and in splendid condition, an extraordinary survival. The Museum has two riding habits of the 1740s (T.26-1923, T.12-1957), and a 'redingote' (T.670-D-1913) of the 1780s; but they do not have their matching skirts. Short jackets were much worn towards the end of the 1780s. They helped to emphasize the shorter waist which was introduced at the end of the 1780s and the beginning of the 1790s. Some were based on the French peasant jacket, the 'caracot'. It is interesting to compare [23] with [3] of the 1730s and with the earlier 'waist-coats'. One type of tailless jacket, the 'Spencer', was introduced by George, second Earl Spencer, in the mid-1790s and continued to be fashionable for the next two decades.[36] [33] is an example from about 1818.

Fashion underwent its own revolution in the 1790s. As in France, inspiration stemmed from the alleged ideals of classical antiquity. One of the aims was the pursuit of liberty, at least for the body; for advanced opinion had been critical of tight corsetry since the time of Rousseau. The new style of light, usually white, straight dresses worn over a natural figure soon proved, however, to have certain disadvantages. Whether equality was also an aim is more debatable, though Sir Nathaniel Wraxall, looking back on the 1790s in his *Historical Memoirs*, seems to have had few doubts:

Dress never totally fell till the Aera of Jacobinism and of equality in 1793–4 . . . a Drabery, more suited to the climate of Greece or Italy, than to the temperature of an Island situate in the fifty-first degree of latitude, classic, elegant, luxurious and picturesque, but ill calculated to protect against cold, damp or fogs; finally levelling and obliterating almost all external distinctions between the highest and lowest of the sex . . .'[37]

Wraxall overstated his case: he did not mention the shawls in which the ladies wrapped themselves. Those imported from Kashmir were made of the finest goatswool and were very expensive. These were soon copied in Edinburgh and Norwich—and in Paris. Moreover, Wraxall

[25]

The ingenious shawl dress, fashionable in the 1790s, was made from a printed silk and wool shawl lightly stitched together and then carefully pleated onto a lining to hold it in the shape of the body.
T.217-1968   [25]

This high-waisted English evening dress of 1810–11 is made of silk machine-made net and embroidered in chenille.
T.194-1958   [30]

ignored the importance of deportment. Such simple clothes were not at all easy to wear. Style was set in England in the 1790s by a beautiful, slender eighteen-year-old, Lady Charlotte Campbell, later Lady Charlotte Bury, and in France by the more mature Madame Tallien.

The origins of the classical robe lay in the one-piece chemise dress popularized by Marie Antoinette in 1783, the *levette*, and the gown with a closed front. Unfortunately, the Museum does not have an example of the earliest type of muslin dress without a waist seam, though there is one in the Gallery of English Costume, Manchester.[38] [27], with its softly gathered bodice and skirt, dates from the 1790s; while [29] is a later version with less fullness. Suitable light cottons presented no problems for the English because of the technological developments in cotton spinning and, alternatively, the finest Indian cottons were available. According to the Duchesse D'Abrantés, however, it was something which Napoleon did not care to see French Court ladies wear.[39]

White remained fashionable from about 1795 to 1810. As late as

1808 *La Belle Assemblée* was asserting: 'the white robe will ever obtain our suffrage'.[40] There were, of course, alternatives to the classical robe. Plain white gowns were worn for informal dress in England in the 1790s. Open robes, coloured and usually with trains, were still worn for formal occasions, and of these the Museum has a large collection. All have a high waist and most, long sleeves [24, 25, 26; see opposite and catalogue]. The back pleats are arranged in various ways: the most ingenious is the shawl dress [25] which was made from a printed shawl, treated with great care by the owner. The length of fabric is only lightly stitched together and then carefully pleated onto a lining to hold it to the shape of the body. From 1794–1806 Nicklaus von Heideloff published his *Gallery of Fashion* with detailed recommendations of suitable wear for fashionable ladies in every circumstance, each issue illustrated by meticulously detailed plates. Significantly, the frontispiece of the first one displays a composition of gaily coloured ribbons. When plain white and simple lines were so fashionable the accessories which accompanied the dresses were all-important.

From about 1800 the one-piece dress was accepted for most occasions. For informal wear it was made with a high neck or with one into which a chemisette could be inserted [28] and the sleeves usually short. For formal occasions the neckline was low and the sleeves usually short. Elements of eighteenth-century cut were retained in some dresses which were made like the rare closed-fronted dress with the front panels of the skirt attached to a waist tape that fastened at the back. In others, the bodice front was cut almost like the bib of an apron and was pinned in place over the over-lapping flaps of the lining that covered the bosom. A draw-string was run through the top of the bib to control the fullness and, when the dress was made of fine, draping material (as in [29]), this worked well. By about 1807, however, attempts were being made to achieve a smoother fit over the bust. In June 1807 *La Belle Assemblée* mentioned bodices in the 'gored corset form' and in September it announced again that 'French gores are replacing gathers'. A comparison of the bodices of [29] and [30] demonstrates the difference. In general, the waistline was midway between waist and bust, although it did fluctuate slightly. Skirts were cut straight with a gentle fullness all round; although shortly after 1800 the front became tighter and the fullness was concentrated at the back.

During the opening years of the nineteenth century, fashionable inspiration was drawn from many sources. Although classical antiquity remained the most important, the titles of the styles recorded in the fashionable magazines suggest that women were finding current events in Europe equally engrossing. In June 1807 *La Belle Assemblée* mentioned Hungarian vests, the Spanish mantle, the Cossack spencer, the Grecian scarf and the French coat. Within two years, however, geography had been deserted for history: *Le Beau Monde* reported in 1808 that: 'The modern rage for studying the production of the old masters has inspired a considerable portion of taste . . . there are some attempts to introduce the embellishments of an earlier time of our own country.'[41] The Tudor period was one that was particularly favoured, although it was to be some years before the romantic interpretation of historical styles was to affect dress radically. The emphasis on novelty

[32]

[35]

Pink silk dress with a figured leaf
design.
English, about 1823
T.28&A-1983 [37]

reflected a *nouveau riche* competitiveness at the spas and in the ballrooms which was expressed in a letter written by an anonymous Young Lady and published in *Ackermann's Repository* in 1810: 'The only superiority one can obtain arises from a quick invention and a fine taste, [for a] commercial country is a great foe to commercial singularity, for money will buy everything.'[42] Yet the dresses surviving from this period show little variety.

Only after the conclusion of the Napleonic wars in 1815, when it was once again possible to visit Paris, was there a decisive change in English fashions. The caricatures in *Le Bon Genre* stressed the differences that had developed between the French and English styles.[43] English dresses were comparatively long-waisted, straight and scanty. French dresses had a higher waistline and were loaded with trimmings concentrated at the upper arm and at the hem of the smooth flared skirt. These features, which had their origins in the puffed sleeve and triangular skirt of the sixteenth century, were to dominate the style as it was developed in England.

The romantically inspired dresses of the later 1810s and 1820s include some of the finest examples of craftsmanship in the collection. In particular, they are decorated with three-dimensional motifs finely finished with facings or piping. Most of these trimmings match or tone with the main colour of the garment. Most fashion plates show a greater unity of design than is apparent in some of the clothes in the collection which show a rather eclectic choice of motifs; [35], for example, has rather naïve floral shapes of indeterminate origin on the bodice and Gothic crenellations on the oversleeves. This outfit is an example of the new *pelisse robe* or coat dress, which was to remain a fashionable item of wear until the mid-1820s. Another feature of this period was the use of sheer fabrics to make transparent overdresses, often in a contrasting colour, for formal clothes. Woven gauze and hand-made lace were popular, as was machine-made net. [32], which is made of Heathcoat's bobbin net, illustrates the way in which applied or embroidered decoration could be used to provide the necessary weight to achieve the correct drape with this light material.

The waistline, which had reached its highest level, just below the bust, in 1815–17, gradually descended to reach its natural level by the mid-1820s; by the late 1820s there were occasional examples of dresses with pointed waists. Women had worn corsets which flattened the hips and raised the bust throughout the early years of the century but, by the 1820s, tight lacing had become a necessity [37 and 75]. The small-waisted effect was emphasized by the exaggeratedly large sleeves. These were to reach their largest size across the shoulders in about 1830 [38; see overleaf], but then the fullness began to slip down the arm so that it swelled out from above the elbow [39]. In the early 1820s the skirt was still gored and was made with a back panel tightly gathered at the waist. Some form of padding or hem decoration was usually incorporated to hold out the skirt at the bottom. As the waistline descended to its natural level, the gathering at the back was gradually extended round the sides of the skirt, while the panels became less tapered and began to fall in soft folds rather than form a stiff cone. Although trimmings at the hem were fashionable until the end of the 1820s, they were wider and softer.

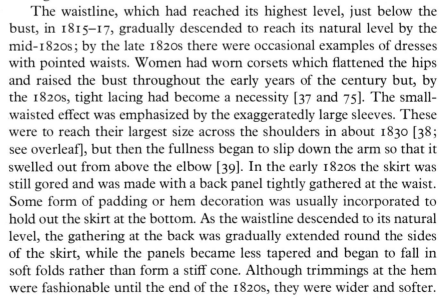

1]

4]

In the 1820s the fashionable small-waisted look was emphasized by exaggeratedly large sleeves. This dress of printed cotton, dating from about 1828, is shown with a fine whitework collar, and a printed silk reticule produced to publicize the work of the Ladies' Society for the Relief of Negro Slaves.

T.151-1968   [38]

Small bustles were worn to give a gentle roundness at the hips. Fabrics with an all-over pattern became increasingly popular after applied decoration went out of favour.

Much importance was attached to accessories at this time. Most striking were the hats and bonnets which became much larger and more elaborate after 1815 when direct contact with French styles was resumed. In the 1820s and 1830s hairstyles grew higher and more complex and headgear similarly increased in size. The difficulty of arranging the hair may explain the great popularity of caps for both formal and informal occasions. Shawls were still worn, as were mantles, while fine whitework collars in a variety of styles were a striking feature of day-time dress.

The change in fashion from Regency ebullience to Victorian restraint was a gradual one which did not happen overnight on the accession of Queen Victoria. For example, despite comments in *Townsend's Monthly Journal*, 1836, about the battle between large and narrow sleeves no final decision was reached until well after 1840.[44] Fullness on the forearm can be found in the fashion plates until about 1842 and also in photographs of the period—a new and useful source which show what people were actually wearing as opposed to what the fashion journals thought they should wear.[45] However, by 1842, the new restrained line was established. [41] is a good, typical example; the bodice is long and close-fitting, with a deep point reaching well below the waist. Under their trimmings, the sleeves are narrow and curved, as well as being set into a low armhole which restricted movement even further. The decoration is minimal and refined. The skirt is full and tightly pleated. The dress is characteristic of its time, with its romantic recall of the mid-seventeenth century, a period more appealing to the sentimental ladies of the 1840s than the brash exuberance of the sixteenth century.

At the end of the 1840s, a depressed and stressful decade, there were signs of a change of mood to which fashion responded. Dresses which had drooped began to spread, and lighter, crisper fabrics replaced the soft, heavy stuffs of the 1840s. The waistline rose and lost its deep point and the sleeves began to broaden at the wrist. Frills at the bottom of the skirts made them look wider. Because so many dresses were altered in response to these developments [42], it is difficult to find good examples of late 1840s–early 1850s styles for the collection. Fortunately [44], a very fashionable dress of 1849, was a nursing dress and its limited function has preserved it unaltered. In general, the most striking survivals from the 1840s and 1850s are white wedding dresses, and of these the Museum has a large collection. For reasons of sentiment and family pride they were usually the most splendid gown that a girl ever owned and ecclesiastical criticism had little effect on fashionable ostentation. Wedding dresses have a further historical advantage in that it is usually known when and by whom they were worn.

During the mid-1850s two industrial developments occurred which were to be of importance to dress. The one with the greatest long-term effect was the introduction of a cheaper and more efficient sewing machine which was suitable for the domestic market. Although invented earlier in the century, it was many years before the sewing machine became reasonably efficient. Its main use had been in factories and, before 1855, the lack of agreement on patent rights had made it very

expensive. Even after 1855 it did not reach the average woman very quickly; although the *Englishwoman's Domestic Magazine* for 1867–68 published a survey of most available models,[46] the consciously up-to-date *Cassell's Household Guide* of 1868[47] did not even mention the sewing machine in an article on dressmaking. By the 1877 edition, however, it was taken for granted.[48] The second key invention was the lightweight dress support made from circles of spring steel, which did not collapse no matter how large the circumference of the skirt [76]. They held the skirts clear of the legs and were capable of replacing the large number of starched and horsehair petticoats which women had been wearing. To those who had grown up in the 1840s and 1850s, this represented a great increase in comfort. Crinoline-making became an important industry, and the largest firm, W. S. and E. H. Thomson, the makers of the Crown crinoline, became in modern parlance a multi-national company, with factories in England, France, Germany and the United States. When they diversified to make bustles, corsets and then ready-to-wear clothes and even gloves, they did much to standardize the appearance of the later nineteenth-century woman. Another, rather different, development of the mid-1850s was the reintroduction of the high-heeled shoe, which had been out of fashion since the 1780s.

The Museum possesses two splendid dresses of the mid-1850s. One (T.324-B-1977) is made from flounced green plush trimmed with fringe, the other (T.325-E-1977) is of golden-brown taffeta trimmed with black velvet; both have matching mantles. Unfortunately, they have the defects of their quality and are too large to display in a restricted area. The magnificent embroidered Court dress of about 1860 [48; see p. 11] is from the same source. They form part of one of the most important gifts that the collection has received in recent years, given by Madame Tussaud's, who, in the mid-nineteenth century, had included tableaux of the latest fashions among their historical waxworks.[49] In their advertisements the firm stated that many of the dresses came direct from the finest dressmakers in Paris and London.

French *couture* was dominated at this period by an Englishman, Charles Frederick Worth (1825–1895).[50] He had opened his *salon* in 1858 and made clothes for the Empress Eugénie and for most of the European Courts. His was the largest and most successful dressmaking house in Paris and, to contemporaries, his name was synonymous with high fashion.[51] He may have introduced the crinoline-supported skirt and the narrower one of the mid-1860s which briefly replaced it. He is also credited with the introduction of the 'short dress' for walking. This had an ankle-length skirt, and the Empress Eugénie is said to have favoured it. The Princess-line dress without a waist seam also originated with Worth, as did the bonnet with no frill at the back. Worth's rise was confirmation of the importance of Paris as an international fashion centre. He was not the only *couturier*, although he was the most publicity-conscious and influential. All built on the prestige that French luxury goods had established at the international exhibitions but, although expensive dresses were sold to private clients, equally important were the models purchased by retail shops in order to copy and adapt from them [69; see p. 47]. Designs were also reproduced in fashion plates, which were influential both in their own right and through their links

Fabric with a pattern woven or printed so that it complemented the shape of the dress when made up was popular in the late 1850s and the 1860s. This cotton day dress of about 1858 has a printed design; and it is trimmed with whitework embroidery.
T.702-1913   [45]

[50]

[53]

Historic costume inspired many late-nineteenth-century fashions. This silk dress of about 1870, with a *polonaise*-like overskirt supported by a bustle, is characteristic of the period.
T.182-1914   [54]

with the paper pattern industry, which was to expand very greatly after 1870.[52] The co-ordination of all these activities was the responsibility of the *Chambre Syndicale de la Couture Française*, founded in 1885. Perhaps because of the stimulus of Paris, the dresses of the 1860s in the Museum's collection show great diversity. [46] has almost all the fashionable features which the magazines recommended to their readers in 1861–62: it has double puffed sleeves, a bolero-like trimming, a triangular 'Swiss' belt and a slightly gored skirt. Gored skirts became increasingly common from about 1866 onwards as a smoother line was adopted; the skirt no longer sprang out all round from a tightly gathered waist, but spread gently to form a triangular shape with a straightish front and an extended back. [49] is a good example of this development. The dresses of the mid-1860s were comparatively severe, with little decoration; but this plainness was short-lasting and by the late 1860s, as the very large skirt reached the end of its development, many decorative features were introduced, most of which emphasized the back of the skirt [50]. The late 1860s also saw a return to elaborate hairstyles; and some experiments were made with the use of cosmetics.

In 1869 the *Englishwoman's Domestic Magazine* reported on a visit to a *couturière en vogue* who stated: 'Each lady comes to ask me not *what is worn* but what has not yet even been seen or worn . . . so I open an album of historic costumes and copy.'[53] The strength of the late nineteenth-century interest in historic costume is reflected in the fact that almost every dress in the collection which dates from after 1870 owes something to the study of 'the models of the past'. According to the anonymous *couturière en vogue*, the 'marquises of the Pompadour period' were an important source of inspiration although, when translated into something which a dressmaker could reproduce from a pattern or magazine illustration, the eighteenth-century original was reduced to a simple bodice with a short waist and a full gored skirt with a *polonaise*-like draped overskirt supported by a bustle [52, 53, 54]. The effectiveness of the style depended on the trimmings—the pleats, frills and insertions—and on the use of colour, although few dresses in the popular pastel shades seem to have survived. The most ostentatious example in the Museum's collection (T.118-B-1979) is by Madame Vignon of Paris, an accredited dressmaker to the Empress Eugénie. It has two bodices, which, together with an assortment of extra peplums and bows, made it extremely adaptable. It is made from magenta silk, lavishly trimmed with pinked and pleated bands. Unfortunately the magenta dye is too fugitive to permit its display.

By the mid-1870s skirts had been considerably reduced in size. The waist had lengthened and many bodices, which were tightly boned, untrimmed, and reached to the hip, looked rather like corsets [57]. The thoughtful were aware of the contradictions implied by so revealing a fashion: in *Art and Ornament* (1875, trans. 1877) Charles Blanc, the French art critic, wrote: 'To hide and yet to display, or rather to indicate and yet not disclose, are the two objects of the bodice. . . . It must not be forgotten that what is concealed is yet that which it is most wished to display.'[54] As [59; see p. 120] illustrates, the trimming tended to be concentrated round the legs. The skirt, which in any case was narrow, was kept close fitting with elastic and tapes and was sometimes extended to

French *couture* was dominated in the mid-nineteenth century by an Englishman, Charles Frederick Worth, who made clothes for the Empress Eugénie and for most of the European Courts. This silk dress, designed by Worth in 1881, is made in the Princess-line style he originated, with no waist seam.
T.63&A-1976 **[61]**

form a rather unwieldy train [see 58]. It was an extremely restrictive style and considerable ingenuity was spent in devising underwear which would be sufficiently sleek and yet supportive [77]. Dressmakers also became clever at using trimming to distract from a shape which might be considered too revealing. In [60], beads, chenille, fringe, gathers and pleats have been deployed to produce a dress of rich sobriety. The earliest dress by Worth in the collection [61; see p. 42], illustrates another way of softening the outline with lace borders. Worth's use of both machine-made lace and embroidery was typical of the period. The developments of the 1870s also led to the replacement of the enveloping shawl by the more closely fitting mantle.

A reaction against these tight, draped dresses set in during the 1880s. The aesthetes and the dress reformers disliked them and found a useful platform for their views at the International Health Exhibition of 1884. There was also a growing interest in active sports, one aspect of the trend towards the emancipation of women. Except for a conventional riding habit, the Museum has none of these early sports clothes, but even ordinary day wear was affected by the change. [63], for example, has a shorter bodice that gave slightly greater flexibility at the waist, and the higher-set sleeves gave a little more room for the shoulders. The skirt was still cut straight, but it was not as tight as it had been; the fullness which was concentrated at the back, was supported by a bustle placed just below the waist. Drapery and trimmings, often in some quantity, were mounted over the skirt rather than being an integral part of it. At the very end of the decade, there was a return to a straighter, more severe line inspired by men's fashions of the Directoire period (see [65]).

By this time the consciously non-fashionable could shop at Messrs Liberty. The firm had been founded in 1874 and specialized in goods of Far Eastern origin which appealed to the aesthetes and those who had rejected contemporary design. It was there that the young sculptor, Hamo Thornycroft, purchased the material for the dress which he designed for his wife in accordance with the principles of the Dress Reform Movement [62].[55] In particular, the gathered bodice was un-boned and the sleeves were wide and softly draping. After E. W. Godwin, the architect and designer, joined Liberty's in 1884, the firm opened a department for the making of artistic and historic dress. Some of Godwin's sketches are in the V & A's Department of Prints and Drawings, and with the sequence of Liberty catalogues in the National Art Library they illustrate the wide range of periods from which he drew his inspiration. Whatever the source, the dresses were made so that they flowed over the figure and restricted neither the arms nor the waist. Nonetheless, to judge from [70] and [73] (see pp. 141 and 142), they were firmly made; they may have been worn over an uncorsetted figure but in these examples, the linings are boned. Both these dresses were made for a member of the Liberty family and they are both in the 'greenery-yallery' colours which were so popular with the artistic fraternity.

The most obvious development of the 1890s was in the shape of the sleeve. This had begun to broaden at the shoulder at the end of the 1880s when the extra material was arranged in a slight 'peak' [66; see p. 45]. Expansion was more rapid in the early 1890s, and sleeves reached their most exaggerated size in about 1894–95 [69; see p. 47]. The decline

A linen suit made by the French couture house, Doucet, in about 1894. When it was washed by the Museum's Conservation Department, it shed quantities of red-brown dust, possibly the souvenir of an Egyptian tour.
T.15&A-1979   [68]

[64]

of the sleeve was similarly rapid and by about 1898 its former importance was indicated only by the presence of an added frill or epaulette [71]. The growth of the sleeve was balanced by an increase in the size of the skirt. In about 1892, flared skirts were introduced and as they grew to their widest extent in about 1895 they were known by a series of self-explanatory names: 'the bell', 'the fan', 'the umbrella skirt'. The fashion journals took great pains to show how they should be cut using the bias of the fabric. Skirts continued to be cut on the cross throughout the 1890s but, by the end of the decade, they were narrower and consequently clung more closely to the hips [71]. By this time softer, more frilly trimmings and a preference for pastel shades foreshadowed the developments of the early twentieth century.

    The clothes of the 1890s in the collection tend to fall into two main categories—tailored suits and ball dresses; and in some respects this reflects the way of life of the leisured classes. Several examples [64, 66, 69 and 72] were worn by Americans, among them Lady Fairhaven and her sister. A selection from their wardrobes made a welcome addition

to the series for the late nineteenth and early twentieth centuries. By this period, French *couture* was finding a high proportion of its clientèle on the other side of the Atlantic. Since, in the main, Americans bought in quantity and tended to accept styles without alteration, their clothes are often among the best examples of high fashions of the period.

Although the wonders of the new century were acclaimed in the popular press, although the Paris exhibition of 1900 was a triumph for *art nouveau*, in fashion there were no immediately discernable changes in styles or colouring, as we shall see. The well-dressed lady of December 1899 could still drive out in her carriage without provoking ridicule in January 1900.

1 Rev. Daniel Rock, *Textile Fabrics in the South Kensington Museums*, 1870

2 Registered Papers Isham V. 26085, 5 July 1899

3 Many of the white wedding dresses in the collection are described in Madeleine Ginsburg's *Wedding Dresses, 1740–1970*, HMSO, 1980. Where non-white dresses have been received with the information that they had been worn at a wedding, this is recorded in the catalogue entry.

4 J. L. Nevinson, *Men's Costume in the Isham Collection*, The Connoisseur, Vol XCIV, No 313, 1934; *New Materials for the History of 17th century Costume in England*, Apollo, Vol XX, 315, 1934; *Catalogue of English Domestic Embroidery of the 16th and 17th centuries*, Victoria and Albert Museum, HMSO, 1938, reprinted 1952

5 Madeleine Ginsburg, *Rags to Riches, The Second-Hand Clothes Trade, 1700–1978*, Costume, No 14, 1980, pp 121–135

6 Fynes Moryson, *An Itinerary*, containing 'His Ten Yeeres Travel through the Twelve Dominions of Germany, Bohmerland, Schweitzerland, Netherland, Denmarke, Poland, Italy, Turky, France, England, Scotland & Ireland', 1607–15, 1617, reprinted 1907, Vol 14, p. 231.

7 Vol 4, p. 231. A pattern of this gown is published in Norah Waugh, *op cit*, diagram 1. In general the pattern is correct in outline, but there should be three gores at each side, not two, with square, not pointed tips. A newly drawn pattern will be published by Janet Arnold in her forthcoming volume on 16th and 17th century dresses in the Patterns of Fashion series, and one of the white satin bodice (172-1900), see below.

8 For the use of this technique see J. Arnold, Decorative Features:
pinking, snipping and slashing, Costume, No 9, 1975, pp 22–26.

9 Examples of embroidered bodices from the Museum collection are described in the *Catalogue of English Domestic Embroidery, op cit*; G. Wingfield Digby, *Elizabethan Embroidery*, 1964, also contains material from other collections.

10 See N. Waugh, *op cit*, diagram III

11 *The Private Correspondence of Jane, Lady Cornwallis, 1613–1664*, 1842, p. 248

12 Mrs Bury Palliser, *A History of Lace*, 1902, p. 349

13 See N. Waugh, *op cit*, diagram VI, also J. Arnold, *A Silver Tissue Dress, circa 1660*, The Costume Society, Vol 1, No 2, Winter 1965–6

14 These gowns are described in Margaret H. Swain, *Men's Nightgowns of the 18th century*, Waffen und Kostumkunde, 1972, Heft 1, pp 41–48; *Nightgown into Dressing Gown—a study of Men's Nightgowns in the 18th century*, Costume, No 6, 1972, pp 10–21

15 Madeleine Ginsburg, *An Introduction to Fashion Illustration*, 1980

16 *Mundus Muliebris; or the Ladies Dressing-Room Unlock'd and her Toilette spread. In burlesque. Together with the Fop Dictionary compiled for the Use of the Fair Sex* (by J. Evelyn), 1690. Edited by J. L. Nevinson for the Costume Society Extra Series, No 5, 1977

17 J. Arnold, *A Mantua c. 1708–9 from Clive House Museum, College Hill, Shrewsbury*, Costume, No 4, 1970, pp 26–31

18 J. M. Beattie, *The English Court in the Reign of George I*, 1967

19 Mary Granville, Mrs Delany, *The Autobiography and Correspondence*, Ed. Lady Llanover, 1861–2, Vol 1, p. 70: Mrs Pendarves to Mrs Anne Granville, 22 January: 1739–40

20 Published by J. Arnold as *A Court Mantua of c. 1740*, in Costume, No 6, 1972, pp 48–52

21 It is not possible to identify exactly which member of the families, Leconte or Gil(l)es, was responsible for the red and silver mantua, but the Huguenot Society, Vol 26, *Régistre des Eglises de la Savoye de Spring Gardens et des Grecs*, 15.10.1707–8, records the birth of Marie Magdelaine Leconte, daughter of Thomas, embroiderer of the Parish of St Martins in the Fields and of Magdelaine. Godparents, Jacques Debat, Marie Gal(?)eron; 24/2/1723 birth of Marie Madelaine Gilles, daughter of Jacques and Marie; 19/3/1723 birth of Madelaine Garneron, daughter of Natanael and Marguerite, godparents Madelaine Leconte and Pierre Menan.

22 *Royal Archives 55440*, 1 May 1750, lists the tradespeople to whom payment has been made for supplying items for the wardrobe of Augusta, Princess of Wales. Among them is 'Mary Magd. Johnson, formerly Leconte', who supplied embroideries 1746–7. In *RA 55441* there is a statement from Magdalen Garneron for supplying embroideries to a total of £200. Reference cited by gracious permission of Her Majesty The Queen.

23 S. Richardson, *Clarissa : a history of a Young Lady*, 1748. 1811 edition, Vol III, pp 290–1, Vol V, pp 302–3, Vol VIII, pp 214–5.

24 Bath City Council, Museum of Costume, *Guide*, 1980, p. 5

25 Sophie von la Roche, *Diary of a Visit to London, 1786*, 1933. Entry for 22 September, pp. 217–8

26 P. Thornton, *Baroque and Rococo Silks*, 1965, illustrates several similar dresses. Ed Donald King, *British Textile Design in the Victoria and Albert Museum*, 3 Vols, Tokyo, 1980; dated 18th-century dress silks and the designs for them are illustrated in Vols 1 & 2.

27 Ed Mrs V. D. Broughton, *Mrs Papendiek, Court and Private Life in the Time of Queen Charlotte*, 1887. P. Clabburn, Costume 6, 1979, p. 100 quotes and comments on all the references to the puce satin dress and its alterations.

28 A. Buck, *Dress in Eighteenth-Century England*, 1980, illustrates some pages of and comments on the Barbara Johnson Album, pp 77–79.

29 The Victoria and Albert Museum collection of dolls is divided. Those whose clothes have particular points of interest are in the Department of Textiles and Dress, others are in the Museum of Childhood in Bethnal Green.

30 *Encyclopédie méthodique ou par ordre de matières par une Société de Gens de Lettres, de Savans et d'Artistes*, tome 192: Paris, Liège, 1787, 82–19 Manufactures; arts et métiers Vol 1, p. 223

31 *Encyclopédie méthodique, op cit*, Vol 1, p. 92

32 London, British Museum, Department of Prints and Drawings, Div 1. *Political and Personal Satires*, Vol V, 1771–83, Nos 4839–6360, 1935, include prints which satirize the dress and hairstyles of the period, for example, in 1776, 5330, 5335, 5394, 5395, in 1778, 5517, 5518.

33 London, British Museum, Department of Prints and Drawings, F. M. Donoghue, H. M. Hake, *Catalogue of Engraved British Portraits*, 1908. Elizabeth (Gunning) Duchess of Argyll, 1734–90, (mezzotint) Vol 1 69: K. Read, published J. Finlayson, 1770. Used as a frontispiece to Jesse's *Selwyn and his contemporaries*, 1843

34 *Encyclopédie méthodique*: op cit. Vol 1, p. 225

35 J. Arnold, A Pink Domino, c. 1760–70, at the Victoria and Albert Museum, Costume, No 3, 1969, pp 31–34

36 London, British Museum, Department of Prints and Drawings, *op cit*, Vol VIII, 1938, No 8192, p. 967

37 N. William Wraxall, *Historical Memoirs of My Own Time*, 1771–1784, 2nd edition, 1815, Vol 1, p. 139

38 Norah Waugh: *op cit*, diagram XVII

39 Laure Junot, Duchesses D'Abrantes, *Memoires de Madame la Duchesse D'Abrantes, ou souvenirs historiques sur Napoleon, la revolution, le directoire, le consulat, l'empire et la restauration*, 1831–5, English edition, *Memoirs of Napoleon, his Court and his Family*, 1836, Vol 2, p. 46

40 La Belle Assemblée, 1808, July, p. 47

41 Le Beau Monde, 1808, July, p. 47

42 Ackermann's Repository, 1810, p. 242. Fourteenth Letter from a Young Lady in the Gay World to her sister in the Country.

43 Bon Genre: a good series of illustrations from this publication are to be found in Gretel Wagner's *Aus besten Kreisen*, 1983.

44 Naomi Tarrant, *The Rise and Fall of the Sleeve, 1825–40*, Royal Scottish Museum Studies, 1983. This is a detailed study of the period.

45 The relationship of fashion to photography from 1826–1900 is dealt with by Madeleine Ginsburg in *Victorian Dress in Photographs*, 1982. A. Gernsheim, *Fashion and Reality*, 1962, contains some very useful photographs, as does Sara Stevenson, *David Octavius Hill and Robert Adamson*, Edinburgh, National Galleries, 1981

46 Englishwoman's Domestic Magazine, 1867; July, pp. 354–9; August, pp. 402–4; September, pp. 483–5; October, pp. 539–541; November, pp. 586–588; December, pp. 626–627; 1868: July, p. 104; September, p. 157; 1869: August, p. 81

47 Cassell's Household Guide, 1868, Vol IV p. 235

48 Ibid., 1877, Vol. IV p. 252

49 A typical advertisement for the Madame Tussaud fashion display from Le Follet, January 1866: 'In accordance with the season, Madamme Tussaud's Exhibition has been entirely re-embellished. The whole of the ancient court dresses, of the most splendid description, selected from the first houses in Paris and London, and probably never equalled or surpassed are on view.'

50 D. de Marly, *The History of Haute Couture 1850–1950*, 1980; *Worth, Father of Haute Couture*, 1980; E. Saunders, *The Age of Worth*, 1954; J. P. Worth, *A Century of Fashion*, 1928.

51 Many of the designs from the House of Worth dating from the later 1860s to the 1950s, when the house was finally closed, are in the Department of Prints and Drawings and Photographs. Record photographs of the dresses made between the 1890s and the 1920s are in the Archive of the National Art Library.

52 M. Walsh, *The Democritization of Fashion : the emergence of the Women's Dress Pattern Industry*, Journal of American History, Vol. 66, 1979

53 The Englishwoman's Domestic Magazine, 1869: January, p. 35.

54 Charles Blanc, *Art and Ornament*, French edition, 1875; English edition, 1877, p. 151

55 Reform Dress is considered in S. M. Newton's *Health Art and Reason*, 1974. Liberty's clothes are described in the exhibition catalogue *Liberty's 1875–1975*, Victoria and Albert Museum, 1975; see also A. Adburgham, *Liberty's : A Biography of a Shop*, 1975.

This American evening dress of about 1894, made in blue-black silk velvet, has the exaggerated sleeves that were fashionable at the time. The dress is trimmed with bead and sequin embroidery and bead-embroidered net in a design of butterflies.
T.272&A-1972   [69]

Opposite :
One of the most important items in the collection, this superb suit of about 1630, consisting of doublet, breeches and cloak in slashed and braided satin, came to the Museum with other clothes from a Dorset farmhouse. It is typical of its time, the doublet with a high waist and long skirt, the breeches tapering to the knee.
T.58 to B-1910   [79]

BOY'S SHIRT, fine linen embroidered with silk in cross and double running stitch with overcast edges and seams worked in knotted and buttonholed insertion stitch
English, 1540s
The shirt may be compared to those shown in portraits painted by Holbein and his contemporaries between 1535 and 1555.
T.112-1972

Men's Dress

AVRIL HART

The acquisition policy for men's fashionable dress and accessories follows the same principle as that for female dress and other decorative arts throughout the Museum: to acquire a comprehensive and international collection of objects of the highest artistic merit and quality. This is made possible by gifts, bequests and purchases, very occasionally supplemented by loans when the objects concerned are of considerable aesthetic or national importance.

The collection spans a period of four centuries. The earliest item illustrated here, and the only one dating from the sixteenth century, is a fine and rare embroidered boy's shirt of about 1540. The seventeenth century is particularly well represented by five complete suits and three important accessories—two cloaks and a doublet—about a third of the collection. The eighteenth-century collection is altogether larger and more comprehensive, although it includes a higher proportion of elaborate dress suits, worn for ceremonial occasions, than fashionable everyday dress. The nineteenth-century collection is small. Most of the outfits date from between 1800 and 1830; they are all very stylish and mostly consist of formal dress suits and coats, as well as some overcoats and a great variety of waistcoats. In the twentieth century again certain decades or fashions are better represented than others. The weakest periods are the 1920s and 1950s, both post-war decades—which may account for the shortage of clothes.

Because of the unevenness of the V & A collection it is impossible to discuss the history of men's dress by reference to it alone. Other collections, especially certain ones abroad, and other media—prints, paintings, literary sources and manuscripts—are needed. Curators, collectors and donors have in the past had quite firm but idiosyncratic tastes. Antiquarian collectors, for instance, sought objects of historical interest because of an intellectual wish to bring to life a period through its surviving objects. It is possible that a nineteenth-century donor, the Reverend Robert Brooke, was such a person, although he seems to have collected only from within his family 'the accumulated memorials of one family from the seventeenth to the eighteenth century'. [1] In 1864 he gave a number of items to the Museum, one of which was a very fine man's

SEMI-CIRCULAR SHORT CLOAK, silk, satin slashed and embroidered with floss and twisted silks in satin and padded satin stitch, French knots and knotted chain stitch. Lined with silk taffeta
Italian, 1600–20
The collar is missing. The cloak is made from two parallel lengths of satin. The slashes are criss-crossed and radiate from the shoulders to the hem, increasing in size towards the hem.
378-1898

Opposite:
Here a 1670s circular worsted cloak embroidered with silver and silver-gilt thread is shown with a coat and open-kneed breeches which were donated with the Isham Collection from Lamport Hall, Northamptonshire. Some of the clothes in the Isham Collection, including Sir Thomas Isham's wedding coat, had been altered for masquerade costumes, but the coat and breeches (worsted trimmed with silk and silver gilt thread) have survived intact.
T.62-1978&191&A-1900   [82]

velvet eighteenth-century suit [94]; in the following year he made a further and much larger gift including jewellery, books, lace and costume. He made several rather singular requests prior to confirming the gift, one of which was that the collection be referred to as 'The Brooke of Gateforth Gift', and the other that:

'Mr and Mrs Brooke, and the future possessor of the "Gateforth Estate", provided that they bear the name and are of the present family of Brooke, to have the privilege secured to them (by memorandum recorded in the Books of the Museum, and by the possession of a Free Pass Ticket) of entrance into the Museum and Library, and the Horticultural Gardens attached, on the holding of any scientific or other meetings, and on all other public occasions.'

Apart from large family collections, many single items such as suits or waistcoats which have descended from one generation to the next have been presented to the Museum from time to time. Quite often a family would find that with changing circumstances they no longer had room to store an heirloom, and so they would offer it to the Museum, wishing it to have 'a good home'. There are a great many of these gifts and over the years they have formed the backbone of the collection. This has been particularly true of the collection of men's eighteenth-century dress. This means of acquiring costume from known sources—from Englishmen whose social standing has varied from that of the aristocrat to the country squire—has proved to be most revealing.

In recent years the people who would formerly have offered their clothes to the Museum have been sending them to the sale rooms for auction instead. This has meant that the Museum has been in competition with other museums and private collectors from home and abroad. In 1980 a seventeenth-century suit which was of considerable significance as an item of fashion as well as being of national importance was bought at auction. This was the suit of the 1660s reputed to have belonged to Prince Rupert [81]. The Museum failed at another recent sale to acquire a nightgown of a type not as yet represented in the collection. The successful bidder is believed to have been an American museum.

The Seventeenth Century

This collection is particularly fine and includes a number of complete outfits as well as more than twelve doublets of 1600–40, six cloaks (one matching a suit) of 1600–70, a 'Brandenburg' overcoat of the late seventeenth century, two leather coats, one of which is a loan, and two pairs of open-kneed breeches from the 1640s. At present about a third of this material is displayed in the Gallery of Dress and illustrated here. The items on display have been chosen not only for their quality but also for their condition: the objects that remain in store are mostly very fragile or incomplete.

The doublet and trunk hose [78; see p. 144], dated about 1604 and lent by the Grimsthorpe and Drummond Castle Trust Ltd, has been in the possession of the Earl of Ancaster's family since the seventeenth century and is traditionally believed to have belonged to James I. It was thought to have been acquired as a Coronation perquisite by an ancestor

DOUBLET, ribbed silk trimmed with silk and silver thread
English, 1620s
The doublet is high-waisted and lined with red taffeta. The only stiffening is at the collar and in the two belly pieces inside each lower front. Around the tops of the skirts are eyelet holes (47 in all) for the points that were laced through to support the breeches. These were supplemented by twelve metal hooks on the breeches and twelve metal eyelets stitched to the inside waist of the doublet.
268-1891

SHORT CLOAK, silk damask embroidered with silver-gilt thread and cord inlaid and couched work with a raised border
Spanish, second half of the 16th century
The cloak is three-quarters of a circle and has an upright collar. The cut may be compared with a cutting diagram, for a semi-circular cloak called a *ferreulo*, in the tailoring book by Juan de Alcega, *Libro de Geometria, Practica, y Traça*, Madrid, 1589. The tailor has had to increase the pattern by half.
T.202-1965

of the family, the thirteenth Lord Willoughby de Eresby, who succeeded to the title in 1602. The suit has been in the care of the Museum since 1937. At that time the curator responsible for textiles and costume, John Nevinson, in consultation with the 2nd Earl of Ancaster and A. R. Wagner, Portcullis Pursuivant of the College of Arms, concluded that the link with James I could only be traditional. Lord Willoughby de Eresby would not have been eligible to receive Royal perquisites and was not in a position to do so until the reign of Charles I, when he became Lord Great Chamberlain. Although the original wearer cannot be positively identified as either James I or a member of his family, it is

[82]

This 1630s suit—doublet and breeches of white satin—is of particular interest because it is decorated all over with small motifs stamped onto the silk in a manner which was popular in the late sixteenth and early seventeenth century. The doublet has the remains of decorative ribbons around the waist. 348&A-1905   [80]

possible that Lord Willoughby de Eresby himself wore it to the Coronation of James I and that the tradition began there and subsequently became confused with perquisites received when he was Lord Great Chamberlain. In any case the question of identity in no way affects the historical importance of the suit as the earliest one known to be in any collection in this country. The suit is made from Italian uncut plum-coloured velvet. The doublet is cut with a slight peascod, a style which at this time was becoming obsolete.

Another complete suit (not illustrated) dated 1615–20 (T.28& A-1938) was given to the Museum in 1938 by Lady Spickernell.[2] It formed part of the collection of heirlooms belonging to the Cotton family of Etwall Hall, Derbyshire. Other items from the collection had been given in 1937 [see 96]. The suit consists of doublet and breeches of slashed and pinked cream satin, now very fragile, with a correspondingly slashed blue silk taffeta lining mounted over ivory silk taffeta. Fortunately, a pattern has been taken by Miss Janet Arnold, who was able also to date the suit to 1618 and to confirm the association of the suit with the Cotton family by identifying a portrait of Sir Richard Cotton wearing it.[3]

The collection contains four suits of the 1630s–1640s, although only two are strong enough to be shown. Two suits were acquired by purchase in 1905 including [80]; and a third was bought in 1910 [79; see p. 48], together with other seventeenth-century clothes from a Dorset farmhouse. Both the suits illustrated are typical examples of their time, with high waists and lengthening skirts to their doublets, while the breeches are tapered to reach the knee. The three-piece matching suit of slashed yellow satin [79] is one of the most important items in the collection. It can be compared in style with the portrait of Henry Rich, 1st Earl of Holland (1590–1649) from the studio of Daniel Mytens (about 1590–before 1648), inscribed 1632–33, National Portrait Gallery, London. The treatment of the slashing is similar to that shown in a portrait of Sir Philip Sidney (1544–86) by John de Critz, about 1585.[4] The other suit of the same period and similar style [80] is of additional interest because it is decorated all over with small motifs stamped on to the silk.[5] This decorative abuse of expensive textiles in dress was popular in the late sixteenth and early seventeenth century. The doublet of this suit also has the remains of decorative woven ribbons around the waist. Several have survived, from which it is possible to discern their quality and design. There are no ribbons for the seventeenth century in the Textiles collection except those on costume.

The third suit (not illustrated) is very similar in style to no. 80 and is made of white quilted silk. It is believed to have been made up from a quilt because of the style and distribution of the pattern. The fourth, a doublet and breeches of about 1630–40, was also given by Lady Spickernell in 1938. This is made of brown woollen twill and lined throughout with looped cotton shag for additional warmth; but it is now very fragile and the wool is rotting. Deterioration is normal in any textile of that age, but the process is being accelerated by the mordant used in the dye.

Although the main collection of children's clothes is in the Museum of Childhood at Bethnal Green, adult fashion is represented in miniature in children's clothes until the middle of the eighteenth century. Hence the importance of a child's suit dating from the 1630s which is made from

apricot silk with a doublet and open-kneed breeches. There are no complete costumes for the Commonwealth period (1649–60) although there are several individual objects from the 1640s including a doublet and two pairs of open-kneed breeches. These breeches reach but do not fit the knee. One of the most important recent acquisitions has been the suit reputed to have belonged to Prince Rupert, dating from the 1660s [81]. This had formerly belonged to Lord Craven and his family since the seventeenth century. It consists of a doublet and matching cassock and a pair of breeches. The breeches do not match the rest of the outfit, nor are they of comparable quality. Moreover, they are too big at the waist to fit the doublet. Originally the breeches for the suit would have been hooked inside the waistband of the doublet. (It has eyelet holes to take the hooks, which would have been stitched to the waistband of the breeches.) The present breeches have some of the original hooks left, and one replacement.

It is remarkable that any clothes survive at all from this period, but a number of things have prevented the destruction of costumes in private collections. Associations with royalty, weddings, christenings and death may all be significant. Probably the most common reason for preservation has been the popularity of old clothes for amateur theatricals or fancy dress. Professional theatrical costumiers of the past and present have also collected original costumes, and artists collected old clothes for their models. Such uses are a mixed blessing, since the clothes have often been damaged or altered to fit different people. Sometimes, however, clothes have been preserved because of their historic as well as their family interest. This was the case with the Isham Collection from Lamport Hall, Northamptonshire [82]. Negotiations for the purchase of this collection took place in 1899 between Sir Charles Isham (and later Captain Vere Isham) and Seymour Lucas, who acted as a specialist consultant to the Museum. In his report[6] Seymour Lucas referred to an undated memorandum in the family archives:

'In the store room over the kitchen commonly called the Wardrobe are two chests filled with old clothes which the last Sir Justinian and Sir Edward being both lovers of antiquity set a value upon as showing the Fashions of the time; among them are the clothes made for Sir Thomas Isham's Wedding, but Sir Justinian's Lady altered the form of some to make masquerade habits.'

The truth of that last observation has recently been demonstrated. The cuffs of the wedding coat (not illustrated) are of pink silk satin brocaded with silver-gilt threads. The coat itself is white silk brocaded with silver-gilt threads. The white silk can be dated to 1680, Sir Thomas died in 1681, and the pink satin can be dated to the mid-1680s. On examination it can be seen that the pink cuffs have been loosely tacked over existing cuffs which are properly made and finished and which are the same silk as the coat. In addition there is a lady's jacket of the same pink satin as the cuffs which can be dated to the late seventeenth century.

Another advisor to the Museum, Walter Crane, the artist and designer (1845–1915) gave this report in 1900:

'I have seen the Isham Collection of costumes and agree that they are of remarkable historic as well as artistic interest and value, and that such good specimens of the time of Elizabeth are undoubtedly

very rare. The garments are interesting both for their cut and make as well as for the patterned silks and other stuffs of which they are made. They would form a very valuable addition to the specimens of costume already in the Museum and would make possible an instructive exhibition of costumes in the Museum.'

It would be appropriate at this point to acknowledge the importance of textiles in dress. When clothes are acquired for the V & A collection their textiles are given as much consideration as the date and style. Costume specialists are not necessarily fully aware of the significance of textile design and its techniques. The knowledge and expertise of the textile specialist has proved invaluable in dating and giving provenance to both historic and modern dress.

The Eighteenth Century

The eighteenth-century collection includes 102 major items, of which about one-fifth are on display. Although the collection is large it is not evenly distributed: the period 1700–60 is represented by only seventeen objects.

The most characteristic dress for men in the eighteenth century was the suit. The coat, with a method of construction derived from seventeenth-century tailoring, remained basically the same in cut throughout the century. It always consisted of two fronts and two backs, with no waist seam. Only the shape of the coat skirts changed noticeably: they were very full for the first half of the century and later were trimmed away to become what is known today as the 'tail-coat'. Fashion was clearly evident from the material the customer chose. Patterned silks or wools, whether embroidered or woven, changed from season to season.

Until quite recently the only early eighteenth-century man's costume in the collection was a plain light grey wool coat of about 1700. In 1980 and 1982 the Museum was able to buy at auction an early eighteenth-century dress coat and a boy's dress suit. The dress coat is English, about 1700–10 [84], made of buff wool embroidered in silver-gilt thread. It was associated with a Gentleman of the Bedchamber to William III (1689–1702), Thomas Severne (1644–1737). Unfortunately, both the waistcoat and breeches are missing, and the cuffs on the coat have been altered to follow the fashions of 1715–20 or, possibly, much later for fancy dress or amateur theatricals. This coat can be compared with a small portrait figurine, shown here (F.E.32-1981), of a European gentleman made in China at about the same date, 1700–10, and wearing a very similar style of coat, with matching waistcoat and breeches. A shirt was acquired at the same sale which is associated with Henry Watkins, a Gentleman of the Bedchamber to William III, and which is the earliest eighteenth-century shirt in the collection (see also *Shirts and Ties*, pp. 118 and 119).

The other purchase was a suit [83] consisting of coat and breeches of red wool embroidered with silver-gilt thread and made for a boy of about thirteen or fourteen years of age (see opposite). It is English, about 1700–05. The style of the coat and cuffs is similar to that worn by Prince James Francis Edward Stuart in the portrait by François de Troy, 1701, Scottish National Portrait Gallery. The cut of the suit had not been altered even though the coat had had extensive but skilful

PORTRAIT FIGURE of a European, painted composition
Chinese (Canton), about 1720–5
The embroidery on the coat is clearly delineated as well as other details such as the side vents. The figure's campaign wig is more easily seen from the back.
Height: 11½ inches
FE 32-1981

This boy's dress suit of 1700–05 was acquired in 1982. Made in wool embroidered with silver-gilt thread, the coat has been extensively and skilfully repaired, but the cut has not been altered.
T.327&A-1982   [83]

[85]

[86]

Opposite :
The opulent fashions of the early
eighteenth century were characterized
by rich dress silks for suits and
particularly for waistcoats, which were
usually the most colourful item. The
brocaded design of this tabby silk
waistcoat is woven to shape.
T.147&T.148-1964   [87]

repairs at a later date. It complements the man's coat of 1700–10 as it
shows the probable style of the cuffs and breeches.

There are no coats in the collection of the style which is typical of the
1720s, with cuffs shaped to the elbow. For the 1730s–40s there are two
items: a coat and a complete suit. The coat has wide boot-cuff sleeves
that reach the elbow and is of buff corded silk.[7] This coat and the suit are
both very fragile, particularly across the shoulders. The coat is kept in
reserve, but as the suit is of considerable importance it is illustrated here
[85]. It is a unique example of textile design woven to shape for clothing
—a technique which came into use sometime in the early eighteenth
century. (There is a panel for a waistcoat woven to shape in the Royal
Ontario Museum, Toronto, which can be dated to about 1710, and a
waistcoat of about 1720 worn by Colonel Ebenezer Storer and now in
the Museum of Fine Arts in Boston, Mass.) The V & A suit, which is one
of the earliest known examples of a suit made using this method, was
acquired by purchase in 1902 and is complete. The breeches have been
altered or totally remade, possibly early in the nineteenth century. The
silk is identical with the rest of the suit, and there are traces of identical
decoration woven to shape on the pocket flaps. The breeches are cut
with broad front falls and have braces buttons on the waistband.
(Braces were not introduced until the 1790s.) The suit was made
originally for a large man but the breeches were intended for someone
even larger. Both the buff silk coat and this suit are similar in style to
those worn in the painting 'A Group of Virtuosi' (1735), by Gavin
Hamilton, National Portrait Gallery, London.

The 1740s are represented by two superb dress suits of the finest
quality. One is complete and made of wool with contrasting waistcoat
and matching coat and breeches [86]. The other [87; see opposite] consists of a coat of shot silk and a brocaded waistcoat with the decoration
woven to shape. Each suit represents typical fashions of the period. The
wool suit can be compared with that worn by the young man in one of
the illustrations to Samuel Richardson's *Pamela*, 1741, painted by
Joseph Highmore in 1745.[8] The fashion for wearing a rich waistcoat
with a plain coat is seen to advantage in the portrait of Thomas, 9th Earl
of Cassilis, dated 1746, by William Mosman.[9]

The Museum has a comprehensive collection of waistcoats acquired
in their own right because they are of interest as woven or embroidered
textiles as well as fashion (see pp. 117 and 118). At least half a dozen
waistcoats have been dated and identified as being of English design and
manufacture from the pattern book of Maze and Steer of Spitalfields
dating from 1786 to about 1790 (Warner Collection T.384-1972).

There are three eighteenth-century undress nightgowns; two early
ones in the short style and one very late eighteenth-century long gown
(see p. 149). The nightgowns of rich dress silks lined with equally rich
silk or fur which were fashionable from the late seventeenth century are
regrettably not as yet represented in the collection.

Other items of dress are also sparsely represented. There is only one
great coat, from the 1760s, one plain wool coat for everyday wear of the
1770s, and one fustian sporting coat of the mid-eighteenth century.

There are at least twenty-four full dress suits for the period 1770–
1800. Except for their colour and design they appear to be almost in-

This elaborate dress coat and waistcoat of sprigged red silk velvet, embroidered in silver-gilt thread, purl and sequins, would have been worn for ceremonial occasions. It is probably French and dates from the 1760s.
T.28&A-1952   [91]

distinguishable from each other. Throughout this period the full dress suit was becoming more stereotyped in both its cut and its embroidered decoration [99; see p. 60]. The designs for the embroideries were of trailing plants and sprays of flowers which sometimes became very fanciful and were often enriched by the addition of coloured foils and pastes. A vivid description of this type of embroidery is quoted by Anne Buck:

'Lord Sheffield's daughter saw the Arrival of the Duke of Bedford at court in 1791, so grand that, "when he arrived the Guard stood at Arms taking him for the Prince of Wales". The dress he wore on this occasion was a coat and breeches of brown striped silk shot with green, with a white waistcoat. All were embroidered in silver, blue foil and stones in wreaths of flowers for the borders and seams and the ground covered with single brilliants and silver spangles and it was estimated it cost him £500.'[10]

Fashionable colours of the late eighteenth and nineteenth centuries were dark, at least for men's dress. This is reflected in the collection: the suits of 1770–80s are of light shades whereas those of 1790s and early nineteenth century are uniformly of rich dark colours. The decoration became increasingly elaborate and the floral designs more formalized.

Dress and full dress suits are worn by several of the men in the painting 'The Tribuna of the Uffizi', 1772–7/8, in the collection of Her Majesty Queen Elizabeth II. The suits are mainly silk or velvet and some are very elaborate. Some of the men are wearing swords. This was a formality rather than a necessity: the wearing of swords had been discouraged socially and at public gatherings from the 1760s in England, when Beau Nash banned them at the Assembly Rooms in Bath after a series of fights had occurred between some of the wilder young men.

The late eighteenth-century coats are an interesting and varied collection. They date mostly from the very late 1780s to the late 1790s. One may be as late as 1795–1805 [101; see overleaf]. Another coat is the only example which shows the influence of the exaggerated style called 'Incroyable'. This was a fashion much affected by the young and required a rather unkempt and raffish appearance. The coats had very high collars, wide revers and tight sleeves. They were more like great coats in style, being cut straight to meet down the front, and reaching the knees. The coat [100; see overleaf] is cut away in the front in the style of a morning coat but has the exaggerated high collar and wide revers. Unfortunately, it is very faded and although the silk appears to be olive green, inspection of the seams showed that it used to be a shot blue and pink silk. According to Museum records and an article written by the costume historian Francis M. Kelly in 1925,[11] the coat was at that time unfaded, for he describes it:

'We have in the cut-away coat of shot red and blue silk (940-1902) a perfect example of a fashion beloved of the Incroyables of Paris about 1797 . . .'

In another part of his article Mr Kelly compares the display of costume at the London Museum and the Victoria and Albert Museum:

'We have in London accessible to all, two exceptionally fine series of costumes, exemplifying the fashions affected by our forefathers in the seventeenth and eighteenth centuries, with portions of even

This English suit of the 1760s, made from silk which is probably French, is of very fine quality. It was probably worn in the summer for formal occasions.
T.137 to B-1932   [90]

earlier date. I refer of course to those in the Victoria and Albert and the London Museum. The latter has the great advantage of being exhibited in a very large, well-lighted room, with plenty of space; the exhibits, too, are pretty satisfactorily set up, so as to afford a fair general idea of the proportions and forms of the costume

Full dress suits of this type (which is probably French, 1790s) were worn for ceremonial occasions. The silk embroidery on the suit, mainly in satin stitch, is considered to be among the finest in the collection, and its design probably dates from the 1780s.
T.148 to B-1924   [99]

as worn. A very different state of affairs rules at South Kensington, although the collection is in many respects the finer of the two. Here all the pieces, irrespective of rarity or interest, are displayed in overcrowded cases along a narrow, ill-lighted gallery. Coats, doublets, waistcoats and breeches are mounted on wholly inadequate dressmakers' dummies. It is impossible in their present crowded arrangement to get a comprehensive idea of the dresses;

form and proportion are nowise suggested, while the cross-lights upon the glass cases further impede a good view . . . At South Kensington, however, the element of costume *qua* costume appears always to have received what the Germans call 'stepmotherly' treatment, and to have been relegated to the darkest corners and least favourable setting.

It would be a real boon if the authorities could see their way, at least occasionally, to exposing a selection of their finest and rarest pieces in one of the more brightly-lighted halls. Properly mounted in a good light, with plenty of elbow-room and (if possible) so as to be visible from back to front, they would be of great interest and practical use to those who, for one reason or another, are interested in costume.'

It seems that between 1925 and 1962 the authorities heeded Mr Kelly's suggestions with regard to 'brightly-lighted halls', for apart from this coat there are a number of costumes that are now irretrievably faded as a result of being placed in too bright a light for display. It takes only a few weeks for a textile to fade in any bright light. The brighter it is the faster the colours fade. It is for this reason that the level of lighting in the new display is so carefully controlled.

The Nineteenth Century

The collection of nineteenth-century dress is neither large nor comprehensive. The Museum is fortunate in having a fairly wide range of suits and coats for 1800–1850, but there are barely half a dozen for the remainder of the century. The collection is no different from other public collections in this respect.

In September 1908 Mr P. B. Trendall, a representative of the Museum, reported on a visit he made to Mr Francis Coutts, great-grandson of Thomas Coutts (1735–1822), the famous banker. 'I called on Mr Francis Coutts by appointment last Saturday as the Director wished me to ascertain whether he intended to present this Museum with the selected suit of clothes and articles of costume worn by his great-grandfather, which are now exhibited here on loan.'[12]

This cautious reminder resulted in a unique and generous gift not only to the Museum but, ultimately, to other museums in Britain and overseas. (They were the Metropolitan Museum, New York, USA; the Royal Ontario Museum, Toronto, Canada; The Royal Scottish Museum, Edinburgh; Bristol Museum and Art Gallery; and the Bootle, Ipswich, Salisbury, Cheltenham, Leicester and Halifax Museums. All received a black wool suit with a certain number of accessories, except Halifax, which was the last museum to receive a part of the gift.)

The collection came to the V & A in 1907 so that a selection could be made for the loan. It was described by Mr Trendall as consisting of:

'the considerable number of cloth costumes, articles of hosiery and underclothing left by Mr Thomas Coutts at the time of his death, 24th February 1822 . . . The cloth suits are all of plain black and of precisely the same cut,[13] so that only one is necessary for exhibition. The underclothing is interesting as a record of the period, and the items are quite unrepresented in the Museum; the shirts in particular are of fine cambric delicately made . . . The set selected for the

Opposite:
This morning coat of shot silk is a most interesting example of the exaggerated styles of the late 1790s, and with its broad revers and very high collar was possibly influenced by the fashion referred to as 'Incroyable'.
940-1902&T.1082-1913   [100]

[105]

Opposite right :
This fashionable woollen dress coat of
the late 1820s is of particular interest
because of its exaggerated styling,
having thickly padded fronts and sleeves
to accentuate the chest and shoulders.
It is shown here with a very fine pair of
silk 'Cossack' trousers—a style which
was introduced after 1814 when the
Czar came to London.
T.683-1913&T.197-1914   [108]

Museum would be very acceptable representing the domestic costume in England about the time of the Regency and Waterloo. We have only one suit (English; early 19th century) on view, no. 355-1903.'

The Coutts collection was very large and quite comprehensive and for this reason was exceptional. It represented the entire wardrobe of a gentleman of the early 1820s or possibly slightly earlier. There were at least twelve suits, [see 105], forty-six shirts, both with and without frills, fifty-seven items of underwear made of either linen or wool, four 'spotted' nightgowns, [see 103], two plain nightgowns, thirteen pairs of gloves of both wool and leather, ten wigs and three beaver hats. The collection was distributed in 1908 and 1912, so that the Museum finally acquired three suits, several sets of underwear, two of the spotted nightgowns and a variety of accessories.

In retrospect it is frustrating to realize that the Museum authorities calmly divided up a complete and therefore unique wardrobe of clothes. This even-handed behaviour, although highly commendable as an act of disinterested generosity, did result in the loss of an irreplaceable record. Admittedly, the information still exists so that a description of the clothes can be consulted; and, of course, the energetic researcher can visit twelve other museums. But it was rather like having a complete dinner service, the only one of its kind, and dividing it up in the manner of distributing souvenirs.

The clothes worn by Mr Coutts were probably not the height of fashion but rather conservative. There is no mention of any trousers, for instance, in the full list of his clothes. All his suits had breeches. The cut of his coats is consistent with the current fashions: his tailor was probably as conservative as his customer. None of his coats has a waist seam.

The advances in tailoring techniques of the early nineteenth century were concentrated on fit rather than style—which had been the preoccupation of eighteenth-century tailoring. Waist seams evolved from a dart made at the waist to eliminate the crease which appeared when coats lengthened in the body between 1810–20. There is one coat in the collection [107; see opposite] of about 1820 which does have a waist seam. Another innovation which followed as a natural development from the waist seam was the under-arm seam. This allowed for a much better and easier fit to the body of a coat and was introduced between 1820 and 30. The frock coat of about 1828–30 reputed to have been worn by Lord Petersham [109; see overleaf] has both these seams. He was noted for his fashionable tastes and patronized the best tailors, who would have adopted the new methods of cut and fit. The coat is of brown worsted, the waistcoat of brown plush and the 'cossack' trousers of brown striped cotton. Captain Gronow[14] in his reminiscences refers to Lord Petersham's apparent fondness for brown:

'His carriages were unique of their kind; they were entirely brown, with brown horses and harness. The groom, a tall youth, was dressed in a long brown coat reaching to his heels, and a glazed hat with a large cockade. It is said that Petersham's devotion to brown was caused by his having been desperately in love with a very beautiful widow bearing that name.'

The collection of coats and great-coats of the nineteenth century date from 1820–1870s and are very varied, ranging from long cloaked styles to short fitted frock coats. Only one is illustrated here [106; see overleaf], the 'pearl' of the collection, a very dressy caped wool frock coat of the finest quality, about 1820. It is cut with a waist seam but no under-arm seam. Similar styles are illustrated in fashion plates of the time.[15] A very fashionable dress coat of the late 1820s [108; see below],

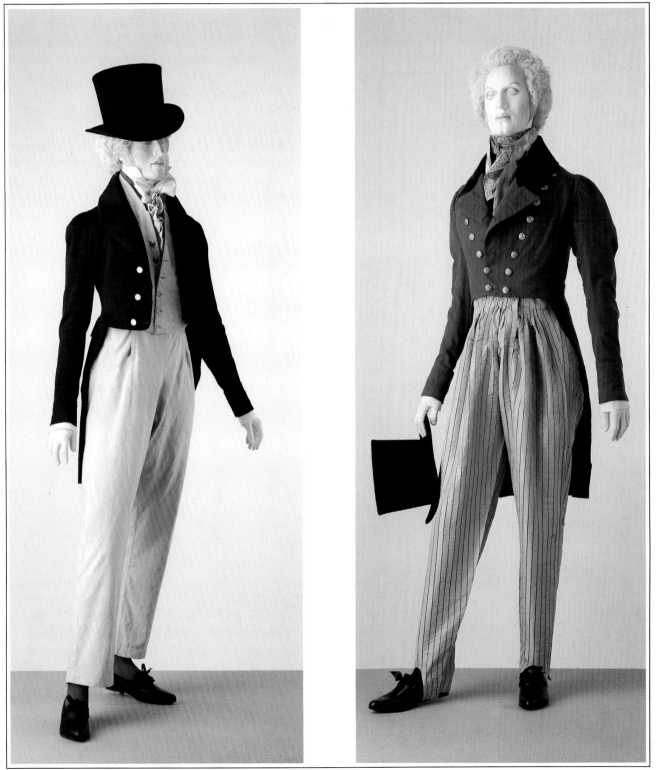

] [108]

[106]

[109]

although of inferior quality to the other 1820s items, is of interest because of its exaggerated styling, having thickly padded fronts and sleeves to accentuate the chest and shoulders. The collar has been deepened to conform to the broad roll of the 'shawl' collar popular in the late 1820s and early 1830s. Worn with this coat is a very fine pair of silk 'cossack' trousers. The Museum has a number of these trousers, the best examples being nos [103], [108] and [109] (pp. 150, 63 and 64).

Most of the early nineteenth-century trousers in the collection are made of cotton in light colours and date from the 1820s and 1830s. They are high-waisted and supported by braces. The style is derived from boys' skeleton suits of the late eighteenth and early nineteenth century. A skeleton suit for a child consisted of a tightly-fitted jacket with decorative rows of buttons down the fronts from shoulders to waist. The ankle-length trousers buttoned onto the jacket around the waist; they usually had whole or split-falls and were often made of cotton.

Children's fashions from the 1760s had become very simple and, as a result, sensible and comfortable to wear. This reflected one aspect of the social revolution which was taking place at the end of the eighteenth century, when established traditions and ideas were being challenged. Jean Jacques Rousseau's *Emile*, 1762, had a profound influence on children's upbringing and dress in England. These styles proved to be so attractive and comfortable that as boys grew into men they preferred to continue wearing them. Trousers were worn for informal daytime occasions and were not accepted as formal dress until after 1817.

Both the dress coat and trousers of [108] and [107], respectively, formed part of a very large and generous gift of Messrs Harrods in 1913. In May of that year Baroness d'Erlanger drew to the attention of the V & A's Director, Sir Cecil Smith, the fact that a large collection of mainly English costumes was at that moment being offered for sale to an American by an English portrait painter, Mr Talbot Hughes. In a long and explicit report in August Cecil Smith wrote:

'The American in question whose name I am not allowed to disclose but who is a well-known owner of a large store in America was intending to visit London for the purpose of purchasing the collection. It was his intention to exhibit it in his store in America and subsequently to present it to the Metropolitan Museum of New York. It was obviously of the greatest importance that this unique collection of English costumes, which are very difficult to find and can probably never be replaced, should not be allowed to leave the country. As we have no funds available, I tried to interest private benefactors, but only with partial success. At the last moment, however, it occurred to me that what could be done in America might equally be done in London, and I approached Mr Burbridge (Messrs Harrods' manager), with the result that Messrs Harrods' directors expressed themselves willing to consider the proposal favourably. I learnt, however, that a difficulty would present itself to them in that by their articles of association they are precluded from making presents, and at first they wished to offer it to us as a permanent loan. After some discussion I persuaded them to withdraw this and to make the gift absolute. . .[16]'

Smith summed up this report with some very pertinent comments

concerning the importance of historical dress in museum collections:

'The history of English costume as a study is engaging more and more attention today. The series we already possess is in constant use by students, not only for purposes connected with literature and the drama, but also by practical workers in the trade. The scientific study of dressmaking is now taken up, I understand, as a subject in schools and institutions, and there is a growing tendency to adopt old forms for present-day wear. For these reasons I regard it as essential that our collection should be as complete as possible, and should be given adequate space in the Museum.'

Negotiations progressed, complicated by the agreement to allow Messrs Harrods to exhibit the collection in their store before officially handing the costume over to the Museum. In November 1913 Cecil Smith wrote another report:

'I called by appointment on Mr Burbridge today. He showed me in the exhibition of costumes a large series which Messrs Harrods have acquired since the exhibition was first mooted, and which are independent of the Talbot Hughes collection. I understand from him that a firm in Bond Street formed this series with the intention of having a rival exhibition and Messrs Harrods bought the whole series largely in order to prevent this.'

The Talbot Hughes collection numbered over 800 items and the other collection over 100. These were offered by Messrs Harrods for inclusion with the rest of the collection and the Museum duly accepted both. The additional group of costumes proved to be of considerable importance and the Museum was very appreciative of the great generosity of Messrs Harrods.

In a further act of generosity, Messrs Harrods donated the funds received from the sale of their catalogue of the collection to the Middlesex Hospital.

Considering the trouble the Museum went through to acquire this collection, Francis M. Kelly's comments in his article for the *Connoisseur* twelve years later are rather unfortunate:

'The fullest acknowledgement, of course, was due from the authorities to Messrs Harrods for their generous gift; unfortunately, however, the importance of this latter was, inadvertently no doubt, unduly magnified at the expense of the already existing collections . . . item for item, the Hughes collection is far inferior to its companions.'[17]

Mr Kelly was perhaps too stringent in his opinions. It would be fairer to say that much of the Hughes collection had been well-worn. Nevertheless, it includes some rare examples of very stylish men's dress which the Museum is very pleased to have in the collection. For instance, of the two pairs of fashionable late eighteenth-century knitted breeches in the collection, one pair came with Messrs Harrods Gift [101].

The quantity of men's dress in the Hughes and Harrods collection was comparatively small. The costumes were mostly from the eighteenth and early nineteenth centuries, and there were none at all from the second half of the nineteenth century. The Museum authorities were not as alert to the importance of contemporary dress as they were to

[113]

[114]

Opposite :
A variation of the morning coat, the
so-called 'University' coat, with
sharply-angled fronts, was introduced
in the 1870s. This one, in cotton
velveteen, and shown with tight-
bottomed woollen trousers, dates from
1873–5.
T.3-1982&T.58-1933   [112]

historic dress. This partly accounts for the unrepresentative collection of men's dress for the period between 1850–1970. Most examples of fashions for this period were not acquired until the 1960s and 1970s.

The collection lacks any examples of the early lounge suit styles which appeared between 1850 and 1900. The usefulness and comfort of this suit must account for its scarcity in most costume collections. There are no examples of any of the suits advocated by the Healthy and Artistic Dress Union founded in 1890,[18] or the 'Sanitary Woollen Suits' designed by Dr Gustav Jaeger. A notable follower of Dr Jaeger's principles was George Bernard Shaw.[19]

The mid-nineteenth century is represented by an American outfit, a dress coat and trousers, given by Captain Raymond Johnes in 1965, a descendant of the original owner [111; see p. 151]; the waistcoat is not associated with it. There are several more coats and one pair of trousers in the reserve collection. The only coat of the 1860s and two short morning coats of the 1870s [including 112] were acquired as recently as 1982 and are the first examples of these styles in the collection. There were already frock coats for 1871 [113], acquired in 1947, and another for 1874 which also had a matching waistcoat was acquired in 1960. Neither outfit has its original trousers. There is one evening suit for the 1880s [114]—the earliest evening suit in the collection. It illustrates the fashion of silk-faced lapels which still had the button-stand around the edge. This was a feature on early nineteenth-century dress coats where a separate strip of cloth was added along the edges of the lapels and fronts to take the buttons and buttonholes. It gradually became obsolete but the stand remained on evening dress coats until the 1890s.

The 1890s are represented by a cream striped flannel suit of the type worn for informal summer dress. These light-coloured flannel suits became popular at the end of the nineteenth century and continued to be worn in the early twentieth century.

The Twentieth Century

As has been pointed out already no attempt was formerly made by the Museum authorities to collect contemporary clothes. The bulk of the men's dress collection for the twentieth century has been acquired since the 1960s. In future the Museum hopes to maintain as up to date and representative a collection as possible.

The clothes for the period 1900–20 are rather sparse, consisting of three day suits, several morning and evening coats or suits and an interesting range of very good quality overcoats. There is a very stylish overcoat for 1906 [116; see overleaf], which was acquired by the original owner as a driving coat. He was Paul Cocteau, the brother of Jean Cocteau (1889–1963), and, according to the donors, Sir Philip and Lady Joubert, he preferred to buy his sporting clothes in England as he considered them to be of the best quality. The interest in driving at this time had influenced the design of such overcoats. They were usually very long and often made with pleats at the sides with double overlaps at the front and back vent. All were intended to keep the driver warm and dry. Elizabeth Ewing writes:

'It was in the early 1900s that the motor car made its first inroads into the "carriage trade". It was as significant an event in social

[116]

Right :
Light coloured suits became popular
from about the 1890s, and matching
coat and trousers ('dittos') were
accepted dress for summer sports and
holidays. The cut of the double-
breasted striped flannel suit of 1904 is
derived from the earlier 'reefer' coat,
usually worn for sailing.
T.159&A-1969   [115]

history as in scientific and mechanical development. Its effect on
clothing was immediate and long lasting. As the first cars were open
to the elements they called for new kinds of protective outerwear,
the most important of which were new varieties of fur coats for
both men and women.'[20]

The Museum's collection does not have any fur motoring coats. There are two overcoats with fur-trimmed collars of beaver and astrakhan, and one of them is also lined with black seal musquash; but neither of these is a motoring coat. It is possible that complete fur coats have not survived, subject as they are to attack by pests when both the fur and the skin dry out.

The earliest suit, acquired in 1969, is a cream striped flannel summer suit [115] similar to the one for the 1890s but double-breasted instead of single-breasted and in better condition. In 1960, the Executors of the estate of Lady Beerbohm gave items of dress which originally formed part of the wardrobe of Sir Max Beerbohm (1872–1956). These included various accessories and two of the earliest lounge suits in the collection, both of about 1918. A superb overcoat of black wool dated 1902 may be the one worn by him in the portrait painted by Sir William Nicholson, dated 1905, now in the National Portrait Gallery, London. The lounge suits are both of the same cut, one of grey wool pin-stripe [118] and the other a brown wool stripe. They can be compared in style with one illustrated in *The Tailor and Cutter*, August 15, 1918, p. 407, figure 9488. These clothes are of very good quality and although they have been well worn they have been most carefully looked after.

From the 1920s there are just two full evening suits [including 119]. This may be a rather old-fashioned suit since it has a black waistcoat instead of the usual white one which has been worn with evening dress since the late nineteenth century. There is one gentleman's city suit by Leslie and Roberts, 1929. The only other item is quite informal, a punting outfit of about 1929 by 'Carefree', worn and given by Mr Aubrey Esson-Scott, who had been World Punting Champion 1929–34 and was a member of the Thames Punting Club. He also gave a number of other items from his wardrobe. All these clothes came under the 'umbrella' of the Beaton Collection and were shown in the exhibition 'Fashion: an Anthology' which celebrated Cecil Beaton's gift to the Museum of an enormous collection of what he considered to be fashionable dress of the very best quality and design. The exhibition is described more fully in the next essay. The number of men's clothes was small but significant and represented a range of styles from 1910–1967.

The 1930s were represented by one shooting suit, before Mr Esson-Scott donated a lounge suit by Ward and Co. of 1932, and two very fashionable evening suits of 1930–33, both by Anderson and Shepherd. One is made of blue-black barathea; this colour was introduced for men's evening dress in the early 1930s instead of black because it looked better in artificial light. The other suit comprises a white mess jacket, waistcoat and evening trousers, a fashion which appeared in the early 1930s. Mr Esson-Scott also gave another shooting suit, including the boots, and a superb black wool overcoat dating from 1931, by Pleydell and Smith, as well as a morning suit from the same year, the coat made by Leslie and Roberts and the trousers by Pleydell and Smith. For his shirts Mr Esson-Scott went either to Turnbull and Asser or to Morgan and Ball.

There were no other major acquisitions of clothes from the 1930s between 1972 and 1983, when the Museum accepted separate gifts of two dinner suits of the early 1930s. Clothes of the 1920s and 1930s are

[120]

[121]

not very common in dress collections. The gift of Mr Esson-Scott was therefore not only generous but most significant. Now and again a light-weight summer suit survives, but rarely in good condition. The same can be said of that traditional English garment, the Harris tweed suit. These do survive but have become so worn and faded either by the original owner or by succeeding generations that they cannot be accepted.

A typical accessory of the 1920s and 1930s only recently acquired is the knitted pullover. These garments became very popular from the 1920s and were mostly worn for informal or sporting occasions. The Museum now has a sleeveless pullover in a Fair Isle pattern given by Mr Lamb, a Friend of the V & A, in 1980. A long-sleeved Fair Isle sweater which had belonged to General Sir Walter Kirke, who wore it in the 1920s when playing golf, was given by Mrs Kirke in 1982. The sweater is worn with the suit of 1940 [120].

There were no men's clothes of the 1940s before 1971–72, when Cecil Beaton received a gift from HRH the Duke of Windsor while collecting fashionable dress for his exhibition 'Fashion: an Anthology'. This was a startling but fashionable mustard-coloured check wool suit, needless to say, in the Glen Urquhart or Prince of Wales check [120]. Since it had been made before rationing restricted quantities of material used in clothing, the trousers had turn-ups.

When rationing was introduced in 1942 Hugh Dalton, President of the Board of Trade, announced a series of measures to take effect from 1 May that year. All men's jackets were to be single-breasted, with no more than three pockets and only three buttons at the front; buttons on the cuffs, whether of metal or leather, were banned, and so were fancy belts. Waistcoats could only have two pockets; trousers had to have nineteen-inch wide legs and elastic waistbands were forbidden. All this was accepted, but the prohibition of turn-ups caused an outcry from the tailors. Norman Longmate writes:

> 'In March 1943 a nation-wide deputation begged Dalton to restore men's trousers to their former glory and immaculately-turned-out M.P.s voiced in Parliament "the serious dissatisfaction the regulations were causing to business and professional men".'[21]

Dalton remained firm: 'There can be,' he said, 'no equality of sacrifice in this war. Some must lose lives and limbs; others only the turn-ups on their trousers.'

Clothes had to be purchased with coupons and from 1 June 1941 everyone received sixty-six coupons to last twelve months. A man's raincoat or overcoat was valued at sixteen coupons, a coat or blazer at thirteen; trousers or a shirt at eight; underpants at four; and handkerchiefs one or two. As the war progressed rationing became more stringent. Whereas the first issue of coupons lasted twelve months the next issue was adjusted to sixty and had to last for fifteen months. By 1945 the allowance was reduced to just forty-one for a year.

The Museum now has a number of Utility suits, all acquired either by gift or purchase since 1981. Except for one suit they have never been worn and still have their manufacturer's tickets stitched to them. The exception is a blue wool pin-stripe [121] purchased by the donor's

mother in April 1945, at Selfridge's sale. Mr Neuhofer continued to wear the suit until he gave it to the Museum in 1982. There are also various accessories with the Utility label, such as shirts and one pair of practically unworn shoes originally purchased by the donor, Mr Austin, just after the war.

In 1949, two years after the arrival of the New Look for women, clothes rationing controls were lifted for the majority of garments. The relaxation of tiresome restrictions also stimulated men's post-war fashions for they, like women, were ready for a change from shabby austerity. A so-called 'Edwardian' style evolved which favoured a high-buttoned, tightly fitted jacket with narrow tapered trousers, a short fitted overcoat with velvet collar, a bowler hat and an umbrella. It was thought to be the antithesis of both uniforms and Utility dress. In fact, it bore a great resemblance to the civilian dress usually adopted by Guards officers of the foot regiments, with some sartorial innovations such as cuffs on the jacket and trousers. The 1950s is represented in our collection by three suits, one of which [122; see p. 153] is in the distinctive 'Edwardian' style. Dated 1951, it is a considerable rarity, since very few appear to have survived. The fashion is supposed to have influenced the clothes worn by 'Teddy Boys', although their interpretation required a much looser fit and had accentuated shoulders—to present a 'masculine' image. The other suits of 1955 and 1959 were gifts of Mr Hubert Viti in 1970 in a collection of clothes mainly of the early 1960s. The Executors of Cecil Beaton gave some of his own outfits, one of which was a suit of 1959. The remainder were all from the 1960s and include the only Pierre Cardin Boutique overcoat in the collection. Despite the considerable importance of Cardin as an innovative designer for men's as well as women's dress there is only one other item of his in the V & A collection of men's dress.

The period 1960–80 is well represented, with a wide range of styles and garments from traditional bespoke tailoring of the early 1960s to the colourful designer styles of the late 1960s and continuing into the more mature and sober early 1970s through to the relaxed casuals of the early 1980s. This covers the time when international *couturiers* first entered the field of men's clothing and turned it into fashionable dress. Previously, it had been the realm of the tailors and to a certain extent the chain store and wholesale manufacturers. They had produced well-made but conservative clothes suitable for the professional and business man. The first sign of this change in men's fashions came in the early 1960s. Rupert Lycett Green opened his shop 'Blades' in London in 1962. His aim was to combine the excellence of bespoke tailoring with good design. This proved a considerable success, attracting a clientèle of young, fashionable men-about-town who liked the well-designed tailored look. There are several items in the collection by 'Blades', one given by Rupert Lycett Green to the Beaton Collection. This is an evening suit of cream figured silk in the 'Nehru' style, dating from 1968. A very fine cream linen suit of 1972 [128] was given by David Mlinaric (who also designed the interior of 'Blades'). The Beaton Collection includes some important men's clothes of the 1960s. The 'Cosmos' space age outfit of 1967 by Pierre Cardin [123] was considered by Cardin himself to be the most representative of his designs up to 1967. There were also two

This double-breasted suit was made in 1968, when psychedelic colours were at their most popular. The printed corduroy is an American furnishing fabric designed by Hexter; the suit was designed by Mr Fish of London.
T.310&A-1979   [126]

evening outfits by Michael Fish, one given by him and the other by the Earl of Lichfield; both can be dated to about 1969–70.

The importance of the Beaton Collection has been rather over-shadowed in recent years by the number and variety of gifts from individuals who have most generously given their clothes to the Museum. In 1977 Mr Aubrey gave two fine examples of the so-called 'Nehru' suit to the collection [124], both designed by Gilbert Feruch and dated 1967. This gift was followed in 1978 by another splendid collection of the late 1960s and early 1970s from Anthony Powell. Among his suits and accessories was a safari suit designed by Yves St Laurent of about 1970 [127]. This is still the only outfit in the collection of men's clothes by this inventive and distinguished designer.

In the following year, 1979, the collection was enriched by the addition of two separate gifts, one from Sir Roy Strong and the other from David Mlinaric, with more clothes of the late 1960s and early 1970s. These men each have a strong and individual sense of dress yet each is totally different. Their collections are too large to itemize here, but in the selection given by Sir Roy Strong there is a suit by Mr Fish and a midi-overcoat by Village Gate, both of about 1967 [125; see p. 75]. Another suit by Mr Fish, a printed corduroy in psychedelic colours of about 1968 [126] is included in the collection from David Mlinaric. David Shilling made a generous gift in 1983 of most of his wardrobe of the 1970s and some of the early 1980s. This collection reflects the movement towards light-weight, unstructured styles and the popularity of separates and casual clothes which have dominated men's fashions for the past ten years.

The Museum has thus acquired within a few years a unique collection that reflects the variety and richness of men's dress since the 1960s.

Another addition to the collection in 1983 was a selection of both wool and leather sports jackets of the mid-1960s and early 1970s. Included with them was an all-in-one suit of black wool jersey, a short-lived fashion of about 1970. Although the style has subsequently re-appeared as fashionable boiler-suits derived from parachute or sky-diver suits made of cotton, these are mostly worn by women. The all-in-one suit had been conceived by Ruben Torres in 1967[22] and Tom Gilbey predicted that a fashion for 1970 would be a sleeveless one. These designers may already have been aware of the fact that an all-in-one suit had already been designed and worn as early as 1907 by Edgar Jepson (1863–1938). He described it with enthusiasm in his autobiography:

'I had always resented the unreasonableness of men's clothes, especially their unreasonableness in the matter of buttons. No man can cover himself decently from the eyes of his fellows without buttoning over twenty buttons . . . I had the suit made by my own tailor . . . I got a very good line from the armpit to the ankle, and it was astonishing how few people perceived that I was wearing a one-piece suit till their attention was drawn to the fact by the Press. Also I had a like suit made for Selwyn [his son] . . . the suit was carica-tured . . .'[23]

Bringing the collection completely up-to-date are two important outfits given by leading British designers. A lounge suit of 1983 by

Tommy Nutter [129; see p. 155] of grey wool chalk-stripe is made with the stripes horizontal, an imaginative treatment of a familiar fabric. This is in keeping with Mr Nutter's belief in using classical tailoring methods in a creative way. The other, and most recent, gift is a punk outfit of 1982 by Vivienne Westwood.

About a third of the twentieth-century collection is illustrated here, and is as representative as the collection permits. The collection does not yet have any clothes by the important Italian designers who have been leaders of fashion for the past ten years or more. The greatest weakness in the collection however lies in the late nineteenth and early twentieth centuries. These were times when there was little regard for or incentive to preserve contemporary material. The tendency indeed was to despise the artifacts of one's own time. The clothes which are least represented are also some of the most interesting to historians, the useful and practical items of dress—in particular the lounge suit. The earlier periods were preserved to a large extent because of their rich and beautiful materials which commanded a certain interest and respect.

Happily the attitude to dress is being reformed and contemporary clothes are being saved. It is very likely that through the generosity of the public as well as designers and *couturiers* the Museum will be able to acquire a comprehensive collection of fashionable menswear from the 1960s onwards which will demonstrate the development of fashion to future generations.

1 V & A RPs 1865/26195
2 J. L. Nevinson, 'A New Suit', *Connoisseur*, June 1949, pp. 99–101
3 Janet Arnold, 'Sir Richard Cotton's Suit', *Burlington Magazine*, CXV, No. 842, 1973, pp. 236–9
4 Roy Strong, *Tudor and Jacobean Portraits*, HMSO, 1969, 2 vols, plate 574
5 A similar suit can be seen in the painting by Dirk van Sandvoort, about 1635, Rijksmuseum. Illustrated in Mila Contini, *Fashion*, Hamlyn, 1965, p. 150
6 V & A RPs 1899/28199 and 93624
7 Norah Waugh, *The Cut of Men's Clothes*, Faber, 1964; diag. XVIII, p. 64
8 Norah Waugh, *ibid.*, plate 10
9 Ellis Waterhouse, *The Dictionary of British 18th Century Painters*, Antique Collectors Club, 1981, p. 250, left.
10 Anne Buck, *Dress in 18th Century England*, Batsford, 1979, p. 21
11 Francis M. Kelly, 'Costume Collection and South Kensington Exhibits', *Connoisseur*, April 1, 1925, pp. 217–26, p. 218

12 V & A RPs 1907/5535
13 In fact both morning and dress coat styles were represented and are included in the collection acquired for the V & A
14 Abridged by John Raymond, *The Reminiscences and Recollections of Captain Gronow*, Bodley Head, 1964, p. 202
15 Norah Waugh, *op. cit.*, plate 206
16 V & A RPs 1913/4054/3931/4023/5728/ 5816
17 Francis M. Kelly, *op. cit.*
18 Henry Holiday, 'Men's, Women's and Children's Dress', *Aglaia*, No. 2, Spring 1894, pp. 9–20
19 Alison Gernsheim, *Fashion and Reality 1840–1914*, Faber, 1963, plate 163
20 Elizabeth Ewing, *Fur in Dress*, Batsford, 1981, p. 119
21 Norman Longmate, *The Way We Lived Then*, Arrow, 1971.
22 Illustrated in Rodney Bennet-England, *Dress Optional*, Peter Owen, 1967, pp. 95, 226
23 Edgar Jepson, *Memories of an Edwardian*, Richards, 1937, pp. 87–8 and plate facing p. 87

Midi and maxi-coats, worn by both men and women, were introduced from 1966. The style was derived from military coats at a time when there was a craze for wearing second-hand uniforms. The herring-bone tweed overcoat of 1967, designed by Village Gate, is shown here with a Mr Fish gaberdine suit, a Take Six kipper tie and a Herbert Johnson velours hat. T.190&T.192&A-1979   [125]

Women's Dress since 1900

VALERIE D. MENDES

The Museum's collection of fashionable dress is particularly rich in its twentieth-century holdings, including as it does thousands of clothes and accessories, the very best of which are now on permanent display. It would be an impossible task to explore the collection's wide-ranging diversity in any detail in the space available here, but the following selection is intended to outline the development of modish dress from 1900 to the present and to offer a survey of the growth of the Museum's collection, pointing out its strengths and weaknesses. As might be expected this part of the Department of Textiles and Dress has a relatively recent history. It pivots on two major collections – the Heather Firbank Collection of clothes dating from about 1905 to 1920, purchased in 1960, and the Cecil Beaton Collection, acquired in 1971, with its emphasis on post-1920 *couture*. In 1979 the collection was given a boost by the gift of twenty-five outfits for winter 1979 by leading British designers.

The collection of twentieth-century trimmings and dress fabric samples is not as extensive as the dress collection but it is a vital adjunct. Swatches and sample books, often usefully annotated, reveal the entire range of patterns and colours and have the added advantage of being compact and fairly easy to store. The records show that, in spite of occasional experiments with man-made fibres, top designers favour natural fabrics, especially costly silks, wools and linens. The collection has been improved recently – for example a group of woollen pattern books from the 1920s to the 1960s from William Brown and Sons Ltd was acquired in 1981; a selection of *couture* lace sample books, mainly of the 1960s, was given in the same year, and, since 1975, Liberty's have given their dress fabric swatches on a seasonal basis.

Since 1971 the Department has continued to fill gaps and expand the early areas of the collection as well as to acquire contemporary dress on a regular basis. The present policy is to continue collecting fashionable clothes by established designers. This approach is guided by various considerations, principally the practical question of storage and display space and the existence of other British costume museums with complementary policies.

This 1905 travelling gown, worn by Viscountess Brackley after her wedding in St Margaret's Church, Westminster, shows how designers of the period lavishly adorned plain cloth with a variety of rich laces and trimmings. T.421-H-1977

The Early Twentieth Century : 1900–World War I

Unfortunately, the early 1900s collection, with a few notable exceptions, is neither extensive nor outstanding. This is the result of a number of factors, but is mainly due to acquisition policy and availability of objects. The Department was not collecting systematically in this area during the period before 1914. An opportunity was lost in 1913 when Harrods brought their exhibition of the Talbot Hughes collection of historic dresses up-to-date with a sequence of modern clothes; these were not included in the collection when it was presented to the Museum. Female clothing from 1900 to about 1907 continued the late nineteenth-century outline with its dependence on tight corsets. A separate bodice and skirt were usual, and although numerous bodices have survived, the accompanying skirts have often vanished. They were composed of many yards of material which could be unpicked and re-styled to suit later fashions. In contrast, the bodices, attached to complex, boned foundations, were intricate constructions with decorative insertions or overlays. It was unrewarding to dissect these garments – at best one could re-use the elaborate trimmings—but the small, shaped pieces had to be discarded. Occasionally the Museum benefits from those who have abandoned laborious re-workings. Attempts had been made to unpick the bodice of the 1905 travelling gown [133; see p. 76], and the skirt's pleats had been opened, but there the operation stopped. It was vital to save this unique and fully documented example, and after consultation with the Textiles Conservation Department it was decided to return it to its former glory. Mrs Marion Kite devoted over three months to its painstaking conservation and now once again it is a supremely graceful Edwardian costume.

Sadly, twentieth-century dress does not mean more durable dress. Fragile materials favoured at the beginning of the century have proved especially vulnerable. Even cherished clothes for special occasions, such as the two Royal ball gowns [130 and 131], are not immune. The figured silk and the velvet of the main garments are sturdy, but much of the frail trimming has vanished, necessitating careful replacement. Weighted silks prove a great problem. They were popular for petticoats and linings though, fortunately, they were employed less frequently for dresses themselves. Soaking in a compound of tin gave these silks a fuller 'handle' and increased their weight. Low levels of weighting were accepted by the trade but, in order to make a quick profit, some unscrupulous manufacturers exceeded the amounts, resulting in weakened silks which eventually disintegrated. Many dresses from the first quarter of the twentieth century in the collection have had their shattered linings replaced or sandwiched between layers of fine crêpeline. In view of these problems it is always exciting to acquire unaltered, complete garments. In 1960 the Museum was given an excellent collection of twentieth-century dress which included such a rare survival—the teagown [132]. Entirely intact, it offers insight into luxurious 'at-home' wear of about 1900. Teagowns were essential to gracious living; most reliable fashion journals carried regular reports on the latest designs and how they must be worn: 'at five o'clock they will don the picturesque teagown and adopt an air of drooping languor which savours of mystery,

[130]

[131]

while striking an Oriental note of passion and colour.'[1] Teagowns make frequent appearances in Edwardian fiction, while biographies of those who were young during the early 1900s abound with nostalgic references to these garments: 'But she spent a long time each day in her boudoir, in a loose negligée, or teagown, without stays, smoking a Turkish cigarette and putting her feet up. "In a teagown one feels less pursed up," she would explain. She would become petulant when the time came for the maid to squeeze her into her tight dress.'[2]

The nucleus of the pre-1920 collection is the collection of high quality clothes worn by Miss Heather Firbank (1888–1954), daughter of the affluent M.P., Sir Thomas Firbank, and sister of the novelist Ronald Firbank. In 1960 the Museum acquired a large cross-section of her wardrobe—well over one hundred items including dresses, costumes and all types of accessories. In 1921 her expensive clothes, bought from leading London houses such as Lucile, Redfern and Mascotte, were packed into trunks and put into storage, where they remained for the next thirty-five years. It was later the Museum's good fortune to gain this record in excellent condition of a modish and wealthy woman's taste extending over a period of some fifteen years, from about 1905 to

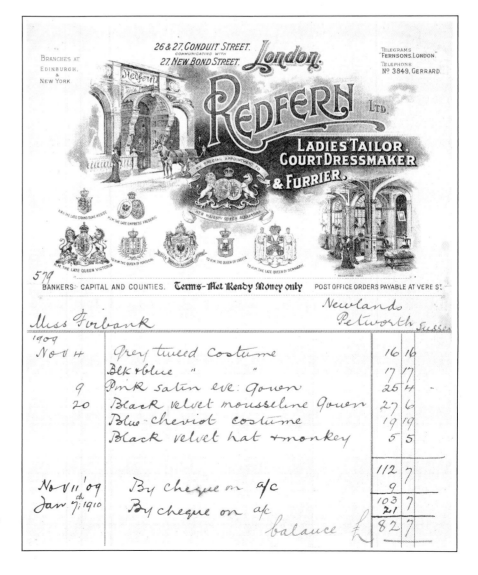

Bill for various items bought by Miss Heather Firbank from Redfern Ltd., 1909–1910.

[135]

[140]

Opposite left :
Lucile (Lady Duff Gordon), the
designer of this draped satin evening
dress of 1912–13, wrote: 'For me there
was a positive intoxication in taking
yards of shimmering silks, laces airy as
gossamer and lengths of ribbons,
delicate and rainbow-coloured, and
fashioning of them garments so lovely
that they might have been worn by
some princess in a fairy tale.'
T.31-1960   [143]

1920. In 1960 the bulk of the collection, supplemented by Ronald Firbank manuscripts, bills and family photographs, was exhibited in the Museum.[3] Miss Firbank was young, 'had beauty, and she adorned it with exquisite clothes of a heather colour to complement her name.'[4] She was devoted to good clothes and amassed a fashion file of clippings from newspapers—among them the *Evening Standard and St James's Gazette* and *The Sketch*. Her taste was excellent but restrained, and mainly London-based. The avant-garde was avoided: for example she did not indulge in any of Paul Poiret's innovatory creations, although doubtless she could have afforded his prices.

The strength of the Firbank Collection lies in the distinctive sense of style which Miss Firbank brought to its acquisition, and to which she remained dedicated. No object appears to be a mistaken purchase or a reckless experiment, though Miss Firbank was never a prudent 'follower of fashion'. Her bills are evidence of the large amounts of money she spent, and her extravagant love of fine apparel sometimes led her into excesses. In October 1924 her brother 'assisted her in the payment of an overdue bill of £40 owed to her dressmaker, Lucile'.[5] One of the earliest dresses in her collection is the unlabelled striped cotton summer gown, 1905–6 [135], worn when she was about seventeen. It established the style of simple uncluttered lines which her later clothes follow; and for summer wear she remained faithful to under-stated pastel-coloured linen and cotton day dresses. The striped gown is the type of crisp, fresh-looking dress that women's magazines recommended for those apparently idyllic Edwardian leisure activities—country picnics, beach promenades or water-parties. It is the epitome of early 1900s fashionable dress. Underneath, a tight-laced, straight-fronted corset would have curved the body. These sinuous lines are exaggerated by the bodice which pouches over the waist, and by the skirt's top-stitched pleats which follow the contours to the thighs and then fall freely to a wide hem—which is above ground level, as this dress was intended to allow some freedom of movement. The high, uncomfortable, boned collar ensures that the head is held alert and aloof.

Well-connected, fashionable women had to own a bewildering array of clothes in order to be dressed *à la mode* for every occasion—visiting, travelling, walking, boating and shooting; they needed gowns for races, garden parties, receptions, dinners and balls; teagowns for 'at home' wear and, of course, a multitude of accessories and under-garments. Miss Firbank possessed such a wide-ranging wardrobe which included some magnificent hats and handsome tailor-made costumes. The 1911 grey worsted ensemble [140] was purchased from the famous Lucile, as was the draped satin evening dress of 1912–13 [143]. Lucile (Lady Duff Gordon) was an accomplished self-publicist: 'I had a message for women I dressed. I was the first dressmaker to bring joy and romance into clothes, I was a pioneer.'[6] Before the outbreak of World War I she had established branches in London, New York and Paris. She had a long and successful career which is represented in the Museum by a small but varied collection of her work. Among her early triumphs were the stage costumes for Lily Elsie in *The Merry Widow* which created a widespread vogue for her 'Merry Widow' hat. She held mannequin parades of her models and calling them 'gowns of emotion' she 'gave

[148]

Right :
Fortuny's distinctive creations were
worn by *avant garde* beauties in Europe
and America from the 1910s to the
1930s, and there has been a recent
revival of interest in his work. This
satin 'Delphos' dress of about 1920 is
inspired by the Ionic chiton.
T.423&T.424-1976   **[148]**

them all names and personalities of their own'. We do not know the
names of the meticulously finished worsted costume or the satin evening
dress but they serve to illustrate Lady Duff Gordon's immense versatility.

Three dresses of the years 1908–13 [136, 139 and 144] indicate the
pre-war development of luxury evening wear. The first [136; see over-
leaf] is a gown which bridges the gap between the pronounced curves and
tiny waist of the high Edwardian silhouette and its replacement—the
pillar-like form with a high waist popularly described as 'Empire' and

[136]

[139]

'Directoire'. Many elements, including the pouched bodice and the full, trained skirt, belonged to the early years of the century; but the waist was starting to rise and deepen. This change culminated in the vertical lines of the 1910–11 Worth evening dress [139]. The gown was no longer divided into two parts but, in spite of the tubular broad-waisted outline, corsets were still worn by all except the most advanced women. Bodices remained structurally complex and boned. This dress has the usual sturdily woven twill waist stay with the Worth signature in grey.

Waist stays were, and still are, vital dressmaking aids. Throughout the twentieth century they vary in type, but basically they remain woven bands which usually fasten with hooks and eyes and anchor the garment, preventing it from becoming dislodged by movement. They also assist in the garment's hang, and take part of the weight of the skirt. They are often a boon to curators because they provide designers with an area to attach a house label easily and sometimes the model number, date and owner's name, without causing an unwelcome bump.

Lacking a label, but nevertheless a top quality product, the silk chiné evening gown [144] sums up many characteristics of pre-1914 dress. Its costly fabrics are supple, varied and layered (with diamanté highlights) and they have the soft pastel tones that were essential before the fashionable few turned to brighter hues.

Much of the early work of the pioneering designers Paul Poiret and Mariano Fortuny falls outside mainstream fashion developments; the Museum owns a number of their key designs. 'Sorbet' [142] is an ensemble of 1912 which employs the fashionable overskirt, but Poiret renders it extraordinary by wiring the hem, giving it a lampshade shape which stands away from the body. Poiret made the most of the then current fad for Middle Eastern and Indian exotica, but only his most intrepid customers adopted his more outrageous designs. In about 1910 he visited the Victoria and Albert Museum and made a careful study of a group of turbans in the Indian Section. A few weeks later his copies were selling well in Paris. A great deal has been written about the rôles of Leon Bakst and Paul Poiret in the movement away from pastel shades to bright colours, not least by Poiret himself: 'There were orange and lemon crêpe de Chines which they would not have dared to imagine . . . I carried with me the colourists when I took each tone at its most vivid, and I restored to health all the exhausted nuances.'[7] Bakst's designs for the Russian ballet, especially *Schéhérazade* (1910), and Poiret's highly coloured clothes, came as a welcome change to the fashionable élite. The sherbert colours of 'Sorbet' are not as intense as other colours used by Poiret but they reveal the trend for clear, bright colours set against black backgrounds that was taken up and developed in the 1920s. The hobble evening dress of 1917 [146] owes much to Poiret's innovations, especially to his emphasis upon Eastern themes.

Fortuny's abundant skills are represented in the Museum by a comprehensive range of items, some worn by the famous Italian actress Eleonora Duse, as well as an interesting group of furnishing and dress fabrics. They include his long, finely pleated silk robes, printed jackets and tunics, and sturdy cottons hand-printed in subtle colours and gleaming metallic pigments. Although the evening ensemble [148; see p. 81] has been worn it is remarkable for its almost pristine condition,

and it epitomizes his many talents. The cut of both garments is simple—a tubular dress and a three-panelled jacket—but maximum impact is achieved by the inspired execution in finely pleated black satin and gold-printed silk velvet with a dramatic flash of colour from the flame-coloured lining.

The twentieth-century leisure and sportswear section, though not large and lacking in specialist attire (which falls outside the collecting policy), nevertheless encompasses well-made clothes for most popular sporting activities—motoring, riding, golfing, ski-ing, walking, tennis, swimming and sun bathing. Of particular note is a bright red gaberdine ski-suit made in 1932 by Burberrys and worn and given by the Duchess of Argyll. In 1983 a 1930s satin exercise outfit worn by a member of the Women's League of Health and Beauty was acquired. The fully documented riding habit of 1912 [141] was a welcome addition. Redfern was a house noted for its tailoring: this jacket, apron skirt and breeches are superbly constructed and finished.

It is not surprising that dress of the period of World War I is poorly represented in the collection although, despite the shortages and the slaughter, salons and shops continued to provide fashionable customers with suitably chic clothes. A small group of costumes illustrates the revolutionary shortening of skirts which liberated the legs and revealed the ankles. All, including the 1917 costume [147], are in a rather fragile state. The full, flared skirt (eight inches off the floor) is designed for a practical woman who wished to look smart but to move freely. Contrast this costume with the Lucile tailor-made [140; see p. 80] of just six years earlier. Both are elegant and feminine but one is made for gracious ease, the other for efficient participation.

The Inter-War Period: 1920–1939

After 1920 the Cecil Beaton Collection begins to assert its considerable strength. It is one of our most important and most famous assets. It was compiled especially for the Museum by the late Sir Cecil Beaton and exhibited with great success in 1971, accompanied by a catalogue which detailed its enormous range.[8] With great energy and dedication Sir Cecil contacted the well-dressed élite of Europe and America to bring together this lasting monument to the art of dress. It illustrates the work of over seventy top designers and consists of over five hundred outfits of all types, plus accessories, many of which were worn and most generously given by those, male and female, renowned for their taste and elegance. Paris-based and British designers are well represented, and the collection includes certain garments which have proved seminal in the evolution of twentieth-century fashionable dress.

Taken as a whole the 1920s collection is somewhat erratic, but star items illustrate the main silhouettes with their fluctuating skirt lengths as well as vital details such as luxurious beadwork and cloche hats. Many of these examples belong to a fine collection of elegant clothes worn by Miss Emilie Grigsby. She was a wealthy and independent American who 'came to England from New York, a mysterious and beautiful figure'[9] and established a *salon* frequented by writers and the military. An international beauty, she purchased her clothes from *couturiers* in London, Paris and New York. Apparently her colouring

[152]

[151]

was remarkable, and the 1927 mustard georgette evening ensemble [152] would have enhanced her pale, almost transparent skin and golden hair.

The early 1920s dress by Callot Soeurs [149] is a masterpiece, constructed of the highest quality lace and beaded silk such as only France produced. Silk dress panels were stretched over frames and tamboured to shape with beads and sequins, and dressmakers assembled the shaped panels, adding embellishments as necessary. The house of Callot Soeurs was well known for its sumptuous and feminine designs incorporating exquisite fabrics. Official aid and encouragement was given to the luxury industries in France, and the *Exposition Internationale des Arts Décoratifs*, Paris 1925, revealed the supremacy of French textile designers, manufacturers and *couturiers*. Each season textile firms, based mainly in Lyon and Mulhouse, produced lavish decorative fabrics especially for Paris *couturiers*. Much of their output is recorded in pattern books and samples belonging to the Musée Historique des Tissus at Lyon and the Musée de l'Impression sur Etoffes at Mulhouse. Leading artists, notably Raoul Dufy, and design studios provided stunning patterns for printed and woven textiles and embroideries throughout the 1920s and beyond.

Dress, accessory and textile designers were quick to gain inspiration from Howard Carter's discoveries in Egypt's Valley of the Kings. Some designs were poor pastiches hastily produced to catch the market, but not so the high quality 1924 short evening dress [151]. Although it is without a label, it bears the unmistakeable hallmark of a top French designer, its heavily beaded pattern being a harmonious and lively interpretation of Egyptian decorative art. It comes from an excellent collection of twentieth-century dress given by Lord and Lady Cowdray in 1970, and it illustrates the tubular look which became the 1920s ideal. Although no longer in the limelight, Paul Poiret remained one of the top 1920s Paris *couturiers* and continued to produce inventive clothes for a faithful clientéle. In his 1924 day dress 'Brique' [150; see opposite] the machining is not immaculate and the hem is bound, as in many of his clothes, with rather crude cotton tape; but, taken as a whole, it is a successful realization of his ideas. The 1928 ensemble [153] has two elements most commonly associated with 1920s dress. The coat is fastened at hip level, giving the typical waistless look, and the matching cloche hat, pulled straight down to eyelid level, became *de rigueur* in the 1920s. The Museum frequently acquires objects from its temporary exhibitions and this outfit was originally lent to the 1975 Liberty & Co. centenary exhibition.[10]

An anonymous gift, the 1930 printed georgette dress [154] from La Samaritaine (one of the *grands magasins*), again shows superb French workmanship and has the fluid lines which were to be the dominant features of fashionable dress until 1938. 1930s evening wear is one of the collection's strong points. Here, the Cecil Beaton Collection comes into its own and, with other substantial gifts, the collection now offers a comprehensive coverage of the decade. After the catastrophic drop in sales caused by the collapse of the American stockmarket in 1929, fashion houses struggled on. The thirties saw the success of many designers, notably Chanel, Schiaparelli, Vionnet and Mainbocher. In 1933 Paul Poiret designed a collection for Liberty's Model Gown Salon.

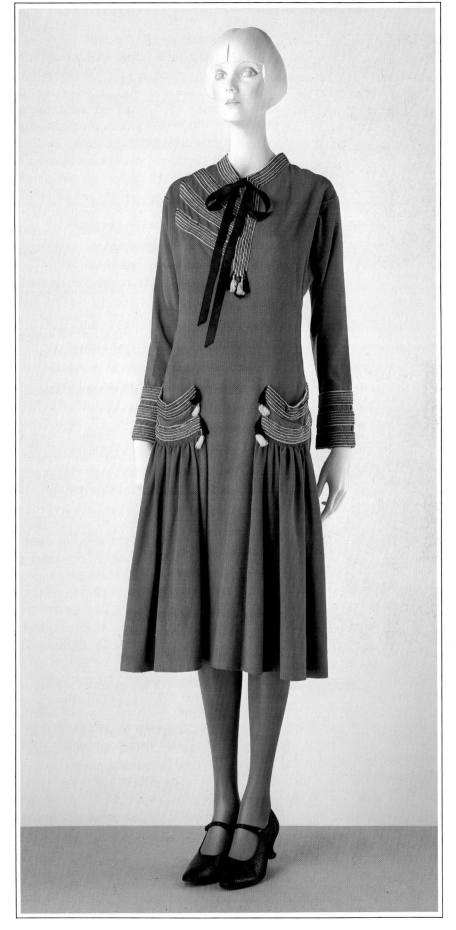

Poiret's 1924 day dress 'Brique', a fairly simple creation, is enlivened by asymmetrically applied braid of bold black and white stripes. Poiret remained one of the top Paris *couturiers* in the 1920s, producing inventive clothes for a faithful clientèle.
T.339-1974   [150]

[156]

[159]

Country Life (18 March 1933) described '. . . the immensely popular dress parade which inaugurated the connection of M. Paul Poiret with this firm. M. Poiret has lost none of his striking originality and individuality, and while, at the same time, his ideas were cleverly adapted to bring out the best points of an English figure, one or two very stately and charming gowns suggested the dresses of the Italian Renaissance.' In a rare survival from this collection [157—another anonymous gift], the plunging back neckline gives way to a cascade of silk velvet ribbons.

In the late 1920s and throughout the 1930s Madeleine Vionnet was the arch-exponent of the art of bias-cutting and diagonal seaming, skills evident in her 1933 evening dress [156] which is typical of the sleeveless, low-backed, clinging gowns worn by attractive, self-assured women throughout these years. Like all her work (the Musée des Arts de la Mode, Paris, has an extensive collection) it is precisely cut and assembled and perfectly finished. Furs become brittle with age and present a difficult storage problem, but one or two outstanding examples—in particular the Vionnet ermine of 1935–7 [159]—represent the thirties methods of handling pelts. Clothes for special occasions such as these conceived by Vionnet tend to be treasured and offered to the Museum, whereas day wear is frequently worn out and discarded. Only a few outfits in the collection illustrate 1930s day attire but, luckily, one is the ultra-fashionable Vionnet jersey ensemble [155].

After seven of his garments were shown in the Cecil Beaton exhibition, Charles James kept in touch with the V & A from his Chelsea Hotel base, giving advice as well as examples of his work. The Museum now has an interesting collection of his output between 1934 and 1976. He constantly explored the sculptural possibilities of cloth, and the late Miss Philippa Barnes (who worked with him in Paris and London during the 1930s) donated a group of Charles James items which included prototype bodices, accessories and swatches of the Lyon taffetas, satins and grosgrains which he employed for his experiments and final creations. The clinging gold evening dress of 1934 [159] is one of the results of his endeavours to transform the svelte female shape admired in the thirties by widening the bust and the hips. The mid-1930s saw a revival in quilted clothing and furnishings, but Charles James took the art to its extreme. His pneumatic jacket [161; see p. 163] has contemporary appeal, and in the 1970s it became a cult object linked with the widespread fashion for voluminous padded coats. The Museum is often asked to lend designer clothes to live fashion shows and this garment shows why such requests are refused. Before it came to the V & A it was modelled for the press, which caused strained and torn seams. These have been repaired (with difficulty because of the feather filling) and the jacket will never be worn again. Damage may occur even in the most meticulously controlled dress show. Frail and ageing fabrics rip easily with movement, and perspiration, which is unavoidable under hot, bright lights, eventually rots the affected areas. These are just some of the reasons why the Museum, in its attempt to preserve examples of fashionable dress for future generations, cannot allow its collection to be worn.

Sequinned and beaded evening attire remained fashionable throughout the 1930s. The all over 'fish scale' method of applying sequins, which made the garments extremely heavy, was particularly popular

and most *couturiers* exploited this technique. Mainbocher was well known for his severe, unpatterned clothes but he also excelled in the creation of beaded dresses and jackets with designs ranging from exotic florals to restrained diagonal stripes [162]. In a letter to the Museum in July 1971 he described these garments as 'a continuation of what I had been doing to bring back embroidered dresses into the mode'. Mainbocher clothes in the Museum are published in the Beaton catalogue, and in 1982 and 1983 this group was supplemented by two mid-1930s, flowing, printed silk garden party dresses, purchased at auction.

Although the Museum lacks work from Chanel's early career (one of her influential jersey cardigan suits would be a welcome acquisition) it has twelve notable Chanel creations. They range from a beaded tunic of 1919 to one of her typically chic and comfortable light tweed suits worn by Lauren Bacall in the 1960s. In contrast to these practical suits are Chanel's extravagant evening designs. Two superb examples represent her 1930s output—a sequinned trouser ensemble (1937) which belonged to Diana Vreeland, and the striking dress and cape of about the same date [160]. In 1979 the black crêpe dress, jacket and hat [181; see p. 169] was purchased to fill one of the gaps in the Chanel collection. It has the severe lines she used for the sophisticated 'schoolgirl' day wear which was rarely absent from her collections. The severity of these suits, usually in navy blue or black, was relieved by her 'chunky' costume jewellery and touches of white at the neck and wrists.

The professional antagonism between Chanel and Schiaparelli has been well documented, and the artistic and fashionable milieu of Paris and London in the 1930s would have been much the poorer without both their talents. In 1965 Madame Schiaparelli gave the Museum a selection of her work, and this was augmented by many outstanding Schiaparellis given by their owners in 1971. Miss Ruth Ford's skeleton dress, circus ensemble, and crêpe evening outfit—with the famous Salvador Dali 'Tears' print—reveal how fruitful the year 1938 proved for Schiaparelli. The Musée des Arts de la Mode, Paris, owns a series of Schiaparelli albums which are invaluable aids to the dating of her work. Sumptuous and amusingly patterned evening jackets epitomize her lively approach to dress design. The 1938 evening ensemble [164] has such a jacket with immense embroidered leaves which further emphasize the wide, padded shoulders. It has a row of leaf buttons. Buttons, which were insignificant fastening devices to other designers, played an essential rôle in Schiaparelli's art: 'King Button still reigned without fear at Schiap's. The most incredible things were used, animals and feathers, caricatures and paper-weights, chains, locks, clips, and lollipops. Some were of wood and others of plastic, but not one looked like what a button was supposed to look like.'[11]

Towards the end of the 1930s the fashionable silhouette altered and the prevailing streamlined shape was gradually replaced by wider shoulders, shorter skirts for day wear, and constricted waists. The Schiaparelli evening ensemble [164] and the 1938 Peter Russell evening dress and coat [163] indicate the lines which were to dominate the clothes of the 1940s. Just before the outbreak of World War II many top designers created eccentric clothes in their attempts to break away from the pervasive, bias-cut line—perhaps these curiosities also re-

Far left:
Throughout the 1930s Norman Hartnell, author of this bias-cut crêpe evening dress of about 1934, designed stage clothes for leading actresses, including Gertrude Lawrence, Evelyn Laye and Gladys Cooper. In 1935 Royalty was added to his impressive list of customers.
T.190-1973   [158]

Left:
The Utility Collection, produced in 1942 by the Incorporated Society of London Fashion Designers, was distinguished by its elegant simplicity. The maximum selling price for this woollen suit, probably designed by Victor Stiebel, was 82s 2d.
T.46&A-1942   [168]

flected the political and social instability of the period. One of their highly impracticable strategies, led by Balenciaga and Molyneux, was a revival of the crinoline [165]. A caption in *Vogue*, October 1938, ran: 'Crinolines bring to the London scene the ample sweep and porcelain femininity of an earlier age. Once more you sail, brave as a full-rigged ship.' Such quirky developments were cut short by the outbreak of war.

Fashion Marks Time: 1939–1946

Inevitably the Department's acquisition books for the years 1939 to 1947 are slender. The most significant gift of these years came from the Board of Trade via Sir Thomas Barlow, the Director-General of Civilian Clothing. It consists of thirty-one garments from the Utility Collection of 1942. In that year the Board invited the Incorporated Society of London Fashion Designers to design clothes within its strict regulations, dictating such factors as numbers of buttons and fabric amounts. The collection which emerged was distinguished by its elegant simplicity. The designers remained anonymous and their patterns were made available for mass production. A fashion show was held to launch the clothes. The Museum was given the designer prototypes modelled in the show, which are made in Utility fabrics of a surprisingly high quality [166, 167 and 168]. The collection nearly left Britain when the Brooklyn Museum asked if they could have it, but, fortunately, Sir Thomas Barlow felt that it should be offered to the V & A as a permanent record of this important experiment. (Contemporary photographs of the collection were given to the Imperial War Museum.) Museum staff in 1942 were, as ever, apprehensive about the storage question but the then Director, Sir Eric MacLagen, reassured them that 'as Utility garments presumably they do not contain any excess of material, and will therefore take relatively little storage space.' The acquisition of contemporary fashions, especially in such quantity, was a rare occurrence, so the acceptance of this extensive gift represented a significant development in policy.

The luxury industries were almost at a standstill in Britain while resources were harnessed for the war effort. Non-essential clothing had a low priority and, along with other commodities, was rationed from 1941 until the last sanctions were lifted in 1952. The coupon system meant that only the prescribed number of coupons together with cash could secure an item. The Museum has an interesting dress fabric printed with various articles of clothing, each inscribed with the number of coupons necessary for its purchase. Women were confined to occupational and service uniform, utilitarian garments or merely altered pre-war clothes: in these straitened circumstances no significant stylistic changes were possible. Throughout the German occupation certain Paris fashion houses remained open, though they were isolated and lacked influence. In *Picture Post*, May 1942, Anne Scott-James chose illustrations from *Album de la Mode Figaro* of luxurious clothes which were available to a fashionable coterie in Paris and pointed out that: 'Most of the pictures that come out of France show rags and squalor—food queues, tearful women, half-naked children. In contrast, here are fur coats, hoods, even handbags for the few.'

Information which reached London showed extremely wide-shouldered, short outfits topped by highly decorative hats worn at precarious angles. Hardy Amies described 'those very tall, elaborately trimmed hats, mostly draped turbans which the French milliners had invented to irritate the Germans,' as '*les chapeaux de la Résistance*'.[12] During this period the rôle of Paris as fashion leader was severely diminished, but after the war it quickly regained its supremacy. In 1945 *The Chambre Syndicale de la Couture Parisienne* arranged an exhibition, '*Théâtre de la Mode*', of small dolls dressed by top *couturiers* which travelled Europe and America. It was sponsored by the *Continental Daily Mail* in London and was shown on behalf of the RAF Benevolent Fund at the Princes Galleries, Piccadilly. Miniature tableaux by famous artists—Jean Cocteau, Christian Bérard, etc.—were peopled by wire dolls about two feet high with moulded faces, wearing clothes by forty-one leading Paris dressmakers.

The shape of these tiny clothes 'was still marked by very broad shoulders, narrow waists and skirts full and short so as to only cover the knee',[13] but in 1946 designers began to promote a softer shape. The square shoulders were rounded off and skirts became longer and fuller. British post-war efforts to revive trade at home and abroad culminated in the *Britain Can Make It* exhibition of 1946, held in the V & A. Fifteen top London designers exhibited in the Fashion Hall and Francis Marshall sketched 'his impressions of the scene: Evening gowns by the great London couturiers revolving on a tall white tower covered casually with mink' for the *Daily Mail*. Unfortunately none of these clothes remained in the V & A.

The Renaissance of Haute Couture : 1947 to the end of the 1950s

The stage was set for Dior's controversial 'New Look' collection of Spring 1947. Bettina Ballard, who had the foresight to buy a Dior dress in 1946, when Dior was with Lucien Lelong, said: 'Paris fashion was waiting to be seized and shaken and given direction. There has never been an easier or more complete conquest than that of Christian Dior in 1947.'[14] In 1960, in response to a suggestion from Cecil Beaton, Christian Dior, Paris, presented the Museum with its first and most important Dior—the New Look suit 'Bar' [169]. The export form described the ensemble as '*Jupe plissée noire, fibranne/laine. Veste shantung grège, soie. Chapeau paille beige.*' A key work in the evolution of twentieth-century fashion, it repeatedly appears in histories of the subject.

Dior, Balenciaga, Jacques Fath, Balmain and Jean Dessès were the leading *couturiers* of the 1950s. Dior and Balenciaga deservedly achieved most of the limelight. Early in the decade Cardin and Givenchy launched their careers. In the 1960s and 1970s there was a spate of memoirs and fashion histories by ex-fashion editors and all seem agreed that the post-war period to about 1958 saw Paris *couture* reach new heights.

Fashionable dress from the house of Dior (Paris and London) is one of the collection's strong points. In addition to 'Bar' the Museum has forty-five works. An important group was purchased by private clients from Dior's own immensely successful and much publicized collections (1947 to 1957). These ranges were published in great detail in 1981.[15]

[169]

After his untimely death in 1957 the Paris house was led briefly by Yves St Laurent, followed by Marc Bohan, and the Museum has day and evening attire which document the years 1958 to 1975. The garments range from a beaded evening dress worn and given by the Duchess of Windsor to a simple black jersey dress from the collection of winter 1975.

Two vital assets from Dior's first year are 'Maxim', a black woollen luncheon dress, and 'Miss New York' a spotted silk day dress with a 'bustle' drape. An impressive, strapless evening dress—a ruched sheath with a flying angular over-skirt—sums up the dramatic, clean lines of his work 1948 to 1950, which has features akin to modern architecture. In the 1950s *couturiers* released well over five hundred new models each year. Some did not sell but, nevertheless, in comparison with this prodigious output, the Museum's holdings are numerically small. Top designers published collection programmes: some, like Dior's, had useful notes about the garments' materials and accessories in addition to the list of outfits to be shown. The 1953 dance dress [171] was part of his spring–summer *Ligne Tulipe* collection. The Museum lacked Dior clothes from 1953 so this dress was purchased at auction to fill the gap. It was not however in excellent condition, for there were some perspiration stains and small tears. The Dior programme explained that the stylized silhouette of 1953 was intended to evoke a tulip in bloom—a somewhat tortuous concept. The bust was raised; an off-the-shoulder neckline gave width at the top; and most of the skirts, except in the dance dresses, were straight to represent the tulip's stem. Fabrics for evening were light and airy and the collection featured many floral printed silks: '*les imprimés impressionistes évoquant les champs de fleurs chers à Renoir et à Van Gogh*'. The Duchess of Windsor selected model number 70, 'Fanny', from this collection.

Dior's seasonal lines, such as *Ligne Profilée* (1952), *Ligne H* (1954) and *Ligne A* (1955), were structurally demanding. The shapes depended upon skilled cut and construction usually involving padding, weighting, interlining, lining and built-in petticoats. All the traditional *couture* skills were employed. The garments, especially for winter, were often heavy, which necessitated large and sturdy fastenings. The pleated skirt [169; see opposite] weighs almost five pounds and is anchored at the back by a row of enormous hooks and eyes. A worsted two-piece suit from Dior's 1952 Sinuous Line has a long bodice which fastens to a heavy skirt with five robust, $\frac{1}{2}$-inch diameter, press studs. A small group of dresses from Dior's penultimate collection—*Ligne Libre*, spring–summer 1957—show that he remained faithful to the laborious *couture* techniques. A bright pink taffeta evening dress with a bell skirt is machine-stitched and carefully hand-finished. It depends upon a long, form-fitting boned corset with suspenders, attached to a many-layered stiffened petticoat.

Until about 1956 two silhouettes prevailed. Both had form-fitting bodices with a defined waist, but the calf-length skirts for day wear could be full or pencil slim. A new breed of professional models emerged with sleek looks which matched the elegant clothes. The well-dressed woman in the 1950s had to be immaculately groomed, with accurate accessories. Magazines ran regular features devoted to handbags, hats, umbrellas, shoes and jewellery. Hats and gloves were worn for all except the most informal events. Millinery had to be of the large flying-saucer variety or of the small biretta type which perched above the front hairline. The fashion press also published details of the latest dress fabrics, and throughout the 1950s sterling efforts were made to improve the sales of British goods. The Cotton Board's Colour Design and Style Centre in Manchester energetically promoted printed cottons and held numerous exhibitions. *The Ambassador, the British Export Magazine* aided the export drive with its lively articles. The Queen wore dresses of British printed cottons on her Commonwealth tour (1953–4) and the Museum has samples of some of these fabrics, designed by Brigitte Dehnert for Horrockses. Zika Ascher injected new life into 1950s dress fabrics from his London headquarters. Paris designers welcomed his textiles, and in 1957 he achieved instant success with an outerwear fabric which was a light yet warm mixture of nylon and mohair. The nylon content gave the cloth durability and prevented it sagging after wear. Lanvin Castillo made it into coats which sold so well that Zika Ascher could hardly keep up with the demand. In the 1960s he presented the Museum with samples of the material.

[173]

Owing to the generosity of Lady Dacre the Museum has an excellent group of works by top designers—including Jacques Fath; and fine day and evening dresses formed just part of the gift of designer clothes worn by Mrs Opal Holt [173, 174 and 180]. In the 1949 Jacques Fath day dress [170; see opposite] rows of functional buttons are used for decorative effect: they are flat and large, unlike the tiny domed buttons employed for a similar purpose thirty-six years earlier [145]. Fath preferred to dress the tall and slender, so Lady Dacre was an ideal customer. Twelve of her chic dresses and a group of hats by Fath are in the permanent collection. His premature death in 1954 robbed the world of *couture* of a considerable talent.

To be smart from autumn to spring in town during the 1950s it was essential to wear a tailored suit or dress, preferably in grey and white tweed. Each year designers showed subtle variations on the theme: trimmings were added or removed and accessories were modified. Mrs Opal Holt's extensive wardrobe of fashionable dress ranges from the 1930s to the 1970s, and over one hundred objects—day and evening wear together with accessories—represent her refined taste. Mrs Holt bought in London, Paris and New York, and her American purchases— 1950s suits and hats from Hattie Carnegie and a Mainbocher coat— have boosted the Museum's small trans-Atlantic collection. Her 1950s day clothes include work by Dior, Balenciaga and Givenchy, and three dresses by Jean Dessès are especially interesting. Dessès has been rather neglected although he was responsible for superbly draped chiffon evening gowns (the Museum has three examples) and restrained, carefully executed day wear [173]. The tailored 'Chesterfield' suit [174] of about 1954 also belonged to Mrs Holt, and Mr Digby Morton has pointed out that he designed it to be worn over a discreetly checked blouse at the races. Similar suits, modelled by mannequins with suitably haughty expressions, were illustrated in glossy magazines, and matching gloves, hats, umbrellas and shoes completed the look. Long, tightly furled umbrellas with extended handles were indispensable fashionable

[174]

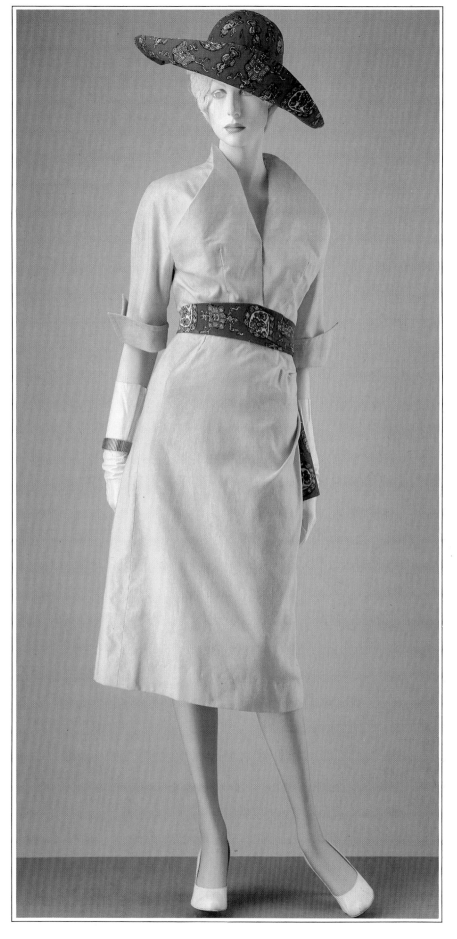

This 1949 Jacques Fath summer day
dress is a forerunner of the elegant,
narrow line of the 1950s. Fath made
maximum use of oblique lines, flying
panels and pointed cuffs for day wear.
T.175-1974   [**170**]

adjuncts at this period. A fine example, which was held by its elegant elongated swan's neck handle [174] comes from Mrs Vere French's collection.

Mr Digby Morton was a founder member of The Incorporated Society of London Fashion Designers, which had its hey-day in the 1950s (Ernestine Carter charts its development in *With Tongue in Chic*, Michael Joseph, 1974). In 1954 Lady Pamela Berry (later Lady Hartwell) became the Society's President, and when interviewed summarized British reluctance to support the fashion industry: 'I expect you've noticed the almost uncanny knack which some of the famous Paris and Rome houses have developed for publicizing their twice-yearly Collections. To compete with this powerful and continuous propaganda from the French and Italian fashion industries, I feel we must make a great blowing of trumpets to launch an international promotion scheme for British Designers. But we are terribly handicapped for lack of money. Compared with that of France and Italy our fashion industry is painfully under-capitalized.' [16]

Strangely enough the V & A's collection of dress by top British designers from the late 1940s to the early 1960s is not as comprehensive as it should be, although it is gradually improving. The list includes Victor Stiebel, Michael Sherard, Peter Russell, Digby Morton and the well known Royal dressmakers Norman Hartnell and Hardy Amies. Three of their resplendent embroidered state gowns were kindly given to the Cecil Beaton exhibition by the Queen and the Queen Mother. In 1966 Charles Creed gave four of his tailored suits (1948 to 1960) and in 1979 the Museum purchased his wife's wedding dress of 1948 by fellow designer Captain Molyneux.

For some at this time there were apparently endless gala events (presentations at court stopped in 1958 but the debutante round continued). A ready market in European and American fashionable centres was provided with lavish evening gowns—either the costly *couture* garments or the somewhat cheaper but, nevertheless, accomplished copies. The Museum has examples of many of these dresses, which came to be perceived as art objects in themselves; but the variety with belled skirts retained by enormous built-in petticoats presents a considerable storage problem.

Schiaparelli closed her house in 1954, so we are fortunate to have the Duchess of Devonshire's ball gown [172] from one of the designer's last collections. She maintained the inventiveness which had brought her fame in the 1930s, and in the early 1950s was responsible for some compelling evening wear. The shocking pink silk and white organza dress with floral patterned swirling circular skirt illustrates a romantic aspect of her later work. At this time designers were preoccupied with elaborate necklines: here Schiaparelli creates a visually effective but impractical neckline with an inverted rippling frill. In direct contrast she also made dramatic and revealing dresses suitable for *femmes fatales*, and in 1965 presented one, dated 1952, to the Museum. It is an extremely tight strapless sheath with an enormous *volant* at the right hip, in mauve and purple taffeta.

The collection of clothes by Alix (later Madame Grès) is small, and the evening dress [175] epitomizes her technical prowess. Though her

[172]

Throughout the 1950s Balenciaga designed a series of extravagant evening dresses based (like this one of about 1955 in fuchsia silk taffeta) upon immense drapes and flounces.
T.427-1967

repertoire is vast, for almost fifty years she has made draped evening dresses adapting the lines slightly to suit the prevailing mode. As Madeleine Delpierre said in the catalogue *Élégance & Création* (Musée de la mode et du costume, Paris 1977): '*Ses créations les plus célèbres sont de grandes robes drapées à l'antique, coupées dans des jerseys de soie très larges, fabriqués pour elle, qui sont inimitables et hors du temps.*'

A number of fifties ball gowns are structurally phenomenal: the Charles James [176] and the Balmain [178] are so constructed that they are almost free standing. Mounting these heavy dresses on display mannequins is an exhausting business, but their precise balance means that when worn the weight was not oppressive. The Charles James evening gown, 'Four Leaf Clover' of 1952, given by the Art Students League of New York, has a more complex configuration than the 'Tree' dress [176], and was originally designed for Mrs William Randolph Hearst Jr.[17]

As well as a group of his ball gowns, the Museum has an important velvet suit (1945–6) created by Balmain for his champion Gertrude Stein. He called his collections 'Jolie Madame de Paris', 'pretty' dresses being his forte. He favoured bouffant skirts [178], and his workrooms were adept at the production of strapless gowns with their necessarily accurate foundations. Vivien Leigh, Moira Lister, and Marlene Dietrich were among the devotees of Balmain. Lilli Palmer chose her wardrobe for the film *Teufel im Seide* at his winter collection in 1955, and in 1981 gave an evening gown from this selection. In warp-printed silk with a floral pattern in pale blues and pinks, it is further embellished with finely worked appliqué in the same fabric. Balmain returned to this successful method in 1957 for a rose-patterned silk dress worn and given by Lady Diana Cooper.

Balenciaga is perhaps the most revered *couturier* of all. Iris Ashley reported: 'As always the subtleties of this connoisseur's collection defeat the writer. Only it is true to say that nobody who attempts to give a true report of fashion would dare to miss a showing at this house.' She praised him 'for designing about two seasons ahead of everyone else' and 'for tailoring beyond the power of description'.[18] The Beaton Collection has over thirty 'Balenciagas', and gradually the numbers have increased— most significantly in 1981 with the gift of eighteen outfits and five hats worn by Mrs Opal Holt. Balenciaga opened his Paris house in 1937. Unfortunately we lack works from the 1930s, our earliest garment being a jacket of about 1948. The strength of the collection lies in his designs dating from the late 1950s and 1960s (his salon closed in 1968) and of particular note are his dramatic evening clothes in silk gazar by Abraham. Gazar—plain woven silk, stiff with finishing—is ideal for creating three-dimensional geometric forms for wearing. Balenciaga excelled at this art. Great care has to be taken with the garments in order to retain the cloth's finishing and thus their sculptural shapes. Balenciaga also used heavily ornate fabrics, but he was most successful with plain silks, wools and linens in cream, black, navy and deep resonant colours. The evening dress of about 1955 [177] and the mid-1960s suit [180] indicate two crucial facets of his sophisticated work. The dress is a lavish and extrovert statement in silk taffeta, whereas the suit is a severe and restrained exercise with the famous Balenciaga characteristics—a long loose jacket with a round neck and gently rolled back collar, over a slightly flared skirt. Most of his departures post 1950 are present: a barrel dress of 1954 and a recently acquired 'sack' dress of 1956–7 are witness to his inauguration of the late 1950s tubular line. In July 1983 a gift of a late 1950s summer coat in green organza was a welcome newcomer to the Balenciaga wardrobes.

The Revolution of the 1960s

The 1960s revolution which affected all levels of the dressmaking trade is clearly reflected in the collection and the chief protagonists on both sides of the Channel are well represented. Top-level Paris fashion was revitalized by the work of Cardin, Ungaro, Yves St Laurent and Courrèges [185]: their youth-orientated output was completely in tune with the times. *Haute couture* was no longer the dominant and profit-making force it had once been, so in order to capture young, less affluent, and more adventurous customers the established houses expanded their ready-to-wear and boutique outlets. They were joined by new *prêt-à-porter* talents including Emmanuelle Khanh, Dorothée-bis, Sonia Rykiel and Karl Lagerfeld.

Courrèges' spring 1964 collection was hailed by the press as a turning point in fashion, much as Dior's 'New Look' collection had been seventeen years earlier. The seven Courrèges outfits made between 1963 and 1967 and exhibited in the Museum in 1971 have been since joined by fifteen other examples from his 1960s collections. They depict variations on the extremely short geometric shapes which were then modish, and exhibit the densely woven fabrics that were essential to maintain these rigid lines.

It is inevitable that the 1960s clothes by Courrèges and Ungaro have features in common. They both worked with Balenciaga, and Ungaro partnered Courrèges for a short period before establishing his own house in 1966. The V & A's Ungaro collection started with clothes worn by the late Mrs Stavros Niarchos and by Princess Stanislaus Radziwill; and, most significantly, they were joined by ten Ungaro outfits of 1966–8 worn and given by Mrs Brenda Azario, whose husband was the Director of Nattier—the Italian firm which wove the dense gaberdines so essential for mid-1960s fashions. A suit with a camouflage print and a dress with one immense circle printed on the skirt front and one on the back indicate the fruitful 1960s collaboration of Ungaro and textile designer Sonia Knapp. A 1967 mini-dress (again with a distinctive print by Sonia Knapp) has a pair of matching shorts, specially designed by Ungaro, which were forerunners of 'hot pants'. Ungaro made tiny replicas of the 1966 suit [183] for Mrs Azario's two little girls, all being photographed for French *Vogue*. Courrèges and Ungaro garments are precisely cut and superbly finished. No detail, from the set of a sleeve to a silk-covered press-stud, can be faulted.

One of the most prolific *couturiers*, Pierre Cardin, is represented in the collection by too few works. In 1967 he was at the head of a work force of 15,000 people, with fifty factories and 1500 shops.[19] Happily he acknowledges 'Cosmos' [186; see frontispiece] to be one of his key creations, summarizing the numerous forward-looking aspects of his sixties output. Mrs Azario's gift includes work of the mid-1960s by Yves St Laurent, Mila Schön, Fabiani, and an embroidered navy and white

[183]

[182]

organza halter-neck, mini-length cocktail dress complete with cape, by Cardin. A month after the re-displayed Dress Collection opened the Department gratefully received another of his works from the mini-skirt era—a triangular, sleeveless shift dress which has a deep hem quilted with a linear geometric design.

Beyond any other designer Yves St Laurent typifies the ever-changing nature of fashion of the last twenty years. The V & A's collection captures only a handful of his inventive moments. In addition to the seven works gathered together by Cecil Beaton, another dress from the 'Mondrian Collection' [182] was purchased in 1981, and in 1979 Joan Juliet Buck gave his influential maxi-skirted loden 'battle dress' suit of 1969.

The V & A collection of 1960s work by the new wave of young British designers is extensive. For a period the international fashionable pace was set by this talented group of London-based designers led by Mary Quant. *Honey* was the magazine which answered the needs of the young and fashionable at this time. In January 1967, in an article entitled 'The Scene Shifters', Mary Quant was described as 'The Fountain Head' and Twiggy as 'The Personality'. In the following April the magazine produced a free sixteen-page booklet, 'On the Quant Wavelength', which was devoted to her work. The collection does not have any of her first designs for 'Bazaar' (1956–57), but a selection of fifteen outfits from her wholesale company Ginger Group [184] illustrate some of the high spots of her career. In 1982 the Department acquired one of the most popular pinafores from the 1963 collection as well as three Ginger Group mini-dresses, in pristine condition, which had been discovered, complete with their original price tags, at the back of a dress shop's stockroom. Garments from other dynamic and sometimes short-lived London boutiques were not especially well made, but were stylistically inventive in a great variety of fabrics—chosen for instant appeal rather than durability. Above all, the mid to late 1960s are known for the 'mini'. Although it was adopted by women of all ages it was really only successful on the very young. The V & A collection includes the tiny white wrap-over mini-skirt which caused such a furore when worn by Jean Shrimpton in Australia. The style [184] was modelled by teenagers with geometric hair cuts by Vidal Sassoon, 'Kewpie doll' eye make-up, and the look was completed by flat, square-toed shoes and sometimes outlandish perspex jewellery—a far cry from the studied elegance of thirteen years earlier. We now have some Biba (Barbara Hulanicki) clothes from her mail-order catalogues and first shop. The colours and patterns of these 1960s garments are diverse, reflecting quick-changing trends such as the Art Nouveau revival and the art movements labelled 'Op' and 'Pop'. Twenty-five brilliantly coloured and amusing 'Pop Art' garments by Mr Freedom (Tommy Roberts) sum up this provocative and iconoclastic period.

1970s and the Future

The Cecil Beaton exhibition provided an ideal opportunity to ask leading British designers for current examples of their work: their response, as always, was speedy and generous [188 and 189]. Marion Foale and Sally Tuffin, Gina Fratini and Thea Porter gave from their 1971 ranges, and John Bates' grey, black and cream ensemble [189] captures the demure

'covered up' spirit of the 1970s. Throughout the decade he made restrained and elegant day wear at prices the less affluent could afford. The transition from the miniscule, starkly geometric, clothes of about 1965 to 1968 to the fluid longer lines of 1969 and the early 1970s fascinates visitors to the present Dress Collection. A mere four years separate the soft pleats of Jean Muir's evening dress [188] and Cardin's cosmonaut-inspired futuristic tunic ensemble [186]. The Museum is fortunate to have a selection of Jean Muir's designs dating from 1967 to 1983. They reveal her fascination with plain fabrics—jersey knit, woollen crêpe, silk, leather, suede and now cotton in 'true' colours. Each season with these materials she creates understated clothes which become classics in their time. An important and extensive collection of her work was assembled in Leeds for a recent and highly acclaimed exhibition.[20]

A number of London designers are best known for their clothes featuring skilled surface decoration, and Zandra Rhodes is the arch-exponent of this art. Her skills are represented in the collection by the screen-printed felt coat [187]; a group of her famous screen-printed silk chiffon evening dresses (1969–78); and one of her 1971 'gipsy' dresses in which quilting further embellishes the printed designs. In 1978 Zandra Rhodes gave the Museum a clinging evening sheath dress from her collection called 'Conceptual chic'. It is a radical departure from the flowing silks with their painterly patterns which are usually associated with her name. She used the heavy elements of street punk dress—black bondage trousers, leather jacket with chains and safety pins—as starting points for a less oppressive variation for a different market. A monograph on her work is about to be published and will prove a welcome addition to the literature of twentieth-century fashion.

Bill Gibb uses patterned fabrics to create dresses which are praised for their romantic appeal. Twiggy gave her 1970 Bill Gibb evening dress, which is so tiny that it demands a specially designed mannequin. Other evening dresses of his now in the collection belonged to celebrities in show business: the evening dress [190] in Liberty prints and colours typical of the 1970s was worn by Sandie Shaw, and a pleated chiffon dress of 1977 was owned by Lynsey de Paul. In 1980 Kaffe Fassett gave a suit of 1976 to represent the immensely successful collaboration with Bill Gibb in the important and ever-expanding area of machine-knitted clothes.

Japanese designers, who are now such a vital force in the world of fashionable dress, have contributed important designs to the seventies collection—the first being a dramatically appliquéd gown by Yamamoto shown in 1971. Yuki gave two of his inimitable draped evening garments [191] in 1979 to mark the occasion of the V & A study day devoted to his work.

In Spring 1979 the Museum received the unexpected and welcome gift of an entire exhibition of twenty-five complete outfits by top British designers, selected by fashion editor Barbara Griggs.[21] The gift was the result of the combined forces of the designers themselves, Simpson (Piccadilly) Ltd and the mannequin manufacturer Adel Rootstein. It was remarkable in many ways: it was the first time the Museum had acquired a wide-ranging collection from one season, and

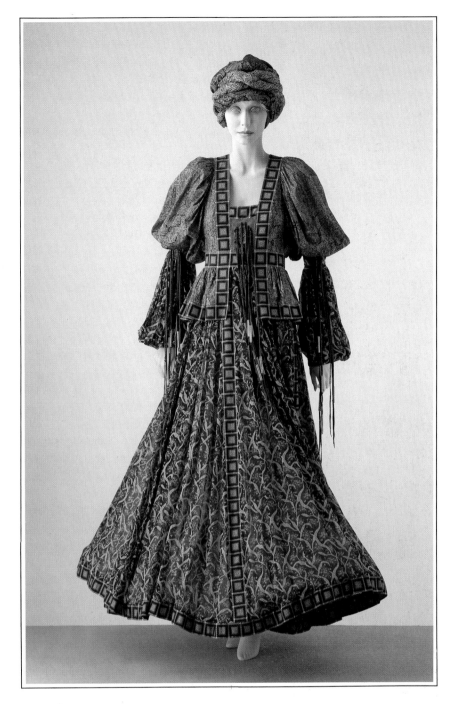

Dress designed by Bill Gibb in 1972 using various Liberty cottons printed with small scale patterns in toning colours. It was worn by the pop singer Sandie Shaw.

T.94-1981   [190]

never before had it acquired contemporary dress with the complete accessories, including make-up and wigs, on special display mannequins. The clothes range from a roller disco outfit complete with skates by Paul Howie to a slinky, almost backless evening dress by John Bates. It is intended that the outfits will be shown in rotation to illustrate British design for 1979, and Wendy Dagworthy's day ensemble [192] is the first to be displayed.

It was decided to complete the re-displayed Dress Collection with an indication of the wide range of clothes from British designers available to fashionable women in the 1980s. Space was limited, which meant that many talents were unavoidably omitted; but four very different

This unisex pirate outfit designed by Vivienne Westwood in 1980, epitomises the 'new-romantic' look. Since then she has explored further original territory in collections which have received international acclaim.

T.334-I-1982   [193]

works were acquired. Zandra Rhodes selected one of her most exuberant 1981 evening gowns [194] inspired by panniers in the V & A collection. In London, youthful street fashions are once again being linked with popular music, notably by Vivienne Westwood—famed for her introduction of punk clothes—whose designs set the pace in this sphere and are now reaching a wider audience. Margaret Howell's straightforward clothes are original and refreshing interpretations of classic British designs [195]. She takes the best elements from the tailor's art and traditional 'country' attire and up-dates them to suit current taste. The first temporary exhibition in the Dress Collection's refurbished gallery, 'The Little Black Dress 1912 to 1983', ends on the high note of a classic jersey dress from Jean Muir's spring 1983 collection.

The twentieth-century collection continues to expand and gaps are gradually filled. For instance, in 1983 the department was given a Paco Rabanne linked paillette mini-dress of about 1968; previously this much acclaimed designer had not been represented in the collection. The group of clothes by artist-craftsmen has improved with the addition of works by Kaffe Fassett, Sasha Kagan and Marian Clayden. The collection lacks examples by the *prêt-à-porter* talents such as Sonia Rykiel, Karl Lagerfeld, dorothée bis and Thierry Mugler, but in 1982 Miss Coco Ettedgui gave two 1970s works by the trend-setting designer Kenzo. A selection of clothes from current American designers would prove a considerable asset. We occasionally have pleasant surprises: after the opening of the Dress Collection, influential Italian designers, including Gianni Versace, offered works from their latest ranges.

The collection has its weaknesses: some designers are over represented and others not at all. There is a preponderance of evening dresses simply because women tend to jettison everyday clothes yet hoard their resplendent gowns. Eventually, these deficiencies will be made good and, in any case, they are far outweighed by the collection's extensive coverage of the art of fashionable dress which has made it world famous. Present policy and that of the foreseeable future is to continue to collect fashionable clothes of distinction and the highest artistic value.

1 *The Lady's Realm*, October, 1901, p. 771
2 Edward Hulton, *When I was a Child*, The Cresset Press, 1952, p. 53
3 *Lady of Fashion. Heather Firbank (1888–1954) and what she wore between 1908 and 1921*, Victoria and Albert Museum, 1960
4 Miriam J. Benkovitz, *Ronald Firbank: A Biography*, Weidenfeld and Nicolson, 1970, p. 129
5 ibid, p. 269
6 Lady Duff Gordon, *Discretions and Indiscretions*, Jarrolds, 1932, pp. 65–6
7 Paul Poiret, *My First Fifty Years*, Victor Gollancz, 1931, p. 89
8 *Fashion: an anthology by Cecil Beaton*, Victoria and Albert Museum, HMSO, 1971
9 Obituary, *The Times*, Wednesday 12 February 1964
10 *Liberty's 1875–1975: An exhibition to mark the firm's centenary* Victoria and Albert Museum, HMSO, 1975
11 Elsa Schiaparelli, *Shocking Life*, J. M. Dent & Sons, 1954, p. 98
12 Hardy Amies, *Just So Far*, Collins, 1954, p. 105
13 ibid, pp. 105–6
14 Bettina Ballard, *In My Fashion*, Secker and Warburg, 1960, p. 225
15 Brigid Keenan, *Dior in Vogue*, Octopus Books, 1981
16 *The Queen*, 25 August 1954, p. 22
17 Elizabeth Ann Coleman, *The Genius of Charles James*, The Brooklyn Museum, 1982, p. 126
18 Iris Ashley, *The Daily Mail*, 4 February 1955
19 Françoise Mohrt, *25 Ans de Marie Claire de 1954 a 1979*, Marie Claire, 1979
20 *Jean Muir*, Leeds Art Galleries and the Leeds Art Collections Fund, 1980
21 Valerie D. Mendes, *A Collection Grows —the Gift of British Fashions for Winter 1979*, The V & A Album, Temple Gate Publishing Ltd. 1983

DOLL of carved and painted wood in
contemporary dress and accessories
English, about 1755–60
T.90-1980

DOLLS

The main collection of dolls belonging to the Museum is housed at the Bethnal Green Museum of Childhood, a branch of the Victoria and Albert Museum. The Department of Textiles and Dress holds a small number, approximately forty, in fashionable dress dating from the late seventeenth century, with two early twentieth-century dolls.

Fashion dolls were originally made by dressmakers to illustrate their skills in miniature for their clients. The practice developed in the seventeenth century and continued until the growth of fashion magazines in the nineteenth century. It has seldom been used in the twentieth century. Such dolls are important, even unique costume documents, rich in detail, providing valuable information for the student of historical dress, especially for the seventeenth century when good visual sources are limited. The earliest and most superb examples in the Museum's collection are a pair of wooden dolls known as 'Lord and Lady Clapham' (see p. 20) dating from about 1695. They were purchased by public subscription, complete with their accessories and the wooden chairs on which they sat.

There is a very good selection of dolls covering the first half of the eighteenth century, in particular a large family of wooden dolls of about 1730, including two gentlemen, a nurse, child and baby, and various ladies with additional clothes. The Museum recently acquired a doll which had previously been on loan (T.90 to V-1980), dressed in a beautiful brown silk sack-back dress of the fashion 1755–60. It is not until much later, however, in the second half of the nineteenth century, that the collection once again becomes comprehensive and includes some French bisque and German wax dolls.

ALINA GRIBBIN

SIX BUTTONS FROM A SET OF 18, satin printed with profile portraits of de Lameth, Lafayette, Mirabeau, Barnave, Volleney and Garat le jeune. The mounts are of glass and gilt metal. *French, 1789–90, given by C. W. Dyson Perrins, T.39B, G, K, F, C & A-1948*

BUTTONS, BUCKLES AND CLASPS

The history of costume fastenings can best be studied in the V & A on original garments. The collection of loose fastenings (which includes buttons, shoe and belt buckles, clasps and dress clips), is large but not comprehensive, the bulk of the material dating from after 1890.

Among the earlier fastenings is a small group of shoe buckles, of silver, cut steel, pewter, paste and ivory, dating from about 1760 to 1810, and several sets of late eighteenth-century coat buttons, one of which, a set of eighteen depicting the leading political figures of the French Revolution, deserves mention here. The holdings of eighteenth and nineteenth-century buttons are small partly due to the popularity of cloth-covered buttons which rarely survive once parted from a garment.

Twentieth-century fastenings are well represented in the collection, and these can be divided into four main groups: the first of French gilt metal and enamel buttons which date from the years around 1900; the second of laminated plastic, glass and base metal clasps and buttons, the majority of which date from the 1930s and which show the 'modernist' style of the decade; the third of buttons made for leading couturiers by François Victor Hugo in the 1930s and 1940s; and the fourth of glazed stoneware buttons made by Lucie Rie between 1945 and 1948 and given by her to the Museum in 1982.

HILARY YOUNG

MEN'S HATS

The collection of men's hats is considerably smaller than that of women's, but nevertheless includes examples of most of the significant styles of the period—a fact that reflects the general conservatism of male taste.

The earliest important pieces consist of a group of plain knitted caps which were fashionable in the sixteenth century, a style that later degenerated into the so-called 'Apprentice Boy's Cap'. High-quality Elizabethan and Jacobean embroidery is represented in a good collection of early seventeenth-century night caps, an important element of informal male dress from the seventeenth to the nineteenth centuries. From the mid-seventeenth century three rare 'sugar loaf' hats may be of beaver felt—a fine beaver or 'caster' being a highly valued, and very costly, possession at the time.

The transition from the seventeenth to the eighteenth century is made with a small group of undress caps in silk and velvet, often decorated with silk or metal thread embroidery. However, that symbol of the eighteenth century, the three-cornered hat, is hardly represented in the collection. Happily, the principal style of the nineteenth century, the top hat, fares better, thanks in large part to a collection given by the Hatters Association in 1937.

The eclipse of male headwear in the twentieth century is reflected in the fact that only the later 1960s, a period when the hat enjoyed a brief return to fashion, is well represented—by a number of flamboyant Herbert Johnson hats from the Beaton Collection.

Peter Giffin

LADIES' HATS

The hat reflects social and economic status and sometimes age as well as high fashion. Before the eighteenth century the coif or cap was the main form of headwear for women and was expected to be worn at all times, indoors or out, for religious as well as social reasons. From the eighteenth century on, the hat as a definite form was adopted by women as well as men, and the variety of styles and shapes have evolved with the changing shape of fashion. Since the First World War, with the increased social and economic freedom of women, a marked proliferation of styles and shapes has taken place. Other influences, notably changing hairstyles, have also affected hat design.

The Museum's collection of hats has been built up in a rather piecemeal fashion which means, regrettably, there are noticeable gaps. However, in the last decade a concerted effort has been made to fill these gaps, particularly with regard to the twentieth century. There is a good collection of seventeenth-century coifs and caps, but the eighteenth century is poorly represented. A characteristic popular style from the 1730s onwards (and again in the 1860s) was the *bergère* or shepherdess straw hat, of which unfortunately there are only two examples. The calash, a large folding hooped hood, was fashionable in the 1770s (and again in the 1820s and 1830s). There are a number of nineteenth-century examples, but none that can definitely be dated to the eighteenth century. Throughout the nineteenth century the predominant style was the bonnet. It reached its extravagant extreme in both size and decoration in the 1820s and 1830s, and gradually diminished in size until by the last quarter of the century it was very small. The main strength of the nineteenth-century collection lies in a number of excellent examples of the large bonnets, and includes a good range of small bonnets, mainly

from the 1880s, a number of which were given in 1923. The very early part of the century and the last decade are not well represented. Only one example of a 'coal-scuttle' shaped hat from 1807, and a few examples of the turban-shaped headdress which was very popular in the 1820s, exist in the collection due to their fragility and also the lack of interest in preserving them once they were out of fashion.

Two large acquisitions form the nucleus of the twentieth-century collection: firstly, part of a purchase of fashionable costume which belonged to Miss Heather Firbank, ranging from about 1905 to 1920; and, secondly, a collection of hats from the Cecil Beaton gift of costumes which date from about 1920 to 1970. Since then the twentieth-century collection has been consolidated by further acquisitions. As well as hats by leading milliners including Aage Thaarup and Simone Mirman, there are also designs by such well-known international couturiers as Jacques Fath, Schiaparelli and Balenciaga.

Although the collection of hats represents most fashionable styles of this century, there are obvious gaps from the very beginning of the century and the last decade. However, examples from two contemporary milliners, namely David Shilling and Stephen Jones, bring the collection right up to date.

Whilst purchases can be made, the generosity of donors has been especially helpful. The hats given by Mrs B. Church, Mrs D. M. Haynes and Mrs M. Clarke, as part of larger gifts of twentieth-century costume and accessories, have greatly enhanced the collection.

ALINA GRIBBIN AND LINDA WOOLLEY

HAIR ACCESSORIES

Women have decorated their hair with feathers, jewels, beads, ribbons and a multitude of other types of ornament since ancient times. The more fragile kinds have largely disappeared, and the collection consists mainly of accessories, such as combs and hatpins, made of more durable materials. The majority of the collection dates from the nineteenth and twentieth centuries, although there are a few examples of earlier combs, one dated 1701 which is on display, and a set of combs in a comb-case from the late seventeenth century.

Hair-combs for ornamentation first appeared in the early nineteenth century with the revival of classical taste, and their decoration often reflects this fashion. There are a number of nineteenth-century combs in the collection, the majority made from tortoiseshell and of varying shapes and sizes, many ornately decorated with paste or gilt. Hair-combs changed quite considerably in shape to suit contemporary hair-styles, as, for example, in the period between 1860 and 1880 when they were fashioned in the style of a coronet to fasten the elaborate *coiffure* of that time. Hair-combs have continued to be used as functional and decorative accessories this century, and the collection includes a small number made from materials ranging from tortoiseshell to plastic, and decorated with paste, artificial flowers or feathers.

In the 1890s hatpins specifically designed to be decorative as well as functional were first introduced, and although there are no examples from the nineteenth century in the collection, the early part of the twentieth century is well represented. Hatpins from this period were used to anchor large hats which perched on top of equally voluminous hair-styles. The decorated tops vary in dimension and ornateness and

HAT of black straw with large curved ostrich feather, *English, about 1913, worn by Miss Heather Firbank*, T.109-1960

BONNET of Dunstable straw trimmed with ostrich feathers, *English, about 1825, given by Mr M. Herbert*, T.91-1957

MAN'S UNDRESS CAP of red silk velvet. The dome-shaped crown has four puckers at the top and an open socket behind, probably for holding a plume or feather. The wide brim is lined with pale blue dotted silk.
English, early 18th century
Bequeathed by the Rev. Dr. N. H. C. Ruddock
T.44-1918

COMB of tortoiseshell, fan-shaped and decorated with pastes, *French, last quarter 19th century, given by Miss D. Gibbon*, T.263-1958

HEADBAND of glass beads and pastes, *French, Schiaparelli, 1938, given by Lady Freida Valentine, The Cecil Beaton Collection*, T.414-1974

HATPINS in various materials, *English, 1953–5*, part of T.66-1983

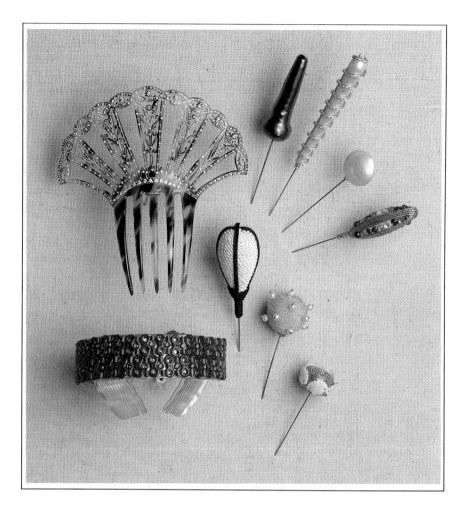

are made from various different materials including glass, ivory, metal and mother-of-pearl. Hatpins of the later part of the twentieth century, in small numbers, are also included in the collection. Examples of the popular bandeaux and headbands of the first three decades of this century include metal headbands studded with paste and head-dresses of diamanté spangled mesh.

The nature of the majority of hair ornaments has dictated that they have neither been considered worthy of preservation, nor been hardy enough to survive accidentally. However, given that this is the case, good examples of the most important types of hair accessory are represented in the collection.

ALINA GRIBBIN AND LINDA WOOLLEY

GLOVES

Gloves, to be both functional and elegant, should follow closely the contours of the hand. In order to do so they must be manufactured from pliable materials—leather, woven fabrics, knitted fabrics or netted fibres. Given these limitations, it is not surprising that there are only two basic types to be considered as fashionable accessories—the glove, with or without a gauntlet, and the fingerless mitten. Both styles are well represented in the collection.

Among the earliest examples are leather gauntlet gloves from the seventeenth century—elaborately embroidered and fringed with silks

A selection of gloves from the collection

and metal threads. It had long been traditional to use such costly gloves as gifts and it is probable that the more elaborate ones were regarded less as practical accessories and more as symbols of esteem or of status.

The richly decorated gloves of the seventeenth century were replaced in the eighteenth by simpler styles. Gloves became an indispensable item of dress and by 1740 it had become common to wear fingerless mittens, frequently made from silk or linen. As variations, both the gauntlet glove and the fingerless mitten proved to be of enduring popularity: the mitten became fashionable again in the second third of the nineteenth century in a wrist-length version made of netted silk, and the collection also includes a satin mitten designed by Elsa Schiaparelli in 1938. The gauntlet glove re-appeared as a lady's accessory in the 1920s and 1930s.

Woollen gloves seldom survive, but the Museum is fortunate to possess a pair which belonged to Thomas Coutts, who died in 1822.

The collection does include many examples of gloves and mittens made from knitted silk, dating from the eighteenth and nineteenth centuries, and cotton jersey gloves of the twentieth century.

JENNIFER WEARDEN

FANS

The Museum possesses a fine collection of some 600 European fans, of which a selection is shown here, including one of the earliest—a rare brisé fan of straw work (*bottom left, about 1620–30, given by Miss Margaret Simeon, T.184-1982*). A French fan (*bottom right, 1670s, T.155-1978*) is, in its sombre colouring, classical subject matter and unadorned sticks, more typical of the predominating seventeenth-century style.

By the eighteenth century, however, domestic scenes, contemporary events or popular plays are regularly illustrated, such as the apotheosis from Racine's Iphigènie depicted on the French varnished ivory fan (*2nd row left, 2304-1876*), a type fashionable from the 1680s to the 1740s.

Folding fans were introduced into Europe through Eastern trade in the fifteenth and sixteenth centuries, and oriental influence remained, as in the chinoiserie details of an early eighteenth-century Dutch fan (*2nd row right, given by Sir Matthew Digby Wyatt and Lady Wyatt, T.211–1959*).

A fine French wedding fan (*3rd row left, about 1780, bequeathed by Mrs C. R. Thornett, T.765-1972*), painted on silk and richly decorated with spangles, mother-of-pearl, straw work and feathers, shows the eighteenth-century fan at its most sophisticated, but a marked change of taste at the end of the century is demonstrated in the austere English fan (*3rd row right, about 1800, bequeathed by Capt. H. B. Murray, T.379-1910*), and the horn fan (*4th row left, bequeathed by H.M. Queen Mary, Circ.243-1953*) fashionable in the early nineteenth century.

Printing largely superseded painting in the nineteenth century, often employing an anachronistic style. The French fan (*4th row right, about 1860, bequeathed by Dame Ada MacNaughton, T.61-1920*) is typical. Commemorative fans—another common type—are represented by that celebrating the 1851 Exhibition (*5th row left, given by Miss Farrah, T.290-1971*).

The fan reached its greatest size in the late nineteenth century, illustrated by Jean de Grandmaison's monogrammed example (*5th row right, 1892, given by Mrs Holland, T.65-1951*). Representing its final flowering as a fashionable accessory are the two early twentieth-century examples, French (*top left, signed Charles Barbier, 1911, T.333-1978*) and English (*top centre, about 1915, given by Major and Mrs Broughton, T.251-1972*).

The fan's last function was that of advertisement, and the 1920s Pierrette (*top right, T.257-1978*) advertises, verso, a Paris restaurant.

Considerable attention was paid to the decoration of the sticks from the early eighteenth century, and three closed ivory fans give a taste of these decorative possibilities. The first (*bottom right, French or Italian, about 1730, T.58-1970*) is carved so that the sticks form a Negro head when closed. The second (*bottom left, French, about 1830, given by Mr O. E. Wise, T.96-1957*) has a guard inlaid with tortoiseshell, silver and ivory; whilst that of the last (*centre, English, about 1850, bequeathed by Emily Beauclerk, T.188-1920*) is carved in high relief with lilies of the valley and forget-me-nots.

PETER GIFFIN

CANES AND WALKING STICKS

The Museum has a collection of only about forty canes and walking-sticks. The standard of design and execution of the decorative knobs and handles is frequently not remarkable, but the collection provides a good cross-section of the types carried in the seventeenth, eighteenth and nineteenth centuries.

The cane was first carried as a fashionable accessory in the fifteenth century, but it was not until the seventeenth century that its use became widespread. The earliest example in the collection is of a native soft-wood, painted in imitation of marbling, which can be tentatively dated to about 1630. All other canes of the seventeenth, and the majority of those from the eighteenth century, are of imported malacca. Almost all have button or pear-shaped knobs of ivory with silver piqué (fashionable at the close of the seventeenth century), pewter, gold, gilt-brass or horn.

In contrast to this uniformity in overall design and construction, those dating from the nineteenth century exhibit great diversity. A number are painted or engraved, or have carved shafts or handles. The materials include Japanese bamboo, native fruitwoods, tortoiseshell, the traditional malacca and in one instance narwhal horn. Several of these are novelties: one, for example, has an ivory handle carved as Andromeda.

The Museum owns very few twentieth-century canes. Canes and walking-sticks have declined in popularity since the beginning of the century and are today rarely carried as a fashionable accessory, this function having been taken over by the tightly-rolled umbrella.

HILARY YOUNG

PARASOLS

The parasol as a fashionable accessory is a phenomenon of the 1830s to the 1920s. Before this time parasols were primarily utilitarian and, consequently, quite plain. The Museum has two dating from the second half of the eighteenth century and a few from the first part of the nineteenth century. They have long wooden sticks with simple decoration, such as a small ivory handle, and covers of green or brown silk twill.

By the late 1830s parasols were smaller, lighter, and had become objects of elegant display. There is a good selection of these in the V & A collection but, unfortunately, many are in a fragile condition and can no longer be fully opened without causing damage to the covers. Sticks and handles range from turned wood to ornately carved ivory and coral. Several of the smallest 'carriage' parasols have folding sticks. Covers are colourful and include examples of woven, painted and printed silks, lace, embroidery, appliqué, beadwork and such novelties as feathers and rafia. A few are in their original boxes.

The late 1860s and 1870s saw a change to larger and heavier designs which in the 1880s became longer and more slender. We have few of these types. The 1890s are only slightly better represented. By this time parasols were large and flamboyant: ruched chiffon and lace flounces were bedecked with ribbons. This style, together with plainer parasols for morning wear, continued over the turn of the century.

The Museum's holdings of 1890 to 1930 are enhanced by a gift of fourteen parasols and umbrellas which belonged to Lady Fairhaven, daughter of an American millionaire. The 1920s are also well covered from other sources, particularly by a group of unused Belgian parasols; these are exquisitely made from the finest materials and epitomize the robust, chunky designs of the mid-1920s.

FRANCES HINCHCLIFFE

CANES AND WALKING-STICKS, left to right: *All items are English unless stated otherwise.*
1, T.1822-1913, malacca with ivory knob, *early 18th century*; 2, 539-1872, malacca with gold cap, *about 1775–1800*; 3, T.62-1935, narwhal horn with tortoiseshell cap, *about 1825–50*; 4, T.18-1949, bamboo, *Japanese, late 19th century*; 5, riding-crop, T.158D-1962, plaited leather, whalebone and bone, *about 1900*; 6, 943-1864, partridge wood with hardwood knob, *Continental, about 1800–25*; 7, 643-1872, thornwood, *19th century*; 8, swordstick, T.15&A-1920, plaited gut sheath, ivory handle and gilt-brass mounts, *about 1800*; 9, T.235-1931, malacca with Chinese porcelain knob, *late 19th century*; 10, 942-1864, malacca with gilt-brass knob, *about 1750–70*; 11, T.232-1972, malacca with ivory knob, *French, late 19th century*; 12, T.90-1965, malacca with silver-mounted ivory handle, *about 1895*. Also shown is a selection of English, French and Belgian parasols dating from the third quarter of the eighteenth century to the 1920s.

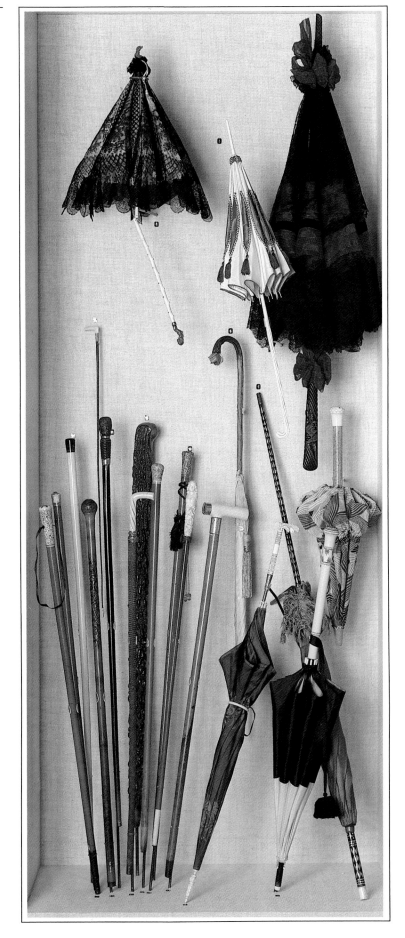

MULE, embroidered velvet, *English, about 1650*, T.631-1972

SHOE, kid, with a stencilled pattern of circles, *English, 1790s, given by Mrs H. P. Mitchell*, T.115a-1933

SHOE, leather, laced with silk ribbon, *English; Hook Knowles & Co., about 1900, given by Mr John Tayleur*, T.246a-1979

SHOE, tulle over satin, with high stiletto heel, *French: Roger Vivier for Dior, 1954, given by Mr Roger Vivier, The Cecil Beaton Collection*, T.148-1974

DRESS WELLINGTON BOOT, black patent leather galosh and red morocco leather leg, *English, 1820s, given by Messrs Harrods*, T.491a-1913

PLATFORM SHOE, patchwork snakeskin, with ½″ stacked sole and 2¾″ heel, *English: about 1972, given by Mr David Shilling*, T.83-1983

SHOES

The collection of women's shoes is reasonably comprehensive for the period from the mid-seventeenth century to the early twentieth century and is far superior to that of men's, where the problem of man's habitual neglect of his clothing is particularly acute. Apart from a number of men's leather shoes excavated from plague pits there are few pre-nineteenth-century examples. With the 1851 Exhibition several model boots and shoes were acquired, and a small later group traces the evolution of the modern classic man's shoe—fully developed by the 1900s. Finally, the adventurously garish late 1960s and early 1970s are represented by examples of the work of Chelsea Cobbler, Mr Freedom and Terry de Havilland.

Among the finest examples in the women's shoe collection is an ornately embroidered mule of about 1650. Clogs are also represented: worn over fabric shoes, they were a necessity in the seventeenth and eighteenth centuries. Tie and buckle shoes illustrate the variety of materials used; brocaded silk, applied silk braid—as on a wedding shoe of 1748—embroidery and couched straw work. A painted kid shoe of about 1760 is a rare example, as leather did not become common until the end of the century. Bright pink and yellow patterned kid shoes of the 1790s with their low heels and pointed toes seem refreshingly different.

By the 1820s heels had completely disappeared. Many shoes survive from this period and the Museum has an unworn pale blue satin pair. Low cut and flimsy, they reflect the dresses of the time. Women began to wear short boots and from the 1820s they became standard wear for much of the century. Examples of side and front lace, elastic and button boots in fabric or leather—or both—indicate the range.

In the last quarter of the nineteenth century heels increased in height and shoes became popular again. With greater social freedom women began to lead more active lives, a tendency reinforced by the demand for women's labour in the First World War. Shoe styles became more practical. Court, Cromwell, bar, Oxfords and lace-ups are all represented in the collection. The bar shoe became typical of the twenties, beaded for evening wear, although high-laced and Russian boots were alternatives for outdoor wear.

The 1930s saw many new developments as, for example, the wooden platform sandal of 1938, developed from beachwear. Utility shoes in the collection demonstrate the priority of economy and functionalism during the Second World War.

The increasing emphasis on casual wear has, in recent years, created an enormous diversity of styles. Although this has meant limitations within the collection, major trends are represented. Roger Vivier's stiletto of 1954 is extreme and elegant, and his satin and plastic creations of the sixties show the increasing use of synthetics in footwear, used in the many copies of Courrèges' white leather boot of 1966, part of the 'space age' look. The revival of the platform sole in the late sixties was an integral part of the nostalgia and colourfulness of the period, and it is represented in the collection by Biba and Mary Quant. A more recent acquisition is a high, red patent sandal by Manolo Blahnik, a far cry from the buckle shoes of the eighteenth century.

PETER GIFFIN AND CLAIRE WILCOX

STOCKINGS

The stocking collection is hardly comprehensive; stockings are seldom treasured and kept for posterity. The Museum, however, is fortunate in possessing two particularly rare survivals, a pair of late sixteenth-century cut cloth hose and a pair of hand-knitted woollen boot hose from the 1660s.

By the beginning of the eighteenth century knitted stockings had replaced cut cloth hose and the use of the stocking or knitting frame was established in Europe. Most of the collection's eighteenth-century stockings are frame-knitted in coloured silks and embellished with sumptuous embroidered clocks.

Examples from the first half of the nineteenth century, both in cotton and silk, are of a finer gauge. The majority are white, then the fashionable colour, and are either plain or knitted in a lacy openwork stitch with self-coloured embroidery. With the development of chemical dyestuffs in the 1860s brightly coloured stockings began to be worn for informal occasions. The Museum has a fair selection from the late nineteenth century, illustrating the enormous variety of colours and decoration, including embroidered clocks, lace inserts and beadwork.

Left to right: KNITTED SILK STOCKING, *English, probably 1860s*, T.209–1928; CUT CLOTH HOSE, linen embroidered with silk, *English, 1660s*, T.126-1938; KNITTED SILK STOCKING, *probably English or French, mid-18th century*, T.34-1969; KNITTED SILK STOCKING, embroidered with sequins and beads, *French, Universal Exhibition, Paris, 1900*, T.53-1962

The early twentieth century is adequately represented by silk, cotton and rayon stockings, both fully fashioned and circular knitted on power-driven machinery. Many of these are the production and gift of I. & R. Morley Co. Ltd. The gradual move towards an ultra-sheer 'no stocking' look was made possible by the wider availability of nylon in the 1950s—unfortunately the Department lacks examples. Thanks to the recent gift of the Nylon Hosiery Company Ltd. there is a good group of fancy stretch nylon tights which were popularized by Mary Quant and Twiggy in the mid-1960s.

FRANCES HINCHCLIFFE

BAGS AND PURSES

Although bags serve many purposes, those which form part of the Dress Collection were acquired as fashionable accessories and bags designed for other uses—items of luggage, document cases, storage bags, etc. are not included.

Examples in the collection range from the small, often ingeniously designed, sweet bags of the late sixteenth century, filled with scented herbs to disguise the odours of inadequate hygiene, to the capacious leather shoulder bags of the 1970s. Between the two are many styles that are instantly recognizable—frame purses, draw-string bags, handbags and clutch bags. There are other styles no longer in common use—late nineteenth-century *châtelaine* bags, eighteenth and nineteenth-century stocking purses and the detachable pockets of the seventeenth and eighteenth centuries, designed to be hidden under the skirts, but often richly embroidered.

Although the splendour of eighteenth-century purses, embroidered with silks and metal threads, is difficult to surpass, several techniques have been employed to decorate bags, from the simple use of printed textiles to the utilization of glass beads, steel spangles, enamels and plastics. The bags and purses in this collection are representative of the many styles popular over the past four centuries and they are made not only of leather and woven textiles, but also of knotted fibres, moulded plastics and alloys.

JENNIFER WEARDEN

POCHETTE, satin embroidered with silk, silver-gilt wire, strip and braid in satin stitch, couching and speckling with french knots. Silver-gilt fringe, strings and tassels. *Italian, early 18th century, bequeathed by Mrs J. R. Lee.* T.46-1950

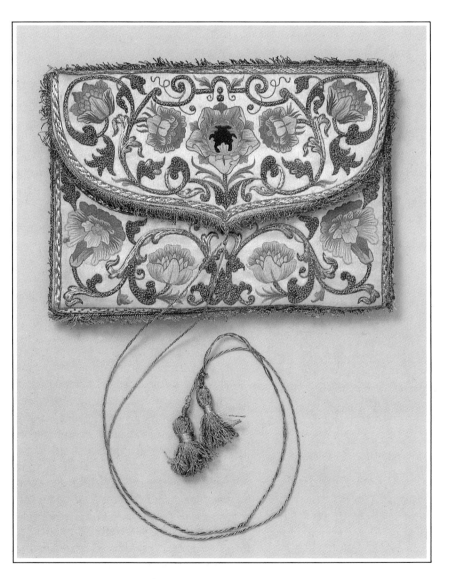

HANDKERCHIEF, linen, embroidered with silk and trimmed with silver-gilt bobbin lace,
English, early 17th century, T.133-1956

MOURNING HANDKERCHIEF, linen, embroidered with silk, with Queen Victoria's monogram
English, second half of the 19th century, given by Their Royal Highnesses The Duke and Duchess of Gloucester, T.48-1957

HANDKERCHIEF, monogrammed. Embroidered cotton edged with Valenciennes bobbin lace
English, mid-19th century, given by Lady Watts, T.95-1959

HANDKERCHIEF, block printed silk crêpe
English; Liberty & Co. Ltd, late 1930s, given by A. I. Stewart Liberty, Esq., T.292-1976

HANDKERCHIEFS

The majority of the handkerchiefs which form the collection have been acquired not as fashionable accessories but as examples of historical styles and of lace, embroidery and printing techniques. Some fine examples from the late sixteenth to the early seventeenth century reflect the importance of embroidery, which included cut work, whitework and needlelace, in a period of ostentatious display in dress.

Over one hundred printed handkerchiefs, mainly British, commemorate and record various subjects, such as a map of England, printed on satin in about 1686. A later example is 'KEEP THE HOME FIRES BURNING', manufactured during the First World War. Among the most interesting are the political satires of the eighteenth and nineteenth centuries, often borrowed from contemporary cartoons. Silk snuff handkerchiefs are well represented; large and ornamental, they were worn hanging from the pocket—a great temptation to thieves.

Whitework flourished in the eighteenth and nineteenth centuries, and embroidered handkerchiefs, often edged with lace, were an essential

WAISTCOAT, canvas embroidered with cotton in cross and vertical tent stitches, the panels of laid silk chenille with couched cord decoration, the waistcoat fronts and pockets edged with silk velvet.
French: H. Creed & Co., about 1900–1905
T.177-1967

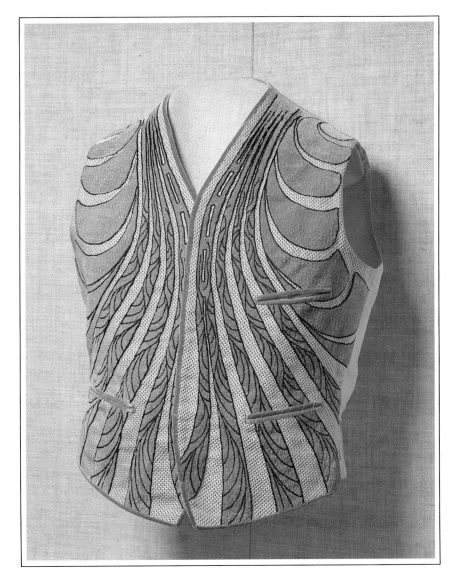

fashion item. There are few examples from the eighteenth century, but the 1840s and the second half of the nineteenth century are well represented. Many are monogrammed and would have been part of a trousseau. Convention also required mourning handkerchiefs; the Museum has some which belonged to Queen Victoria.

Handkerchiefs reflected the general direction of the decorative arts in the first part of the twentieth century. The Museum has several 'Art Deco' inspired printed silk handkerchiefs as well as floral silk squares made by Liberty & Co. Although the collection has attractive handkerchiefs from 1930 onwards, this originally elegant accessory has become an essentially functional item.

CLAIRE WILCOX

WAISTCOATS

The Museum's collection of waistcoats is extensive, numbering nearly 300 examples, excluding those acquired with coats or suits. Waistcoat styles have evolved slowly and, though there are notable gaps in the collection, the overall development of the cut of the garment from the early eighteenth century to about 1875 is well illustrated.

Among the eighteenth-century waistcoats are examples cut from figured silks and velvets, in some instances woven to shape, but the greater number are decorated with embroidery. Of these embroidered waistcoats mention should be made here of a large group, dating from the last forty years of the century, with fronts of ivory silk or satin. Waistcoats with fronts of plain silk were fashionable throughout the eighteenth century but lacking decoration were perhaps not thought worth keeping, have rarely survived and consequently are under-represented in the collection. For the same reason the early nineteenth-century embroidered full dress waistcoats and the 'fancy' and wedding waistcoats outnumber other, less lavishly decorated nineteenth-century types. The 'fancy' waistcoats date from the 1830s to the 1870s and have fronts of figured silks with small patterns, or of velvet, woven to shape, or with the tartan patterns popular in the 1850s.

During the 1870s suits with all three items of the same material became fashionable and the waistcoat, hitherto the most decorative item of a man's dress, suffered a decline in importance from which it has never recovered. The Museum's collection reflects this change and, with the exception of those acquired with suits, includes few late nineteenth or twentieth-century waistcoats.

HILARY YOUNG

SHIRTS AND TIES

The Museum houses a number of rare and important Tudor and Stuart shirts, the earliest being a boy's shirt of about 1540, once reputed to have belonged to Prince Arthur. A shirt of about 1630 is embroidered with motifs traceable to a contemporary needlework manual, whilst a shift of about the same date is copiously decorated with bobbin lace insertions.

From the late seventeenth century the shirt became a more formalized item of male dress, and the collection includes many beautifully made plain linen examples. A number of fine nineteenth-century shirts have fronts embroidered with whitework, but by about 1900 this had largely fossilised into the stiff-fronted dress shirt. A feature of the dress shirt was the detached starched collar; but of the great variety of styles then available, few have survived in the collection. Indeed, the twentieth century, with its growing informality in male dress, is meagrely represented. There are almost no casual shirts prior to the 1960s, and from this period just three or four bear witness to the exuberance of psychedelia.

Apart from a good collection of lace used for cravats and ruffles, ties, as such, are also poorly represented. A few stocks and cravats demonstrate the conservatism of nineteenth-century male dress. More interesting are three batik ties made in 1921 by Ilse von Scheel, an artist associated with the Bauhaus, and a magnificent woven tie designed by Picasso in the 1930s.

However, the 1960s—perhaps the great period for tie design—is well covered; extravagant kipper ties with Pop Art, Op Art and psychedelic designs reflect the optimism of the Peacock Revolution.

PETER GIFFIN

SHIRT of woven striped cotton
English : Turnbull and Asser, 1970
KIPPER TIE of silk printed with
chequer design
French : Yves St Laurent, about 1970,
Given by Mr Anthony Powell
T.353-1979 and T.368-1979

CATALOGUE

Women's Dress before 1900

1 GOWN, cream Italian silk with a brocaded formal, floral pattern in blue, green and pink, additionally patterned with diagonal cuts
English, early 17th century

The gown is straight-cut and flowing, with the fronts extended to form shoulder straps, the fullness held to the figure by pleats tacked loosely onto a strong linen lining which reaches from shoulders to high-waist-level. Inserted under the arms and reaching to the hem are two gores, giving extra flow and fullness. There is a semi-circular stiffened collar with two worked eyelets in the back for the attachment of the *supportasse*. The shoulder wings are tabs, doubled over. Applied narrow dark pink ribbon and traces of silver braid emphasize the cut of neck and shoulders. Stitch marks suggest that the gown was made from re-used fabric. It was also altered; the gores may be additions and the hem has been pieced. The silver braid may in part belong to an earlier state. Because of its condition, it is no longer possible to be certain whether the absence of sleeves is accidental or intentional. Another from this collection, 178&A-1900, otherwise very similar, has hanging sleeves, but a third, 174-1900, has none. Certainly, in contemporary portraits and tailors' pattern books dresses normally have sleeves.

The gown came from a collection of clothes kept by the Isham family of Lamport Hall, Northants.
189-1900

CUFFS, Italian needle lace, *early 17th century*, 281&A-1890, 676&A-1892
HANDKERCHIEF, cut work and detached needle lace (modern centre), *Italian, early 17th century, given by Mrs Charles E. Allen, O.B.E.*, T.247-1918   page 12

2 GOWN, a mantua of pale blue silk brocaded in silver with a large scale design of fantastic fruits and leaves on looped trails
English, 1720s

The back of the bodice is pleated and stitched, the pleats running over the shoulders to form double robings which merge with the skirt draped back in a basque with inner cords and wound silver buttons. The sides of the skirt are folded sides to centre, seamed on face and reverse, so that the train is right side out if turned up to hip level. The sleeves are wide and hang below the elbow, the folds held in position by two lead weights stitched inside the back of the deep, turned-back cuff. The bodice is lined with white and faced with pink silk. The back pleats are un-lined but held in position with two bands of the brocaded silk. This is an early feature, recalling those discussed in 'A Mantua, c.1708-9, Clive House Museum, Shrewsbury' by J. Arnold, *Costume 4*, 1970. Fragments only remained from the petticoat but enough for a conjectural reconstruction based on the portrait of an unknown lady by S. Belle (1674-1734), s.&d. 1718, anon. colln., which had a hip yoke and deep flounce with gauged heading. Similar bodices can be seen in B. Lens, (1682-1740), *The Correct Dress of the Head*, 1724-5, especially plate 25 (V&A E.1662 & E.1677-1926); also in chalk drawings by A. Watteau (1684-1721) of about 1720.
T.88 to B-1978

CAP with LAPPETS, Brussels bobbin lace, *1720s*, 7427, 7428&A-1861 and BORDERS, Brussels bobbin lace, *Flemish, 1720s, bequeathed by Mr L. C. Collier*, T.3-1963, *and Mrs Flora Hill*, T.125-1973   page 16

Waistcoats and heavily-trained skirts were fashionable in the early 1880s. This dress of 1879–81 is made from brown satin trimmed with rose pink and figured pink and green satin, chenille tassels and machine-made lace.
T.238&A-1916   [59]

3 JACKET, silk damask
English, about 1720

A 'waistcoat' woven in buff with an extra yellow silk pattern weft in a design of vertical meandering floral trails. It is a tightly fitting hip-length jacket, the fronts and two-piece back shaped to the figure, and an extra panel, the 'side-body', under the arms. The skirts, cut in one with the body of the jacket, are gored, and overlap and flare at the hips. They are faced with green silk. The sleeves are smoothly set at the shoulders and curved to the arm. They are finished with a flat, open, turned-back cuff in leaf green moiré which matches the robings. The jacket is lined with brownish linen, and boned at the laced-up fastening.

Randle Holme's *The Academey of Armory and Blazon*, 1688, describes unstiffened bodices with gored skirts as 'waistcoats', assigning them to the 'middle and lower sort of woman'. In this context they appear in Gavin Hamilton's (1697–1737), *The Fortune Teller*, (about 1725), anon. colln. But, though this jacket is made from re-used fabric, its excellent cut, fit and finish are such that it is closer to that worn in the anonymous portrait of Anne, wife of Henry Ingram, 7th Viscount Irwin, about 1720, Temple Newsam, Leeds.

Given by Miss D. Gibbon
T.264-1958

PETTICOAT, shot green silk, lined with wool and quilted in a diamond pattern, *English, mid-18th century*, T.306-1982
CAP, *English, mid-18th century, given by Mrs B. H. Davey*, T.194-1915
APRON, embroidered in whitework in a Chinoiserie pattern, edged with Flemish bobbin lace, *English, 1720–1730, given by Mrs Dora Carson Roberts and Miss Tufnell*, T.9-1952
SLEEVE FRILLS, linen, *English, mid-18th century, given by the Earl of Harrowby*, T.352A&B-1975   page 31

4 GOWN AND PETTICOAT, a mantua made from Spitalfields silk (about 1732) with a brown tabby ground brocaded in red, pink, green and dark blue silks and chenille
English, mid-1730s

The back of the bodice is pleated and stitched, the pleats running over the shoulders to form robings. These merge with basques, their top fold emphasized by a run and fell seam, held back with inner cords and brown buttons wrapped in silk thread. The skirt is draped sides to centre and the back panel is turned up and attached at hip level. The bodice and petticoat are lined in silk. The five-breadth

petticoat fastens at the centre back. This was a formal dress and the material is of very high quality. It is illustrated in (Ed) D. King, *British Textile Design*, vol. 1, illus. 161. A dress with similar short sleeves, deep plain cuffs and a draped back is shown in V. B. Sirieff (1709–1785), 'Mrs Charles Broughton', s.&d. 1736, anon. colln.; W. Hogarth, (1697–1764), 'Marriage of Stephen Beckingham and Mary Cox', about 1730, New York, The Metropolitan Museum of Art; and 'The Rake's Progress, He Marries an Old Maid', 1732–4, Sir John Soane's Museum, where the servant can be seen adjusting the train. This was probably pinned, since no stitch marks in this position have been observed on any surviving dress of the type.
T.9&A-1971

CAP AND TRIMMINGS, Brussels bobbin lace, *1730s, given by Miss Mary Gardiner V*, Circ.495-1927, T.121&A-1913, 866-1853   page 19

5 GOWN, cream Spitalfields silk with a brocaded design of pear-shaped fruits and exotic flowers in pink, yellow, brown, green and black
English, about 1735

This is an open robe with a stitched, pleated back, seamed across but continuous with the centre of the skirt, the sides of which are pleated into slanting waist seams. There are double-pleated robings. The sleeves are very wide with deep pleated cuffs which hang below the level of the elbow, a form more characteristic of the early 1740s. An alteration, perhaps during the 1780s, may account for the abbreviated robings, the missing half-panels in the front of the skirt, and some of the pleating at the waist. The dress is lined with white silk.

The portrait of Frances Lane, 1742, anon. colln., by A. Devis (1711–87), illustrates similar bodice and sleeves. The ladies from the series *Male and Female Dress* by H. Gravelot (1699–1773), engraved by T. Major (1720–99), show the dress as it might have been before alteration.
T.23-1972

PETTICOAT, yellow diamond-quilted silk, *English, mid-18th century, given by Mr J. B. Fowler*, T.427-1966
CAP, trimmed with Valenciennes bobbin lace, *French, 1730s*, T.307-1982
NECKERCHIEF, NECK RUFFLES AND SLEEVE RUFFLES, *German and English, 1730s and 1740s. Neckerchief given by Mrs Ethel Hill*, T.67-1972; *sleeve ruffles given by Brigadier General J. Dallas*, T.52&A-1925, Circ.202-1920   page 25

6 GOWN AND PETTICOAT, a mantua made from scarlet ribbed silk embroidered to shape with silver thread of several textures in a Tree of Life design
English, about 1745–50

The back of the bodice is pleated and stitched, double pleats running over the shoulders to form robings which merge with the skirt. These are draped into basques with inner silver cords looped over wound silver buttons attached to the back. The skirt is folded sides to centre; the end, embroidered in lighter style, drapes up and is attached to the low back. The sleeves are elbow-length and narrow with turn-back cuffs, seamed in the bend of the arm, so as to have a slight winged effect. The bodice is lined with white silk. The petticoat is embroidered all over its seven breadths and is shaped to accommodate narrow side hoops, six feet across at their widest point. Under its silver embroidery there are traces of coloured silk suggesting a change of mind, expensive because about 10 lbs of silver were required. The cost may account for the ink inscription under the embroidery on the reverse of the train: 'Rec'd of Mdme Leconte by me Magd. Giles'. These are names listed in the records of the English Huguenot community. Lecontes are mentioned as embroiderers from 1710 to at least 1746 when a Mary Magd. Johnson, formerly Leconte, embroidered items for Augusta, Princess of Wales, (RA 55440). Traceable from baptismal registers are families Gil(l)es and links between Leconte and Garneron, also embroiderers to the royal family.

From its richness and form, this was a Court dress, but it is untraceable before its purchase by Annie, Lady Cowdray from the London couturier Reville, for a fancy dress ball. She was painted in it by J. Macdonald Aitken, s.&d. 1927, Colln. Dunecht. J. Doré, *The Conservation of 18th century English Court Mantuas, Studies in Conservation*, 23, 1978, 1:14, describes restoration.

Given by Lord and Lady Cowdray
T.227&A-1970

FAN, painted leaf, mother-of-pearl and gilt sticks, *French, 1740s, bequeathed by Emily Beauclerk*, T.151-1920
SLEEVE RUFFLES AND DRESS TRIMMINGS, French needle-lace, possibly with Flemish fillings, *1730s–1740s, bequeathed by Lady Ludlow*, T.39 to D-1949   page 21

7 GOWN AND PETTICOAT, a mantua of white ribbed silk embroidered to shape with flowers in natural colours in long

[8]

and short stitches and French knots
English, 1744

The style is rococo, with a distinct
difference in the workmanship between
the top and bottom of the 7-breadth
petticoat. Both the leaves and the
arcaded and shell pattern border are
embroidered with silver thread on a
copper core. The back of the bodice is
pleated. Stitched double pleats run
over the shoulders to form robings.
These merge with the skirt as basques,
draped up by silver cords attached to
silver thread buttons at the back of the
waist. The skirt is folded sides to
centre, but the train would seem to be
missing. The above-elbow-length
sleeves are medium-wide with deep
turn-back cuffs. The petticoat is shaped
to take narrow side hoops, five feet at
their widest. There are traces of a white
silk lining.

J. Doré, *The Conservation of Two
18th century English Mantuas, Studies
in Conservation*, 23 (1978) 1:14,
describes this dress. The discovery of
an inscribed late 19th-century family
photograph linked it with the wedding
at Exeter Cathedral on 14 May 1744 of
Isabella Courtenay, 5th daughter of Sir
William Courtenay, 2nd Baronet and
de jure 5th Earl of Devon, to Dr John
Andrew. Ed. Lady Llanover, *The
Autobiography & Correspondence of
Mary Granville, Mrs Delany*, 1864,
refers to many flower-embroidered
mantuas in the 1730s and 1740s.
T.260&A-1969

CAP AND TRIMMINGS, Brussels needle-
lace, *1740s, bequeathed by Mr Edmond
Dresden*, 605-1904; *given by Mrs R. A.
Chapman*, T.76-1954; 1399&1-1874,
909&A-1901, Circ.321-1927
FAN, sticks and guards of carved and
pierced ivory, *French, 1730s–40s, given
by Sir Matthew Digby Wyatt and Lady
Wyatt*, 2202-1876   page 23

8 GOWN AND PETTICOAT, a mantua of
Spitalfields silk with a pattern of
shaded red, orange and yellow floral
sprays on a cream ground, with self-
coloured *cannelé* stripes between which
are spaced rows of self-coloured
feathers, dating from 1748–50
English, mid-1750s

The bodice has a stitched, pleated back
and attached robings. It continues into
a basque to which is joined a hem-
length tail, pleated sides to centre. The
petticoat has seven panels and is
shaped to fit over side hoops, sixty-four
inches at their widest. Silk fly braid in
harmonizing colours trims the robings,
the frilled cuffs, the pocket openings,
the puffed and gathered waist trimming
and the stomacher. The latter is made
from undulating gathered bands of
brocaded silk attached to a silk
foundation. There has been a slight
alteration at some time to the top of the
petticoat, and the gores at the side
appear to be additions.

The doll, W.42-1922, 'in fashionable
full dress for Spring 1759', wears a

dress of identical cut and provides an
invaluable reference for the style. This
form of dress was fashionable from the
mid-1750s to the early 1760s. Several
museums hold examples, notably one
in the Museum of London, dating from
1752, and another of 1749–50 at Tullie
House, Carlisle.

There are two examples in N.
Waugh's *The Cut of Women's Clothes*,
plates XIII & XVII. A Dutch example
was published by the Gemeente
Museum 's-Gravenhage, 'Een
Galajapon Omstreeks 1760'.

Given by Miss P. Lloyd
T.120 to B-1961

SLEEVE RUFFLES, striped gauze edged
with blonde bobbin lace, *probably
French, 1750s–60s*, T.9B&C-1971
BODICE TRIMMINGS, Mechlin bobbin
lace, *Flemish, 1750s–1760s, given by
Mrs A. Evans*, T.235&A-1914, *and
bequeathed by Mr L. C. Collier*,
T.5-1963
NECK FRILL, Mechlin bobbin lace,
*Flemish, second quarter 18th century,
given by H.M. Queen Mary*, T.85-1939
ETUI of silver gilt, *German, mid-18th
century, given by Dr Joan Evans*,
M.267-1975

9 GOWN AND PETTICOAT, pale blue silk
(French, about 1755), brocaded with a
floral design in maroon adorned with
green foliage springing from linked
silver tendrils with silver flowers
English, 1755–60

A sack adjustable with a laced linen
lining, skirt and petticoat cut to
accommodate a wide, slightly flaring
hoop. The trimming is exceptionally
rich and elaborate. The double-frilled
cuffs, robings, front facings of the skirt
and petticoat are trimmed in silver lace,
and to this are applied artificial flowers
of ruched ribbon with bead centres,

stiffened silk tassels and feathers in colours which harmonize with those of the silk.

Alterations were made to allow the bodice and skirt to fit more closely as well as adjusting it for a hoop which flares towards the hem, features which were fashionable in the early 1760s. Similar changes have been made to another dress of the same date and from the same source, T.253-1959.

The very deep pleats, the unusually short waist and the deeply curving waist seam of the petticoat, which fastens at the back, suggest the wearer was squarely built and slightly stooped. The dress was said to have been worn by Mrs Craster (pre 1707–1778), née Catherine Villiers, wife of John Craster, Northumberland (?–1764), MP for Wembley, 1754–61. Before her marriage in 1726 or 1727 Mrs Craster was said to have held a place at Court.

Floral trimmings were popular in the later 1750s, and similar ones can be seen on A.12413, Museum of London. F. Boucher's (1703–1720) portrait of Mme de Pompadour, 1759, National Gallery of Scotland, illustrates this style at its best.

Shown in the Loan Exhibition of Furniture 1896
T.251&A-1959

SLEEVE RUFFLES, Valenciennes bobbin lace, *French, 1740s–50s, given by Mrs Horace Nevill, T.12-1921, and by Mrs Eugenia Lindsay, T.98-1965. Also 729-1897 and 1053-1905*

10 GOWN, PETTICOAT AND STOMACHER, yellow silk
English, about 1760

Sack with a train made from yellow ribbed silk, trimmed with flounces with pinked edges, fly braid, and matching silk tassels stiffened with parchment. It has a gore inserted below the pocket slit and the main skirt pleating is concentrated at the back hip. The stomacher of similar silk has matching bands of applied and gathered purl-edged ribbon. There are buttons and loops stitched inside each pocket slit to permit the adjustment of the train. The petticoat fastens with a tie at the centre of the back. The bodice is lined with natural linen and there are traces of a former silk lining in the robe and petticoat.

Stitchmarks suggest that the set of the robe and petticoat was altered at the waist and hips and the trimmings rearranged at the front. The petticoat has been much pieced at the back. The loops and buttons may have been added then. Since a sack with a train was conventional formal wear in the later 1750s, the alteration may have been

either to adapt the garment to the smaller, more rounded hoop of the 1760s or to permit a less formal use with a looped-up skirt.

This dress may be compared with the painting 'A Lady in Blue', Tate Gallery, inscribed 'Art. Devis p. 1757' (Arthur Devis, 1711–87), and the fashion plate 'Lady in the Dress of the Year 1759', V&A, Department of Prints, Drawings and Photographs, E.1188–1908. Sacks with trains and applied trimmings remained fashionable until the early 1770s.

Given by John Sterling Williams
T.77 to B-1959

SLEEVE RUFFLES, chenille blonde bobbin lace, *French, 1750s*, 1043 and 1044-1876
page 24

11 GOWN AND PETTICOAT, mid-blue silk damask with a pattern of holly leaves, dating from about 1745
English, about 1760

This is an open robe with a stitched, pleated back, seamed across but continuous with the centre of the skirt, the sides of which are pleated into slightly slanting waist seams. The robings hang loose from the shoulders and the linen-lined bodice fastens across with tapes. The front edges of the skirt are pinked into scallops, as are the borders of the double frilled cuffs. The sleeves are narrow. The petticoat fastens with tapes at the hips.

There is much piecing, especially on the petticoat and robings, which suggests that the dress was at least partly re-made, probably in the late 1750s or early 1760s when frilled cuffs and tight-fitting bodices became fashionable.

Described in (Ed.) D. King, *British Textile Design*, vol. 1 no. 18.

Given by Miss M. S. Mourilyan
T.197&A-1959

APRON AND SLEEVE FRILLS
English, about 1760

These were received with the dress. They are made from silk gauze woven with floral trails on a diamond pattern background, the edges having diaper bands in a scalloped border.

Given by Miss M. S. Mourilyan
T.196, T.197B&C-1959

12 GOWN, a 'sack' of pale green silk *chiné* with a pattern of red flowers with green foliage on a ground of trails of maroon around meandering bands of pink and yellow lines
French, mid 1760s

The pleated robings, continuous with the skirt, are trimmed with pierced, pinked and gathered bands. The skirt is pleated to take medium-wide side hoops. There is a matching attached stomacher which fastens with self-covered buttons. The set of the back seams and the robings has been altered.

The dress is very similar in cut to that described by A. de Garsault, '*Description des Arts et Métiers ... 'Le Tailleur ... L'Art de la 'Couturière ...*', Paris, 1769. There, this form of stomacher is referred to as '*une compère*'.
T.16&A-1961

HAT, straw, *Italian or English, 1760s*, 157-1865
SLEEVE RUFFLES of bobbin lace, *English, 1760s*, T.29&A-1969   page 28

13 GOWN, a *polonaise* of cream silk with a Chinese-style painted pattern in pink and green
English or French, late 1770s

The bodice has a rounded point at the front and is tightly fitting, the centre back seam emphasized with three rows of green braid. The skirt is neatly pleated into the concave waist seam, stay-stitched on the reverse, and gathered into three puffs trimmed with green silk ribbon rosettes. The skirt can be draped higher by looping the green silk cords stitched to the inside of the bodice over the green ribbon bows at the back of the waist. The low, square neck and cuffs of the tightly-fitting sleeves and the skirt borders are trimmed with a frill of pale green silk. The stomacher, a mock lacing of applied green silk ribbon on a bobbin lace ground, is hooked at the side to the bodice, though the fastening may not be original. Former seam lines indicate that the fabric formed part of an earlier dress.

The style, originally French, was popular in England. It is illustrated in the fashion plate, 'Two Ladies in the Dress of 1775', anon. colln., and little changed when illustrated in 'Two Ladies in the Dress of 1779', V&A, E.5528-1902.

In the fashion plate series *Galerie des Modes*, *polonaises* predominate from 1776, remaining popular until 1780. This example is similar to that in the Moreau le Jeune engraving, '*Le Promenade à Marly*' 1778.

Given by Mrs George Shaw
T.30-1910

PARASOL, whalebone ribs, bone tip, green silk cover, *English, third quarter 18th century, given by Mrs F. Beddington*, T.4-1961
HAT, plaited straw with applied straw trimming, *Italian or English, third quarter 18th century*, T.158-1965
NECKERCHIEF AND SLEEVE RUFFLES, edged with Mechlin bobbin lace, *Flemish 1775–80, given by Mrs Ambrose B. Rathbone*, 1528 to C-1900
PETTICOAT, *English, 1760s–70s, given by Mrs O. Furnivall*, T.264A-1966

page 29

14 GOWN AND PETTICOAT, silk lustring with a pattern of shaded pink, maroon and yellow stripes on a ground of cream horizontal bands
English, 1775–80

The robe has a low, rounded neck with a centre-front opening and square tabs at the waist. The back is pleated and stitched, with the central pleat continuous with the skirt, the sides of which are neatly pleated into the concave waist seam and stay-stitched on the reverse. The skirt is cut away at the front corners and can be draped up with internal loops and tapes to a tape inside the bodice. The petticoat fastens with tapes at the hips. The cuffs, shaped to the elbow, are tightly gauged, a style which first appears in an English fashion plate, 'Two Ladies in the Dress of 1775', anon. colln.

The dress is pieced and patched but seems hardly altered. Its precise narrow back pleats, hanging loops attached to the bodice waist lining and to the petticoat waist are unusual features, though they appear on other dresses from the same source.

Given by Miss A. Maishman
T.92&A-1972

CAP, embroidered net trimmed with silk bobbin lace and cherry ribbons, *English or Scottish, about 1770*. Said to

have been worn by Elizabeth Gunning, Duchess of Hamilton and Argyll (1734–1790), *given by Lady Broughshane*, T.219-1964
NECKERCHIEF, silk and embroidered muslin, *English, late 18th century with 19th-century additions, given by Miss Emily Ford*, T.119-1925

page 25

15 JACKET AND SKIRT, a riding habit of crimson woollen broadcloth, the borders embroidered with silver-gilt thread and spangles in a formal floral design
English, early 1770s

The buttons are foil over a wooden core, embroidered with a similar motif. The fitted jacket is hip length and has a turn-down collar and long, curved sleeves. It is seamed at centre back and waist. The skirts are flared and have vents at centre back and hips, where they are also pleated. The scalloped edges are caught together and trimmed with buttons. The jacket fronts button back to suggest a double-breasted fastening, though they actually fasten with metal hooks and eyes. There are vertical pockets with a scalloped welt, which fastens with a button. The

waistcoat buttons left over right and has a V-shaped half belt attached to buttons at each side and to the centre front. The skirt is box-pleated at the front, and flanked by pleats which meet at an inverted pleat at the centre back. The waist, bound with braid, fastens with tapes at the hips, and the hem is bound with black. The jacket is half lined with brown glazed linen, and faced with red glazed wool also used for the back of the waistcoat. Man-tailored jackets and skirts, riding habits or 'redingotes', were popular informal day wear in the 1770s and 1780s, and were used for riding and walking. A similar example is worn by Sophie Masters of Colwick, painted by George Stubbs (1724–1806), s.&d. 1777, Norwich Castle Museum. The outfit is said to have belonged to Alice Thorold of Cuxwold Hall, Caistor, Northants, (1734–1821).
269 to B-1890

HABIT-SHIRT of linen, *English, mid-18th century*, T.27-1969
RIDING WHIP, silver-mounted, whalebone, *English, third quarter 18th century, given by Mrs M. M. Bryant*, T.105-1954

16 REDINGOTE, yellow quilted satin, faced with green silk on the low, rounded collar and the turned-back cuffs on the long curved sleeves
Italian, 1780s

The bodice has a centre-front opening with a concealed lace fastening. The back is pleated and stitched, with the central pleat seamed across but continuous with the skirt, the sides of

which are pleated into the concave waist seams. There is a coarse linen lining.

The style of the garment is fashionable, but the material, a large-scale corded quilting in a floral and diaper design, probably dates from the second quarter of the century and may never have been intended for clothing. Nevertheless, stitch marks suggest that at least two attempts have been made to make it up into a garment.

A redingote with a lobed front to the bodice was illustrated in *Galerie des Modes* for 1787.
106-1884

WALKING CANE, malacca with gilt-brass knob, *English, late 18th or early 19th century, given by Colonel J. I. Melville*, T.234-1931

17 GOWN AND PETTICOAT, a sack made from purple and white brocaded silk with undulating trails of flowers in shades of cream, green and pink. The gown is trimmed with matching gathered serpentine bands of the same material.
English, mid 1770s

The petticoat fastens at the hips. It is trimmed with a band and two flounces, the upper one draped up with loops and buttons, the lower extending around the hem. The trimmings are edged with fly braid in colours to harmonize with the silk. Inside the pocket openings are self-covered buttons which, when fastened to the loops just above the hem, would drape up the train. The skirt is gored at the hips to take a flaring hoop of medium width.

The alterations were very slight; a small adjustment of the waist seam and tucks behind the robings.

The fashion plate, 'A Lady and Gentleman in the Undress of the Year 1771' (V&A E.506-1902) illustrates a similar gown, with serpentine trimming and double flounces.
Given by Miss Mary Hodgson
T.161&A-1961

SLEEVE RUFFLES, tamboured muslin, *possibly English, 1770s, given by Miss S. M. Emery*, T.187&A-1962   page 28

18 GOWN AND PETTICOAT, a sack made from cream *tobine* with blue vertical stripes and trails and sprays of pink and lilac silk and chenille flowers with green foliage
English, mid-1770s

The gown has a square neck with a centre front opening and a deep point

at the waist. There are double-frilled cuffs. The skirt is cut to fit hoops which are medium wide and slightly flaring. The bodice is lined with pieced linen. The petticoat has six breadths and fastens with tapes at the hips. The trimmings of the robe and petticoat are of cream, green and pink silk gauze, plain and chequered, gathered in undulating trails and trimmed with bows. Around the front edges of the skirt is a looped pink and green vellum fringe.

The survival of such a fragile trimming as gauze is unusual. It is interesting to compare this slight but effective material with the more labour-intensive and applied and embroidered decoration of T.180&A-1965.

Given by Mrs E. Bendixon
T.255&A-1973

FAN, sticks of carved and pierced ivory, decorated with silver gilt foil, *English, 1770s, given by Sir Matthew Digby Wyatt and Lady Wyatt*, 2269-1876
LAPPETS, BORDERS AND RUFFLES, Mechlin bobbin lace, *Flemish, 1770s, bequeathed by Mrs Elsie Grant Michaelson*, Circ.169 to 171-1916, Circ.205-1916, T.87-1916, *and by Mrs A. C. Innes*, T.333-1972

19 GOWN AND PETTICOAT, a sack of cream satin embroidered to shape with chenille and silk ribbon chain stitch in an all-over floral sprig design.
French, late 1770s

The borders are trimmed with padded bands of blue satin, chenille blonde, flowers of gathered ribbon, feathers and raffia tassels enclosing sprays and garlands of embroidered flowers in shades of pink and green. Parallels to this rich *mélange* can be found among

sample embroideries at Lyon, Musée des Tissus, nos B.874, 878, 880. The skirt fronts are edged with cream cotton bobbin lace over pale blue ribbon; the bodice is edged with gathered pale blue ribbon. The pointed bodice, with centre-front opening, fits tightly. The side seams mould the figure, lacing under the back pleats, and a waist seam extends to the side back. The skirt is cut to take a medium-wide hoop. Draw ribbons through the pocket slits of the skirt and the five-panel petticoat may have adjusted them to the size of different hoops. Elaborate trimming was a feature of formal dress in the 1770s. J. M. Moreau le Jeune (1741-1814) in the engraving, 'Les Adieux', 1777, (E.472-1972) shows a dress of similar cut and style of decoration.

Given by Miss Louise Band
T.180&A-1965

FAN, embroidered and painted silk, *bequeathed by Captain H. B. Murray*, T.376-1910

BORDERS AND RUFFLES, *French* needle-lace, *1770s, given by Mrs Ambrose B. Rathborne*, 1563A,C,E&F-1900, *and bequeathed by Miss A. C. Innes*, T.305-1972   page27

20 GOWN AND PETTICOAT, cream silk, trimmed with applied trimming of glazed white cotton embroidered with floral garlands in natural colours, edged with heliotrope satin ribbon and a stencilled, shaded fringe
French, about 1785

The bodice has a low, round neck fastening with a draw ribbon, and an opening at the centre front. It has tight curving sleeves shaped by tucks in the bend of the elbow. It is unusual in having the bodice front cut without separate shoulder pieces. There are deep, squared tabs at the front and the back is pointed, with three central boned seams. The skirt is set into the deeply curving side waist in neat, narrow pleats, fanning out inside to accommodate the bones at the centre of the back. This is a feature found more often in French than in English dresses.

The skirt has a train with silk loops inside the back, through which runs a heliotrope ribbon to adjust the length and drape. The petticoat has four widths of material and fastens with a draw ribbon at the waist tying at the sides, its only shaping being at the centre front of the waist.

Given by A. M. R. Kenny
T.98&A-1966

SLEEVE FRILLS, trimmed with Brussels bobbin lace, *Flemish, 1780s*, 554&B-1868 826&A-1868   page 30

21 GOWN AND PETTICOAT, white printed cotton with a dotted ground and a design of small pink, blue and green floral sprays recalling Indian tambour patterns, with blue line in the selvedge
English, about 1785

The bodice is tight-fitting and has a low round neck, tight sleeves with gussets at the elbow and a centre-front opening with deep square-ended tabs. The back, which has three seams with channels for bones, is pointed and the skirt is pleated into the concave waist seam. The petticoat has three breadths and is pleated away from the wide front box pleat and the narrow one at the back towards the hips, where it fastens with tapes. It has a flounce above the hem.

When the dress was received by the Museum the skirt had been restitched two inches higher, covering the pointed bodice back, and it has now been restored to its original level. Such an alteration is often found on dresses of the period, as it would have extended its fashionable life into the 1790s when the waistline was raised.
Illustrated in (Ed.) D. King, *English Textile Design*, vol 2, no. 187.

Given by Miss K. Lack
T.274&A-1967

FAN, printed paper, *French, 1780s*, given by Sir Matthew Digby Wyatt and Lady Wyatt, 2191-1876
KERCHIEF, embroidered cotton, *English, 1780s*, given by Mrs H. E. Talbot, T.285-1977

22 GOWN, brown silk and white cotton *French, late 1780s*

The bodice is made from dark brown silk, opens down the front and has a low, round neck fastening with a draw cord, and long squared-off points at the centre-front waist. The sleeves are tight with a small stitched cuff at the elbow. There is a centre-back seam and closely spaced side-back seams, internally boned. The skirt is made from white glazed cotton with a printed pattern of spiny stems in brown, pine trees complete with roots and cones, lilacs, pink dianthus, brown convolvulus and daisy trails. It is neatly pleated to the concave waist of the bodice, the folds horizontally arranged at the pointed back. The bodice is lined with brown glazed linen.

The gown is an elegant example of the figure-moulding style of the later 1780s. There is a similar example with a close-seamed 'bodice-skirt' in contrasting colours illustrated in the *Galerie des Modes* for 1787. It is captioned '*vêtue d'une Robe Anglaise*', but is nevertheless French rather than English.

Given by Miss L. Wethered
T.232-1969   page 30

23 JACKET, white linen with a small all-over printed pattern of pale purple seed pods and flowers, quilted onto a linen lining
French, late 1780s

The jacket is hip length and front fastening. It is trimmed with a pleated frill and has a low, round neck and tightly-fitting moulded sleeves shaped to the arm. The cut is subtle, departing from the strict convention of the period but beautifully executed. The centre-back seam is flanked by two side-back panels which swoop from the armhole almost to centre back where they spread into a kite-shaped tail, with a central vent. The side-bodies are joined to an overlapping basque and the fronts are cut in one, with the squared points at the lower waist. The jacket fastens with brass hooks and eyes.

Neat, fitted jackets with flared tails appear in the *Galerie des Modes* series of fashion plates from about 1782. They increase in number and in ingenuity until the series ends in 1787. They are usually referred to as 'caracos'.

Given by J. Cyril Nairne
T.219-1966

APRON, cotton, *English, late 18th century, given by Miss Emily Ford*, T.117-1925   page 31

24 GOWN, pink satin with a woven design of cream silk flowers
English: the silk, 1759–60, the dress about 1797

The edges of the wide, deep neckline, the rounded half collar, the front skirt opening and the cuffs of the long, curving sleeves are trimmed with narrow, pleated cream silk ribbon. The bodice has a centre-back seam with closely-spaced side back seams, and was formerly boned. The bodice was pointed at the back, but the skirt, which is pleated from the side to an inverted pleat at the centre, was raised to a higher waist level, completely covering this point. The bodice is lined with white linen. From the stitchmarks and piecing, the dress had two periods of alteration. It may have been made up in the 1760s, but of this little trace remains. It was certainly made up again in the 1780s. The wide stomacher, curving to a shallow point, has been reversed to form the bodice front. The long back bodice point and possibly single remaining button at the back of the waist are typical of 1780s cut. Despite this, in its present form, the dress was fashionable and very close to Fig. 39, Afternoon Dresses, *Heideloff's Gallery of Fashion*, 1795, which clearly illustrates the same arrangement of the skirt. In the caption it is described as a Robe.
T.83-1963

FAN, kid leaf painted in watercolours, *Italian, 1780s–90s, lent by H.R.H. the Duke of Gloucester (loan 11)*

25 ROBE, made from a cream silk and wool shawl
English, late 1790s

The shawl has a printed design in pink and green of formal floral motifs with chiné-like borders. The shawl was halved, seamed up the centre back, then stitched to the shape of the body. Great care has been taken to alter the shawl as little as possible and the borders still remain within the seam at the centre of the back. The front borders are faced with green silk and there is a green silk collar and oversleeves edged with white. The sleeves themselves are made from cream silk, long, tight and shaped to the arm, fastening with covered buttons at the wrist. The bodice is linen extended into bodice flaps.

Oversleeves on similar long robes can be seen in *Heideloff's Gallery of Fashion* for 1794 and 1795. The style was long lasting, for it is illustrated again in the *Journal des Luxus und der Moden*, Vol. XV, March, 1800. Norwich Shawl Dresses from Mr Knight's Manufactory, 1792, are mentioned in P. Clabburn, *Shawls*, 1981.
T.217-1968

FAN, green silk leaf and ivory sticks, *French, late 18th century, bequeathed by H.M. Queen Mary, T.217-1959*

page 32

26 ROBE, glazed cotton with a white ground, block-printed in a design of vertical trails of bell-like flowers in shades of pink, blue and green
English, late 1790s

The robe is high-waisted and has a train. The bodice is low-cut, the sides gathered and held together with draw tapes at neck and waist. There are front bodice flaps attached to the linen lining of the back. There is no waist seam and the front of the robe forms semi-pleated robings. There are stitched pleats at the side and back which shape the gown to the body. These flow into the skirt as inverted pleats, double at the back and single at the front. The front corners of the skirt are turned back in a curve. The sleeves are long, curved and fasten at the wrist with covered horn buttons.

This type of robe may be the kind referred to by Jane Austen in her *Letters*, 1798: 'I believe I shall make my new gown like my robe, but the back of the latter is all in a piece with the tail, and will 7 yards enable me to copy it in that respect?'
Reproduced in (Ed.) D. King, *British Textile Design*, Vol. 2, plate 186.

Given by Mrs P. M. Cooper
T.286-1968

27 DRESS, white muslin with an embroidered design in white cotton, silver thread and gilt spangles of fantastic flowers within a scalloped border, worked in satin stitch, chain stitch, lace filling and French knots.
French, late 1790s

The dress has a low, square neck, long, straight sleeves and a high waist to which the skirt is gathered. The bodice is gathered in the front but plain at the back, where it is shaped with sidebodies and fastens with a draw ribbon at the waist and two buttons.

The embroidery on the dress may be compared with an example of about 1797 in the Musée Historique des Tissus, Lyon, illustrated in the catalogue, *Costumes de Cour et de Ville du Premier Empire, Paris, Musée du Costume de la Ville de Paris*, 1958, No. 4. *Costumes Parisiens* illustrates many high-waisted, low-cut muslin dresses with gathered skirts and bodices during 1797. Bodices with diagonal back seams begin to be illustrated in 1798. There seems no definite etiquette governing the use of long versus short sleeves.

There is a pattern and description in J. Arnold's *Patterns of Fashion*, vol. 1, pp. 48–9.

Given by Messrs Harrods T.673-1913

SHAWL, Indian (Kashmir), *late 18th early 19th century, given by Miss M. Davis*. IM.17-1915
SHOE, leather trimmed with braid, *English, late 18th century, given by Messrs Harrods, T.484-1913*

28 DRESS, printed cotton
English, about 1810

This has a black ground printed with a vertical stripe of pink and green flowers with white diamond motifs interspaced. The dress has a fairly high-waisted bodice, with bust darts and a deep pointed neckline which wraps across at the waist and is trimmed with a faced border. The skirt is straight-cut with side plackets and ties at the waist. It is arranged in narrow pleats at the back. The sleeves are knuckle-length, with faced wristbands. There is a matching belt attached at the back and an inner waist tape. The hem is faced with brown glazed cotton. The material dates from the 1790s, but there is no sign that it has been re-used. Extra long sleeves and bust darts are features of the years after about 1805.

Given by Mrs P. Pengree
T.356-1965   page 33

29 EVENING DRESS, white muslin, embroidered all over in white cotton
French, about 1806

The embroidery is worked in a pattern of French knots, with the collars, skirt border, and centre stripe embroidered in chain stitch, satin stitch and French knots. The design links vine tendrils and acorns. The dress has a low square neck adjusted with a draw cord, and 'stomacher front' closing over inner lining flaps. The waist is high and the skirt cut straight and gathered at the centre of the back, fastening with a tape tie. It extends into a long oval train. The sleeves are short and have a 'vandyke' trimming.

White muslin, classical in effect, was fashionable from the 1790s to about 1810. Dresses of similar shape to this with a stripe down the centre front were in use from about 1806, when an example was illustrated in the *Lady's Monthly Museum*, February 1806, through to 1809, the 'pocket book' plate 'Fashionable Dress of the Year 1809'. The oak leaf had classical connotations but, as one of Napoleon's devices, became even more popular after his coronation in 1804.

Given by Miss M. B. Hudson
T.124-1913

SCARF, printed, knitted silk, *English, about 1810*, 678-1893

30 EVENING DRESS, red silk machine-made net with borders embroidered in chenille with garlands of pink roses in natural colours
English, 1810–11

The dress has a high waistline to which the straight skirt is attached smoothly except for a panel of tight gathering at the back. The neck is low and round, the front of the bodice semi-fitted, with the sides on the cross, and a gathered centre panel. The sleeves are short and slightly puffed. It is said to have been worn over a red silk underdress. The wedge-shaped panels on the front of the bodice had the effect of defining the figure.

There is an early illustration of this feature in *Ackermann's Repository*, December, 1809. It is shown on 'half' or semi-formal evening dress, with short puffed sleeves and a small train in the same journal in January, 1811. Chenille embroidery, from references in the journals, was at its most fashionable between 1807–1810.

Given by Mrs George Atkinson and Mrs M. F. Davey
T.194-1958

FAN, horn brisé pierced and painted, *French or English, first quarter of 19th century, given by Sir Matthew Digby Wyatt and Lady Wyatt.* 2285-1876
page 32

31 COAT, red and blue shot silk
English, about 1808–10

This is mid-calf length, cut straight except for small pleats at the centre of the back of the waist where the matching belt is attached. The fronts are cut without a waist seam and can wrap across to fasten with an inner silk tie, or be held by the belt. The most

White lawn, classical in effect, was fashionable from the 1790s to about 1810. This French dress of about 1806 is embroidered all over in white cotton. It has a high waistline typical of the period, and the neck is adjusted with a draw cord.
T.124-1913   [29]

striking feature is the back bodice, a panel emphasized by braid trimming on shoulder and side seams. It gets its distinctive shape from the sharp slope of the shoulder seams up to the collar and the slightly gathered head of the long straight sleeve.

The coat is half-lined in blue silk. Wrap-over pelisses with high collars seem to have been fashionable in 1810–11. Similar examples are illustrated in the English journal (*La Belle Assemblée*,) August, 1810 and in the *Lady's Monthly Museum* for February, 1810.

Given by Miss M. D. Nicholson
T.24-1946

RETICULE, steel chainwork mounted with steel, *German, early 19th century, given by Mr Charles Gorham*, T.8-1971
DRESS, printed cotton, *English, about 1810, given by Mr J. N. Addison,* T.277-1973

32 EVENING DRESS, hand-embroidered black, machine-made net
English, 1817–18

The dress is trimmed at the hem with padded black satin rouleaux and rosettes. The bodice has a low, square neck and fastens at the back with tapes. It is very short-waisted with slight fullness eased in at the front. The gored skirt is attached smoothly except for a wide panel of tight gathering at the back. The epaulettes are wired and, like the cuffs on the long sleeves, made from satin with an applied cord decoration.

A very similar evening dress with long sleeves, epaulettes and border was illustrated in *Ackermann's Repository*, 11 December 1818, where it was mounted over white satin. Fashionable black dresses for smart mourning were frequently illustrated during 1817–18, after the death of the Princess Charlotte.

Given by Miss Mary Hague
T.175-1922

FAN, mother-of-pearl, brisé, *French, first quarter of 19th century, bequeathed by H.M. Queen Mary, Circ.379-1959*
NECKLET, gilt metal and glass inset with gold and silver leaf, *English, about 1820, given by Miss Kathleen Martin,* M.137-1922
TIARA of pastes set in gilt metal, *English or French, 1820s, given by Mrs R. F. Halpin, M.274-1977*   page 34

33 JACKET, blue velvet
English, about 1818

This is high-waisted and fastens edge to edge with a hook and eye at the neck. The sleeves are long with short puffed oversleeves, trimmed with satin-faced matching bows and fastening with similarly trimmed wrist bands. The rounded collar is stiffened so that it can be worn turned up. It is faced with satin.

Short jackets without tails were known as 'spencers' after George, 2nd Earl Spencer (1758–1834), who is said to have originated the style in the later 1790s. They were worn for 'walking dress' until the mid-1820s. Very similar jackets are illustrated in *Ackermann's Repository* from 1818 to 1820, but this example is almost identical with the illustration opposite p. 77 in C. W. Cunnington's *Englishwomen's Clothing in the 19th century*, 1949, source not stated but probably from *La Belle Assemblée*.

Given by Messrs Harrods
T.890-1913

DRESS, white cotton with a woven pattern and border in blue and pink, *English, 1810–15, given by Messrs Harrods, T.762-1913*
COLLAR, whitework embroidery, *English, early 19th century, given by Messrs Harrods, T.1780&A-1913*

34 DRESS, white muslin, trimmed with openwork embroidery
English or French, 1818–20

The bodice has a fairly high waist

and fastens at the centre back with tapes and buttons. The front is horizontally gauged between two bands of embroidery. There is a double-layer ruff collar. The skirt is slightly gored, gathered at the centre back, and trimmed at the hem with puffed and gathered bands and frills. The sleeves are long with epaulettes, puffed oversleeves and frilled cuffs. The body of the sleeve is gathered into a series of puffs.

In *Englishwomen's Costume in the 19th century*, C. W. Cunnington refers to this type as the 'Marie' sleeve. The dress is a fine example of Regency dressmaking, showing full but unostentatious use of a wide range of texture. The style with ruff and puffed sleeves was introduced from Paris: it was widely adopted and had a long life. In 1815 it was illustrated in *Ackermann's Repository*, and in 1816 in *La Belle Assemblée*, on both occasions with the prefix 'Parisian'. The sleeves appear in a design in the *Allgemeine*, March 1821, and a similar gauged bodice in the issue for September 1822.

Given by Miss Joan Gibbon
T.79-1972

SCARF, yellow woven silk on blue net ground, *English, early 19th century, bequeathed by Estella Canziani,* T.291-1965

35 COAT, golden brown silk
English, about 1820

This is a 'pelisse robe': it has a fairly high waistline to which is attached a slightly gored skirt with a gathered panel at the centre of the back. The collar is stiffened and has a vent at the back, trimmed with a tassel. The sleeves are long with short puffed oversleeves of stepped bands, faced and lined with satin, and wristbands which fasten with a button. The coat is trimmed with applied piping arranged in flower shapes on the bust and at the wrists and in elongated curves on the skirt borders. It is lined with blue silk and padded at the hem. It fastens with loops and concealed buttons.

The garment is well made but unusual in the variety of motif used for its trimming. Most examples in fashion plates have a greater unity of design.

Given by Mrs H. Lee
T.383-1960

BONNET, straw trimmed with wired ribbon, *English, about 1820*, 693-1902
PARASOL, mother-of-pearl handle, silk cover, *English, about 1820, given by Mrs Arthur Evans*, T.232-1914
SHAWL, green figured silk, *English, about 1820, given by Mr J. N. Addison*, T.274-1973
RUFF, edged with openwork, *English, about 1820, given by Mr J. N. Addison*, T.277A-1973   page 34

36 EVENING DRESS, rose pink satin trimmed with self-coloured applied decoration and blond bobbin lace
English or French, 1823–4

The skirt is set smoothly at the front but is tightly gathered at the centre of the back and gored to flare at the hem. The dress, which fastens at the back with hooks and eyes, is a fine example of Regency dressmaking with effective use of applied decoration in high relief, and excellent workmanship. It is typical in its Romantic nostalgia for 16th-century fashions with its puffed sleeves, square neck, and diagonal movement of the skirt trimming. Traces of former seam lines on the back breadth of the skirt include a former vertical pocket slit, suggesting that part, at least, of the material was re-used despite its fashionable style.

The vertical bands of trimming on the skirt began to appear in European fashion journals such as the *Allgemeine Modenzeitung* early in 1823, continuing to appear throughout the year. They do not appear in *La Belle Assemblée* (an English journal) until 1824, disappearing in 1825. The extremely high waist and the details of the sleeves appear in *La Belle Assemblée* in 1822.

Given by the Hon. Mrs Grizell Hastings
T.156-1962

SCARF of Mechlin bobbin lace, *Flemish, 1820s*, T.470-1980
FAN with paste-set metal guard, *French,*

1820s, given by H. M. Howard, OBE, RNVR, T.49-1947
NECKLACE AND EARRINGS, gold inset with paste, *English, 1820s, bequeathed by Mr J. C. Joicey*, M.263-B-1919

37 DRESS, pink silk with a figured leaf design
English, about 1823

The dress has a low, rounded neckline, and a high-waisted bodice which fastens at the back and has an attached belt. The skirt is gored, though the whole breadths are not cut away, and is pleated at the centre of the back. The matching jacket has a turned-down collar and long sleeves arranged in puffs which diminish slightly towards the wrist. It has an attached belt trimmed with loops and a silk waist ribbon. Bodice and jacket are lined with silk. The dress is remarkable for the quality and variety of its faced and applied decoration. There are faced slits which stiffen the collar, leaf shapes on the jacket, petal shapes on the bodice and a deep scalloped satin border with a padded hem. The matching jacket would make the dress suitable for less formal occasions.

Parallels to this dress can be found in a pattern book of the same date (T.385-1972). Sleeves with a series of puffs, more or less in the fashionable 'Tudor' style, appear in the English journal *La Belle Assemblée*, 1 August 1816, described as 'Parisian Walking Dress'. *Ackermann's Repository* illustrates an example with puffs diminishing towards the wrist on 1 September 1824.
T.28&A-1983

RETICULE, netted silk and metal thread, made on a purse mould, *possibly Italian, early 19th century, given by Dr R. Forrer*, T.11-1910   page 34

38 DRESS, printed cotton with a floral pattern on a yellow and white striped ground
English, about 1828

The dress has a low oval neckline and a pleated bodice. There are four straight breadths in the skirt, which is pleated into a waistline placed slightly above normal level. There are two deep flounces above the hem. There are 'leg-of-mutton' sleeves with a deep, pointed cuff. All the main structural seams are piped. The bodice is lined with white cotton and fastens at the back.

A pleated bodice, described as a '*corsage en blouse*', is illustrated in *Ackermann's Repository* in 1824 and again in 1826 where it is accompanied by leg-of-mutton sleeves. This type of skirt, pleated all the way round and trimmed with flounces, was introduced in 1827, and by mid-1828 the *Ladies Monthly Museum* illustrates a skirt shortened to above the ankles. Since the hem of our dress has been cut, it is not possible to be precise about the date.

Given by Mrs K. Ludgate
T.151-1968

BONNET, yellow figured silk, *probably Dutch, about 1830, bequeathed by Mrs Sankey*, T.130–1962
RETICULE, printed silk, *English, 1827–8*. This was issued to publicize the work of the Ladies' Society for the Relief of Negro Slaves, Birmingham, and contained pamphlets relating to Abolition. *Given by Miss E. F. Howard*, T.20-1951
PARASOL, ivory and green silk, *English with Chinese export handle, bequeathed by E. S. Dove*, 435-1896.
COLLAR, whitework embroidery, *English, 1820s–30s, given by Miss H. L. Hermione Unwin*, T.115-1923
CUFFS, whitework embroidery, *English, 1820s*, T.42&A-1983   page 36

39 DRESS, wool printed with a trefoil design, possibly shamrocks, in lilac on a brown and lilac ground
English, 1836–8

The fitted bodice has a low, round neck and a slightly high waistline. The skirt is box-pleated, more tightly at the centre back. The sleeves are set low, tightly pleated below the shoulder.

They have been altered by having the fullness reduced and a frill attached at the elbow.

The former style was comparable with *Townsend's Monthly Selection of Parisian Costumes*, May 1836, plate 647, the latter with that in plate 752 of the July issue of the same journal. In March 1836 Townsend had commented: 'The war of extermination which has been raging these two months between BOUFFANT SLEEVES and TIGHT SLEEVES has not ceased . . .'.

The sleeve puffs are stiffened with calico and supported with tapes. The main seams are faced, the bodice is lined with cotton and the skirt faced with glazed cotton.

Given by Mrs H. M. Shepherd
T.11-1935

BONNET, *English, 1835–40, given by Messrs Harrods*, T.1030-1913
PARASOL, *brown silk, ivory handle, English, 1830s, given by Miss M. Davis,* T.159-1915
COLLAR, *embroidered net, English, late 1830s,* T.43-1983   page 35

40 DRESS, lilac silk
English, 1838–42

The bodice is tightly fitted, fastens at the back and has a long pointed waist. The separate skirt, which has a deep border at the hem, is flat-pleated with a panel of tight gauging at the back. The long, low-set sleeves are medium full, gathered below the shoulder and again above the small, turned-back cuff. The neckline is trimmed with silk blonde. The bodice is faced on the main seams, lined with cotton and boned.

From piecing, stitch marks, and the

many cut but unused pieces, some shaped into vandykes, it seems probable that this dress was re-made from a dress of the 1820s. Similar sleeves and bodices are illustrated in *Townsend's Monthly Journal* from 1838 through to 1840.

Given by Mrs O. T. Wade
T.257&A-1968

MANTLE, deep purple velvet, the borders trimmed with trailing sprays of roses, silk-embroidered in satin stitch in pinks and green.
Probably French, about 1840–45

The edges are faced with narrow green, pink and white satin bands and there are fancy silk tassels in harmonizing colours. The mantle is full-length, with a deep, curved yoke, a pointed collar, holes for the arms and curved vents at the sides. It fastens with tasselled cords at the neck. It is lined with quilted pink satin.

This is a most luxurious garment, beautifully made. A similar example is illustrated in *Townsend's Monthly Journal* for 1840–41.

Given by Miss Lettice Walsh
T.130-1963

HAIR PINS, *glass, gilt metal setting, English, 1820s–30s, given by Miss M. Rathbone,* T.196&A-1961
SINGLE OPERA GLASS, *gilt metal set with mother-of-pearl and turquoises, English, early 19th century, lent by the Science Museum*

41 DRESS, greenish-gold satin
English, about 1842

The neckline is low and oval, framed by a deep collar which, like the flared over-sleeves, is trimmed with matching looped braid and cord. The bodice is close-fitting, with a long, deeply pointed waist to which the full skirt is neatly attached with organ pleating. The dress fastens at the back with hooks and eyes and is lined with heavyweight cotton. The main construction seams are boned, the joining seams faced and there are cambric dress preservers. The hem is interlined and padded and edged with braid. There is a matching cape-collar which would make the dress suitable for less formal day wear.

This is a fashionable and beautifully made dress, the technique still Regency in its precision. Dresses with long pointed waists and deep collars and flared over-sleeves are illustrated in *Townsend's Monthly Journal*, No.981/1842. A similar dress is worn in a callotype by Claudet, Science Museum

Collection, illustrated in M. Ginsburg *Victorian Dress in Photographs*, 1982, plate 78.

Given by Mrs J. P. Friend Smith
T.848&A-1974

SCARF, *striped velvet, English, mid-19th century, associated with Mrs Emma Stanbridge of Hoxton (?–1871), given by Miss P. W. Stanbridge,* T.210-1926
page 37

42 DRESS, striped silk
English, late 1840s

The dress has a high neck and long fitted bodice. The waistline is deeply pointed and the skirt attached to it with tight gathers. The front of the dress is trimmed with a row of motifs in tasselled braid. The dress fastens at the back, the bodice lined with cotton and boned on the main seams. The skirt is lined with stiffened cotton and interfaced at the hem where it is bound with brown wool braid. The side seams have been enlarged and gores have been inserted to widen the sleeves at the wrist.

The dress is said to have belonged to Sybella Frances Cookson, who married in 1847 and died in 1853. The style would be compatible with a dress of the mid-1840s, altered to keep in fashion in the late 1840s–early 1850s. Similar graduated braid trimming appears in *Townsend's Monthly Journal* for 1844, but the plain sleeve and long waistline were not usual until 1845 when they are illustrated in the *New Monthly Belle Assemblée* for April. The same plate also illustrates a dress with a double row of trimmings on the skirt.

Given by Mrs C. R. B. Eyre
T.856-1919

SHAWL, silk bobbin lace, *French, probably Chantilly, mid-19th century, given by Mrs H. C. B. Lethbridge* T.63-1968

43 DRESS, satin with a woven chequered pattern in blue, green and pink *English, mid 1840s*

The dress has a high, round neck, fitted bodice and a waistline with a rounded point to which the skirt is flat-pleated except for a panel of tight gathering at the back. There is a front lace fastening. The sleeves are long with an open epaulette. The only trimmings are the agate stud buttons mounted on black velvet bows above the wrists. The bodice is piped on all the main seams, lined with cotton and boned. The skirt is lined with yellow and white washed and re-used figured silk. The back is softly interlined. There are yellow chamois dress preservers.

Open epaulettes are illustrated in *Townsend's Monthly Journal* in 1843 and continued to be fashionable through 1844.

Given by Lady Lindsey T.169-1959

MANTLE, velvet *English, mid 1840s*

It is made from blue velvet, lined with black quilted silk and fastened with concealed hooks and eyes. It reaches to the knees and has openings for the arms. It has a rounded collar and is flounced from the waist to the hips. The edges are trimmed with matching looped braid and fringe. A similar mantle dated 1847 is illustrated in C. W. Cunnington's *Englishwomen's Clothing in the 19th century*, 1937, p. 149, (source unspecified).

Given by Lady Lindsey T.170-1959

STOCKING PURSE, netted silk and steel beads, *English, second quarter of 19th century, given by Messrs Harrods,* T.1424-1913

44 DRESS, wool with a printed multicoloured shawl pattern of *boteh* on trails, with a blue and white striped ground *English, late 1840s*

The dress material was printed by Swaislands of Crayford, Kent and registered between July, 1845 and April, 1847. The high-necked bodice has drapes arranged from the shoulders to the long pointed waist. There is a basque to which the skirt is tightly pleated. There are pagoda sleeves to which are attached half-sleeves, gathered into a wrist band. The bodice fastens with blue silk loops and buttons, which continue to the hem as a decorative trimming. Narrow bands of blue braid trim the basques and sleeves. The bodice is lined with glazed cotton and boned. Vertical slits over the bust, which are fastened with cotton buttons concealed by the front drapes of the bodice, suggest that this was a nursing dress.
Worn by Susannah Cheale of Uckfield, Surrey. A bodice with basques is illustrated in the Paris Fashions for August 1849 in the *Illustrated London News*.

Given by Mrs Geoffrey Myers T.849-1974

SHAWL, hand-knitted wool, *Scottish (Shetlands), mid-19th century, given by Miss Mary Nicholson,* T.104-1961 CAP, trimmed with openwork embroidery, *English, mid-19th century, given by Messrs Harrods,* T.714D-1913
page 37

45 DAY DRESS, cotton *English, about 1858–60*

The design is printed in lilac and beige and the dress is trimmed with white-work embroidery. The body of the dress has an all-over lilac sprig pattern and the flounce a formal floral design. The bodice has a plain, round neck and extra fullness at the bust gathered just above the waist. It fastens at the back. The sleeves are tight to just above the elbow, and then flare widely. The

This English dress of the mid-1840s is made of satin with a woven chequered pattern in blue, pink and green. It is shown with a blue velvet mantle of the same period.
T.169&T.170-1959   [43]

flounced skirt is gathered onto a slightly peaked waistband.

Dresses with a pattern woven or printed so that it complemented the shape of the dress when made up were popular in the late 1850s and 1860s and there are many examples in museum collections.

Given by Messrs Harrods
T.702-1913

CUFFS, whitework, *English, mid-19th century, given by Messrs Harrods,*
T.1122&A-1913   page 38

46   DRESS, green silk
English, about 1862

It has a woven green and white floral design. The bodice has a narrow band collar and three-quarter length sleeves with double puffs on the upper arms. A bolero is suggested by panels of narrow stitched pleats over the bust, outlined in looped green silk braid. This is also used to edge the cuffs. Pendant crystal beads trim the front, masking a fastening with hooks and eyes. The matching skirt is slightly gored, with pleats running from box pleats at the centre front and back towards the sides. There is a matching belt, trimmed with a bow with pendant ends which has a diamond-shaped panel, and the front and back reinforced with internal bones. The dress is lined with white glazed cotton and boned. It has a padded interlining on the bust, and dress preservers of rubberized cotton which appear to be original. There is green brush braid at the hem.

Bolero trimmings are illustrated in the *Illustrated London News*, Paris fashions for October 1862. *Le Corsage Suissesse*, 'a sort of corselet . . . worn

over high dresses . . . and reaching as far as a low body would', is mentioned in the *Englishwoman's Domestic Magazine* for April 1861. A sleeve of the kind used for this dress, 'perfectly tight at the elbow and finished off at the top with two puffs', is suggested as suitable for ordinary dresses in the *Englishwoman's Domestic Magazine* for May, 1861.

Given by Miss Edith Westbrook
T.222-B1969

47   DRESS, golden-brown corded silk
English, about 1862

It has a close-fitting, short-waisted bodice fastened with black glass stud buttons, and a waistband to which the skirt is attached in deep, double box-pleats. The epaulettes on the medium-wide long sleeves, cuffs, bodice and skirt border are all trimmed with machine embroidery. An interlinked design of leaves and flowers is carried out in black chain stitch and velvet appliqué. The making up of this dress was imperfect. Despite re-stitching at the waist, the pleats were not centred.

From the *Englishwoman's Domestic Magazine*, August 1860, it would seem that dresses with double box-pleats were gored, in this instance impossible, because the panels were embroidered before being stitched together. The embroidery patterns are similar to

several illustrated in *The Queen* for 1862. It is probable from the quality that they were professionally machine-embroidered. The dress itself is hand-stitched. High waists and epaulettes appear in Paris Fashions for October 1862 in *The Illustrated London News* but continued to be worn through to 1867.

The dress was worn by Maria Goodman née Cunliffe, born 1833, married 1858, died 1867.

Given by Dr N. Goodman
T.22-1973

MANTLE, cream silk and woollen cloth with a long nap, woven in a zig-zag stripe
English or French, about 1865

It is knee-length with a graduated hem, the back and front cut on the straight and the shoulder panels on the cross. It is trimmed with stranded wool and braid fringe and black and gold moiré ribbons with an anchor motif. It is lined with quilted silk.

Given by Lord Rothschild
T.220-1981

PARASOL, white silk with wooden handle, *English, about 1865, given by Mrs E. Gibbs*, T.250-1928

48   COURT DRESS, ivory silk
English, about 1860–5

The dress is trimmed with hand and machine embroidery. The bodice laces at the back and has a pointed waistline. The low neck and short sleeves are trimmed with tiers of net, machine-embroidered in yellow chain stitch. This is also applied to the front of the bodice, where it is edged with ruched yellow and white gauze ribbon. A train eleven feet long is attached at the waist. The edges are trimmed with machine-embroidered net insertion with pleated ribbon borders, the remainder hand-embroidered in satin stitch with roses and morning glories in natural colours. The net flounce on the reconstructed skirt is embroidered by hand with the floral motifs and with yellow machine embroidery. The bodice is lined with white silk and boned.

The dress conforms to Court etiquette. *The Habits of Good Society*, 1859, instructs 'The dress . . . is made low and the boddice (sic) is trimmed in accordance with the petticoat and the train. (The train) . . . fastens half round the waist and is about 7 yards in length and wide in proportion . . . The head-dress consists of feathers and comprises a lappet of lace.' (It is possible that 7 *yards* was a misprint for feet. The length in later sources is 3½ yards, which, in practice, trails for 7 feet.) In the mid-19th century, Madame Tussaud exhibited fashionable dress, Court groups amongst them. This dress may have formed part of a display, for there is another bodice of the same fabric.

Given by Madame Tussaud
T.329 to B-1977

FAN, *French, 1860s, painted by Tony Faivre, 500-1869*
FALL, *silk bobbin lace, French : Caen or Bayeux, mid-19th century, given by Mr Sydney Vacher, T.15-1909*   page 11

[49]

49 DRESS, blue and grey striped silk
English, about 1866

The bodice is fitted, fastens at the front and has a slightly high waist, a narrow collar, long, tight sleeves with a slit, and flared elbow-length over-sleeves trimmed with blue silk bows which are bordered with clear glass beaded braid and fringe. A similar line of trimming is stitched across the bodice to suggest a yoke. There are harmonizing glass stud buttons. The separate skirt is gored and has a small train. It is

pleated with the folds arranged so that they run from the centre-front double box pleat with inverted pleats at its sides towards the centre back.

In 1865, the *Englishwoman's Domestic Magazine* notes, 'Dresses incline more and more to the Princess Shape. All the widths are gored, the skirt is scant and short at the front and forms a long sweeping train at the back. The body is plain with a round waist.' The newness of the style may account for uncertainty in the set of the pleats. There is a photograph of Marie Wilton in the play *Ours*, 1886, (Theatre Museum) wearing a very similar dress.

Given by Miss M. Frobisher
T.174&A-1965

SHAWL, *French, probably Bayeux, third quarter 19th century, given by Miss G. M. Redwood, Mrs Z. C. Evans and*

Mrs M. L. Kearney, T.66-1957
BONNET, *English, late 1860s, given by Mr H. C. Andrews, 479-1905*
UMBRELLA/PARASOL, ivory handle, blue silk cover, *English, about 1860, given by Mrs Stewart Dyer, T.97-1915*

50 DRESS, brown wool and blue silk
English, 1868–9

The bodice is made from brown wool trimmed and faced with fine, striped, mid-blue shot silk, the material also used for the underskirt. It fastens with worked silk buttons and has a narrow neckband with a detachable fichu collar trimmed with a bow. The bodice is fitted to shape with darts and has a basque which is short, hip-length, in front but longer at the back where it is arranged to suggest coat tails with patch pockets. The sleeves are long and wide with deep cuffs trimmed with pleating and bows. The overskirt is knee-length, trimmed with a false button fastening down the front, and asymmetrically draped at the back where it is trimmed with bows. There are tapes on the underside to adjust the drape. The skirt is gored, the sides pleated and the straight-cut back pleated tightly into the waistband. The bodice is lined with glazed cotton and boned. The skirt is lined with fine stiffened cotton and there is a tape which passes through strings on the underside of the skirt, from the outside of the waistband so that the train can be gathered up for walking.

The dress is very well made and finished. Similar examples are illustrated in the *Englishwoman's Domestic Magazine*, 1869. This form of cuff remained fashionable through to the early 1870s. There is a pattern in J. Arnold's *Patterns of Fashion*, vol. 2, plate 26, p. 196.

Given by Miss E. Beard
T.6 to C-1937   page 40

51 DRESS AND JACKET, golden brown silk trimmed with ruched matching satin ribbon and fringe
English, about 1870

The dress consists of a loose, waist length bodice which fastens in the front and is worn inside the waistband of the matching skirt. It is lined with glazed linen and held in position with tapes at the waist. The sleeves are a short wrist-length with a trimming of ruching and fringe for the cuffs. The skirt is gored, fitted to the hips with darts and tightly gathered at the back. Inside are tapes and loops to adjust the length and drape.

The jacket is a short hip-length and

loose cut in front. It is longer at the back and is semi-fitted with a central vent. It has a round neck trimmed with ribbons and fringe and fastens with covered, embroidered buttons. The fit suggests that this outfit belonged to an old lady. The unshaped bodice is unusual. The loops and tapes within the skirt are a simple but effective way of adapting a skirt to a bustle.

This is not an unfashionable garment but similar jackets are illustrated in *The Queen*, 16 July 1870, as 'Paletot Mantelet' for an elderly lady.

Given by Miss Wilson
T.152 to B-1966

BONNET, purple ribbed silk and velvet, *English, about 1868–70, given by the Misses Montefiore*, T.110-1919
PARASOL, yellow silk, lined in purple, with a wooden handle, *English, late 1860s, given by the family of Major and Mrs Mackay Mackenzie*, T.220E-1915
CUFFS, whitework with bobbin lace insertions, *English, 1870s, given by Mrs Evans*, T.289-1920 and Circ.712-1920

[51]

[52]

52 DRESS, white muslin
English, about 1869

The dress is trimmed with applied bands of emerald green satin, and insertions of Midland Counties bobbin lace and machine-made white work embroidery.

It consists of a blouse, loose-fitting and below the waist in length, with a high, round neck and a concealed front fastening. The sleeves are long and medium-wide. The matching skirt, which is very full, is straight-cut in front, gored and pleated at the sides and tightly gathered at the centre of the back. It is unlined, but has a deep facing at the hem. Over it is a *polonaise*, arranged in graduated swagged festoons. There is a satin belt trimmed with a rosette.

There are several similar blouses illustrated in *The Queen* and the *Englishwoman's Domestic Magazine* during 1869, as well as draped peplums over full, pleated skirts, and it was a vogue which continued into the early 1870s.

Given by Miss Ada B. Cooper
T.12 to B-1943

53 DRESS, bright green silk
English, about 1872

The silk has a figured pattern of black and white leaves on a speckled ground, and the dress is trimmed with looped green silk braid. The dress has a low, square neckline with a bow at the back and long pagoda sleeves. The waist is round and the skirt gored and pleated with a gathered panel at the centre of the back. The overskirt is hip-length, draped and trimmed with a matching fringe. There is a belt with a bow at the back. The bodice is boned and lined with white glazed cotton, the sleeves faced with white silk and lined with pleated white silk ribbon. The overskirt and belt are lined with black buckram.

Open sleeves of this kind were very fashionable in 1870 and an example with the same squared edge was illustrated in *The Queen*, 6 August 1870.

Given by Miss A. Maishman
T.101 to B-1972

DRESS FRONT AND CUFFS, Honiton bobbin lace, *English, 1870s*. Dress front *given by Mrs Andrew Dunlop*, T.267-1969. Cuffs *given by Mrs M. Tomlinson*, T.180&A-1973   page 40

54 DRESS, bright aniline purple silk, trimmed with matching satin bands, covered buttons and Bedfordshire

Maltese lace
English, about 1870–3

There is a bodice which fastens with domed, fabric-covered buttons and has a narrow collar. The sleeves are long and medium-wide with deep pointed cuffs. The basque of the bodice extends to become a knee-length *polonaise*, draped and trimmed with a bow at the back. The skirt is gored, pleated and tightly gathered at the back, and is trimmed with matching applied bands. The jacket is lined with beige glazed cotton and boned on the main seams. Inside the jacket there is a hanging loop, and three tapes, possibly for attaching a bustle. The hem is faced with black, stiffened cotton and has a border of purple woollen braid.

The dress is said to have been worn by the mother of the donor on her wedding day in 1870. Dresses in this style, with the knee-length fronts of the bodice flowing into the *polonaise*, are illustrated in *The Queen* for October 1871, and continue through to 1873. The applied bands on the skirt appear in *Le Follet* in March 1872 and in *The Queen* for July 1872.

Given by Mr Leonard Shields
T.182&A-1914   page 41

55 DRESS, blue and white striped cotton trimmed with darker blue to which is applied pale blue silk braid, and bone buttons
English, about 1872

The dress is inspired by the sailor suit, and the jacket, which is hip-length, has a square collar with scarf ends. There are patch pockets on the pleated basque. The skirt is gored with a straight panel at the back, gathered at the waist. The over-skirt is pointed with patch pockets and a pocket in the seam. There is also a belt trimmed with a stitched bow with long ends. The outfit is unlined. This is a jaunty, sensible and comfortable though decorative seaside outfit of a kind which rarely survives.

The donors offered it to the Museum as part of a collection of '*good* middle class (clothes) bought at Peter Robinson's, Duncan Smith's, Marshall & Snelgrove or Lewis and Allenby's'. There are several approximations to this style in *The Queen* in 1872. A version of the jacket is illustrated in *The Mousquetaire Bodice*, 24 March 1872.

Given by Miss Julia Reckitt and Messrs G. F. & A. I. Reckitt
T.128 to B-1923

HAT, *English, late 1870s, given by the executors of the late Mr E. W. Mynott,* T.54-1980

56 DRESS, light blue silk trimmed with a darker shade
English, 1872–4

A man's coat and waistcoat provide the inspiration for this afternoon or 'promenade' dress. The bodice is hip-length and fastens at the front. It is darted to shape and has stepped revers, wide, straight sleeves with deep cuffs trimmed with bows and a panel of gauging, and there is a basque with flares and 'tails'. A contrasting waistcoat front is applied to it. The skirt is gored at the front and straight-cut at the back with the material arranged in cartridge pleats at the waist. The train is mounted on a separate waistband and fastened to buttons concealed in the side seams of the skirt. It is gathered into deep graduated contrasting facings and has inner silk ribbons to make extra draping possible. Narrow cross-cut bands with a false button fastening trim the basque. The bodice is lined with white glazed cotton, faced with silk and lightly boned. The skirt, faced at the hem, has a pleated brush frill and braid. The main seams are machine-stitched.

The dress is an excellent example of professional dressmaking. The cross-cut facings are precise and smooth and the finishes firm and well judged. It is disciplined, almost severe in concept, looking forward to the firmer lines of the mid 1870s and away from the frothy haberdashery trimmings of the beginning of the decade. A dress with a waistcoat effect and contrasting facing to the train is illustrated in the *Le*

Follet, 1874. There is a description and pattern in J. Arnold, *Patterns of Fashion*, plate 30.

Given by Miss B. M. Eyre Poppleton
T.112 to B-1938

CUFFS, whitework embroidery, *English, mid-19th century, given by Miss B. Hinton,* T.115&A-1971

57 EVENING DRESS, rose pink satin
English, about 1876–8

The bodice is fitted, laced at the back and has a point at the back and front.

The neckline is low and square with a lace border, and there are tight three-quarter length sleeves. The matching skirt consists of a drape of pink figured silk, tucked up at the hips to show tiers of machine-made lace frills and pleats which are intermingled with ribbon bows. A draped panel of satin forms the back of the skirt. The bodice is lined with white figured cotton, the skirt with pink glazed cotton. It has a hoop and is held in place with tapes and elastic.

This type of bodice was known as a 'cuirasse', which the *Englishwoman's Domestic Magazine* described in 1875: 'cut low and laced at the back, it comes down quite plain over the hips so as very greatly to resemble a corset put *over* the dress instead of under'. According to *Myra's Journal*, 1878, ball dresses with short (untrained) skirts were new and popular.

Given by Mrs Therese Horner
T.130&A-1958

FAN, sticks and guards of mother-of-pearl, *English, 1870s, given by Mrs Lilian Albert*, Circ.1174-1926

58 EVENING DRESS, cream satin with a figured design of vertical stripes and leaves
English, 1879

The dress has a low V-neck and tight three-quarter-length sleeves. It consists of a tunic, fastened with laces at the back, fitted as far as the knees where it drapes back over the underskirt. Applied decoration machine-embroidered with flowers in green and maroon trims the centre front, the tunic borders, and the neck and sleeve

openings. The neck and cuffs are additionally trimmed with pleated net and lace. The bodice is lined with white glazed cotton and boned. The separate skirt is made from cream silk. It is ruched in front and has a train box-pleated into the back. It is faced with cotton and has tapes to hold the breadths in position.

A label is printed in gold on the waistband: 'Mrs Golding Modes and Robes 19 Conduit . . . Bond St., London W.' Kelly's Directory lists her under this title from 1875 to 1882. The dress came from the donor's trousseau, September, 1879.

Given by Mrs W. A. Horn
T.63-1939

MANTLE, maroon silk plush
French, about 1880–5

It has bronze bead embroidery around the sleeve openings, the front borders, and in a triangular panel on the back. The borders are trimmed with brown marabou feathers. The mantle is full-length, and its deeply-set sleeves have wide cuffs. It is fitted and has a vent at the back of the skirt, headed by a brown satin bow. The mantle is lined with pale blue satin and fastens with hooks and eyes.

It is labelled 'Maison Dieu la fait, Boulevard de la Madeleine, Paris'. Similar full-length mantles are referred to as 'opera mantles' in contemporary fashion journals.

Given by Count Adam Zamoyski
T.311-1977

59 DRESS, brown satin trimmed with rose pink and figured pink and green satin, chenille tassels, and machine-made lace
English, London: Halling Pearce and Stone, 1879–81

The fitted jacket-bodice has an attached waistcoat front of figured silk, fastening with self-covered buttons and pleated tails trimmed with ribbon. The bodice is boned and lined with silk. The skirt fastens at the back and has an inner lining with elastic mounted tapes which hold it close to the figure. Tacked and tied inside the train is an additional stiffened cotton lining edged with machine-made lace and frills.

Waistcoats were fashionable from 1879, when *Myra's Journal of Dress and Fashion*, 1 January 1879, comments: 'Paniers, jackets and waistcoats are all in vogue for evening toilette. . . . There are many varieties . . . of waistcoats . . . The waistcoat is a most becoming *vêtement* . . . for dress toilette, of plain or opal brocade satin in rose colour, amber or blue'. But the heavily trained skirts do not appear until 1880–81: a

similar example is illustrated in the same journal for 1 February 1881.

This dress is said to have been made for Mrs Arthur Davey, the mother of the donor, by Halling Pearce and Stone, Waterloo House, Cockspur Street, London. They were established as linen drapers under that name in 1817.

Given by Miss B. M. Davey
T.238&A-1916

FAN of silk painted in water colours, *French, signed Alexandre, D.A.C.(?) Beaumont, 1880s, lent by His Royal Highness, The Duke of Gloucester*, Loan 6   page 120

60 DRESS, dark purple satin
English, about 1880

The dress fastens at the back from the narrow band collar to the hips with silver-plated buttons in a Florentine design. The tight, three-quarter sleeves are entirely gauged, trimmed at the cuffs with two rows of pleated bands. The front is fitted to the figure as far as the hips, and is designed to suggest a jacket. It is trimmed round the edges with motifs in irridescent beads and worn over a pleated and ruched stomacher front with a mock lacing. At the hips it is draped back into paniers which knot over the train. The skirt is ruched as far as the knees, where it is arranged in pleated tabs with pendant chenille tassels mounted over crenelated tabs and bands of pleats. The sleeves and the bodice (which is boned) are lined with white glazed cotton, the skirt with mauve polished cotton. The back breadth is lined with stiffened cotton and held in place with tapes.

This is an excellent example of the varied sewing techniques used by the dressmaker in the late 1870s and early 1880s. It is said to have been worn by the mother of the donor on her wedding day, in 1880, and was purchased in Bond Street.

Given by Mrs A. Nicholls
T.113-1964

61 EVENING DRESS, pale pink satin
French, Paris : Worth, about 1881

The bodice is made in the 'Princess' line, and is seamed and gored for a moulded fit. It fastens with laces at the front and has a deep, square neckline trimmed with pearl-embroidered machine-made lace. The sleeves are elbow-length and narrow but slashed, with the openings filled with lace. The bodice extends into drapes at the hips, merging with the train which falls in inverted pleats from the seams of the bodice. The border of the train is scalloped, trimmed with machine-made lace and mounted over a pleated band. The skirt has a front panel of cream satin with a formal floral pattern machine-embroidered in silk and chenille in shades of pink, bronze and green, the centre trimmed with bead tassels. The dress is lined with white silk, the bodice is boned and the skirt is hooped at the back with tapes for adjustment. 'Worth, Paris' is machine-woven on the waist-tape.

Given by Mrs G. T. Morton
T.63&A-1976

FAN, needle-lace, *Irish, 1880s, bequeathed by Miss Eileen Mary Chatt,*
T.34-1973   page 41

62 DRESS, blue and white striped Liberty washing silk
English, 1880s

The dress has a low, square neck and short-waisted bodice fastened at the back. It is cut fairly full and smocked at the back and front. The waist is round and the skirts attached. These consist of an overskirt, draped with tapes and gathered up to show an underskirt, mounted onto a white cotton lining and tied back with tapes. The sleeves are elbow-length puffs, smocked and gathered. Darker blue silk is used to face the bodice and sleeves.

The dress was made and worn by the mother of the donor, the wife of Sir Hamo Thornycroft (1850–1926), the sculptor, who designed it for her. They were both interested in the dress reform movement and the dress is designed in accordance with the movement's principles so that it did not restrict the waist and arms. It fits a good, natural, uncorsetted figure. The sewing is not professional and it has been altered. Liberty's was a predictable choice for the purchase of material. When opened in 1875, the shop specialized in oriental fabrics which were very popular with the artistic community. This is a thin, probably Indian washing silk, possibly quite cheap, of a type which seldom survives.

Given by Mrs W. O. Manning
T.171-1973   page 43

63 DRESS, white cotton
English, about 1885

The dress has a square-cut neckline, hip-length bodice and tiered, pointed and pleated flounces trimmed with Bedfordshire Maltese lace. The side and back of the bodice are cut and darted to fit the figure. The front panel is gathered and smocked and flared below the waist. The bodice fastens at the side with two rows of buttons for easy adjustment of size. The sleeves are just below elbow-length, and straight. An asymmetric drape with its back points gathered into a bustle and two tiers of flounces are mounted on the under-skirt, which is straight in front and gathered at the centre back.

The dress is machine-stitched and simple but effective in concept. It has fashionable features, bustle drape and copious trimming, but is comparatively tough, light and easy to wear and wash. It is said to have been made in Clifton, Bristol, in 1895 and worn in Burma. Dresses with asymmetric drapes and inserted waistcoat effects were fashionable from 1884. S. Blum in *Victorian Fashions from Harper's Bazaar*, 1867–99, illustrates a similar example on p. 178. Plate 2 from the *West End Gazette*, February 1885, confirms their continuing popularity.

Given by Mrs Phayre
T.224&A-1927

TENNIS RAQUET, *English, 1880s, lent by the Wimbledon Lawn Tennis Museum*
HAT, straw trimmed with ribbon, *English, about 1885, given by Messrs Harrods*, T.985A-1913

64 EVENING DRESS, silk
USA, about 1887

There is a closely fitting bodice of dark green velvet with a pointed front and back extending into a squared-off tail. Applied to it is an irridescent beaded panel. The bodice is low-cut with very short lace sleeves trimmed with ribbon bows. The separate skirt is made from shot cream silk, trimmed with irridescent bead motifs over which machine-made lace is asymmetrically draped. The cotton lining is boned and taped into a bustle shape. The train is made from dark green velvet, tightly gathered at the back, the edges trimmed with a pleated frill faced with white satin. One side is faced with a triangular panel of gold and white figured silk.

According to the *Lady's World*, 1887, 'Skirts now never have two sides alike.' Stamped in gold on the grosgrain waistband is 'E. Wiggins, 52 West 21st Street, N.Y.' E. Wiggins was at this address only from 1886 to 1889. The dress is very similar in cut to a fragmentary one from the same source, now in the collection of the Norwich Castle Museum and marked 'La Ferrière' a well known Paris *couturier*. The make of the V & A dress is not very certain, and it may either be a copy or have been altered.

'A. P. Rogers' is written in ink on a paper label stitched to the waistband. She was a daughter of Henry Huttleston Rogers of New York, and the sister of Lady Fairhaven (see also 66 and 69).

Given by Lord and Lady Fairhaven
T.278 to B-1972

FAN, sticks and guards of mother-of-pearl, *English or French, 1880s, given by Mrs M. Schlesinger*, Circ.226-1953
                      page 44

65 DRESS, brown satin
English, about 1888

The trained overdress has a high collar with notched lapels, and is styled to

suggest a man's coat of the Directoire (late 18th-century) period, but with a train gathered to the back of the waist. The fronts are faced with machine-embroidered panels in an oriental style, and are trimmed with three cast metal Japonaiserie buttons. The dress fastens with a half-belt, with a buckle copied from those of the 18th century. There is a draped waistcoat front in cream grosgrain which fastens with concealed buttons. Collar, cuffs and the front of the separate skirt are made from brown silk with a velvet warp-figured cream stripe. The skirt is mounted on brown glazed cotton and is boned and taped to shape.

The Queen, August 1888, illustrates a very similar 'Directoire' reception dress, and in November comments: 'the petticoat falls in gathers from the waist . . . corresponding with the large revers (and) . . . the large cuffs . . . The sides of the coat hang down plain and straight . . . all the fullness being gathered into a cluster in the centre of the back below the waist.'

Given by Miss Sophie B. Steel
T.164&A-1937

66 DRESS, dark green wool with strawberry-coloured figured satin panels edged with black silk braid
French, 1887–9

The bodice is waist-length, panelled with satin and edged with black moiré ribbon. It is trimmed at the back with a made-up bow with long pendant ends. The dress fastens at the shoulder over a boned green silk bodice lining. The sleeves are long with a high pleated shoulder. Collar and cuffs are faced

with gold beaded tulle. The skirt has a slightly draped front, with the back flared and arranged in deep pleats. It is mounted over a green silk petticoat, and boned and taped to a bustle shape at the back. The skirt may have been altered and have lost a side panel.

The machine-woven label 'WORTH PARIS' was stitched to the waist tape.

The dress is said to have been worn by Cara Leland Huttleston Rogers of New York, later Lady Fairhaven (?–1939). (See also 64 and 69.)

Given by Lord and Lady Fairhaven
T.268&A-1972

LORGNETTE, tortoiseshell, *English, third quarter of 19th century, given by Miss E. M. Haiselden*, T.13-1972   page 45

67 DRESS, printed silk
French or Italian, 1892–4

The silk has alternating stripes of cornflowers on a cream ground and black seed pods on beige. It has a fitted bodice with a pointed waist; the boned silk bodice lining fastens with hooks and eyes under the draped

insertion of cream silk gauze. There are frilled collars and cuffs of the same gauze with a machine-embroidered border. The leg-of-mutton sleeves are long, full, gathered at the shoulders and gauged at the insides of the elbows. The skirt has a straight-cut front, darted at the hips, is gored at the sides and tightly gathered at the centre of the back. It is faced with white silk and the hem is bound with pink velvet. The low collar is an unusual feature, more

common towards the end of the 1890s than at the beginning. Since the dress has been let out, suggesting a relatively long period of use, this may be a later alteration. It was worn by the mother of the donor.

Given by The Comtesse de Tremereuc
T.368&A-1960

HAT, straw trimmed with machine-made lace and ribbon, *English, about 1895, given by Mrs H. Moreton,* T.105-1932
HANDBAG, maroon leather, *English, 1890s, given by Mr A. Weingott,* T.63 to E-1956
PARASOL, *English, late 19th century, given by Mrs J. A. Woodthorpe,* T.38-1958

68 COAT AND SKIRT, beige linen
French, about 1894–5

The jacket is single-breasted, hip-length, seamed and fitted, but with flared and pleated tails. It has curved pockets at the hips. The fancy, stepped collar and the cuffs of the leg-of-mutton sleeves are embroidered in beige silk cord in a formal floral pattern. The skirt has the front panel cut straight and channel-seamed. The back is widely flared with central box-pleats. The fullness is controlled by elastic stays on the inside. The suit is unlined but the seams are bound, and there is stiffening inside the sleeve heads.

A label stitched inside the neck has 'Doucet Paris' machine woven in yellow on a beige ribbon. 'G 0841' is written on a tape inside the skirt waist. Beige was a popular colour for travelling clothes because it did not show the dust. When this outfit was washed by the Museum's Conservation Department, it shed quantities of red-brown dust, previously almost unnoticeable. Possibly this was a souvenir of an Egyptian tour. Linen was popular for hot weather travellers because it was comparatively light-weight and washable.

The *couture* house, Doucet, was founded in Paris in 1824 as a lace and lingerie establishment and they were not noted in the Bottin directory as a couture house until 1883. Jacques Doucet, 1853–1939, was better known for his formal rather than tailored clothes.
T.15&A-1979

HAT, *English, late 19th century, given by the executors of the late Mr E. W. Mynott,* T.55-1980
HANDBAG, *English, late 19th century, given by Mr W. A. Weingott, T.65-1956*
page 44

69 EVENING DRESS, blue-black silk velvet
USA, about 1894

The dress is trimmed with bead and sequin embroidery and bead-embroidered net in a design of butterflies. It is lined with black silk. The bodice, which laces, is boned and has a rounded point in the front, emphasized by bead embroidery. It has a low, square neck and very full, puffed sleeves, tapering slightly to a triangular bead-embroidered cuff just below the elbow. The sleeves have a stiff interlining. There is a tulle frill at the neck, which is also trimmed with a bow and flared tulle epaulettes. The skirt is darted at the hips and in front is slightly flared. It is more widely flared at the back, where it is box-pleated, interlined and caught together with elasticized tapes.

The label, 'Stern Bros., West 23rd, New York', is stitched to the waistband. One of the largest New York department stores of the time, they imported Paris models for copying. The dress has the quality and design of a *couture* model, though not the label. The design cannot be precisely assigned. Butterflies were popular motifs in 1894. *The Queen* in April, 1894, illustrates an example by the *couturier* Felix, and butterfly trimming remained fashionable through 1895. There is an example by Worth in the Brooklyn Museum (65.189.2). A paper label inscribed '1894 A. P. Rogers' is stitched to the waistband (see also 64 and 66).

Given by Lord and Lady Fairhaven
T.272&A-1972   page 47

70 DRESS, silk
English, about 1894

The dress is inspired by the fashions of the late 15th century and consists of a dark green velvet overdress, with epaulettes, a wide 'V' neckline, a high waist and a full, gathered skirt. It is trimmed with bands of satin-stitch embroidery in paler green silk and irridescent beads. The neckline is filled with a pleated front of green and yellow Liberty 'Hop and Ribbon' damask, the design for which was registered in 1892–3. The same material is used for the gathered 'leg-of-mutton' sleeves. The gown is lined with green silk and has a yellowish green frill at the hem. The bodice fastens in the front with hooks and eyes and is boned. The back of the skirt is held with tapes and elastic bands. The black satin waistband is marked 'Liberty & Co Artistic and Historic Costume Studio, 222 Regent St, W.' Liberty's began to make dresses in 1884.

The gown was made for a member of the Liberty family and conforms to aesthetic taste in its 'greenery-yallery' colours. It is close to the Walter Crane designs for aesthetic dress in *Aglaeia, The Journal of the Healthy and Artistic Dress Union* 1893, p. 7. The dressmaking is, however, fashionable and conventional. Dresses of this kind were often worn as 'tea gowns', informal 'at home' dresses for the late afternoon or even as simple dinner dresses.
T.56-1976

71 DRESS, supple, light-weight wool, checked in black and beige on a heather coloured ground
French, about 1897

The waist-length bodice is designed to suggest a bolero jacket, to which is applied bands of black silk braid edged with black and white fringe, worn over a slightly draped high-collared blouse front, with a wide, square yoke extended to epaulettes of white machine-made lace. The sleeves are long and tight with a slightly puffed and tucked sleeve-head. Narrow bands of tucked yellow ribbon are applied to the lace collar and cuffs. There are traces of a wide, draped heliotrope silk sash. The bodice is mounted on and fastens over a front-fastening cotton lining, boned at the main seams. The skirt fits closely and is made from two cross-cut main panels, with a double box-pleat at the centre back held with

internal stays of black ribbon. It is pieced out at the back hem and faced round the bottom with lilac silk.

The dress was worn by the mother of the donor, and is said to have been bought in Paris. It was probably bought ready-made. Boleros and figure-moulding, flared skirts were very fashionable in 1897. *The Queen*, 2 April 1895, illustrates examples with epaulettes, blouse fronts and pointed belts. *Myra's Journal, Our Lessons in Dressmaking*, No. 80, April 1, 1894, *Bell and Gored Skirts*, illustrated a similar example: 'The newest bell skirts are absolutely without fullness at the top . . . It fits closely over the hips and begins to form a series of fluted pleats a little above the knee.'

The soft colours of this dress anticipate the pastel shades of the early 20th century.

Given by Mrs A. Perrot
T.139&A-1961

UMBRELLA, blond tortoiseshell diamond-set handle, brown silk lever, *English, late 19th century*, given by Mrs B. Samuel, T.432-1977
HANDBAG, chromium-plated mount, maroon calf, *English, about 1890*, given by Mr Weingott, T.62-1956

72 EVENING DRESS, pink satin
French, about 1897

The dress is trimmed with machine-embroidered lace motifs in a pattern of carnations, re-embroidered with pastes. The bodice is long and mounted over a boned pink silk lining. The neckline is square and low, edged with pink tulle, arranged into upstanding bows at the shoulders. Deep swags of pink roses are draped over the upper arms. The skirt is fitted over the hips with a side-seam partially concealed under the applied embroidered motif. Swags of pink tulle trim the border of the skirt, which is widely flared and overlaid at the back with a double layer of pink tulle. The machine-woven waistband is marked 'WORTH PARIS' with 97888 written on the reverse.

This is a fine example of the *fin de siècle* ball gown and, fortunately, enough remained of the fragile trimmings to which it owed its effect for them to be restored. Similar dresses with bows on the shoulders and floral trimmings are illustrated in *The Queen* for 1897. Although Worth was fond of tulle and flowers, this model does not appear in the Guard Books of designs. The dress belonged to Miss Anne Thomson of Philadelphia, daughter of Mr Frank Thomson, an early collector of Impressionist paintings.

Given by Mrs Soame Jenyns
T.433&A-1977

FAN, Flemish needle-lace, gilt and mother-of-pearl sticks, *French, about 1890,* Duke of Gloucester loan 10
NECKLACE, silver set marcasites, *English, third quarter of 18th century, given by Dr Joan Evans,* M.75-1962
page 45

73 ROBE, woven silk and cotton, sateen and plush
English, London: Liberty & Co Ltd, late 1890s

This garment was inspired by 16th-century long gowns; it was made in Liberty's Artistic and Historic Costume Studio for a member of the Liberty family. Years later the original Costume Department was remembered in the house magazine, *The 'Liberty' Lamp*: 'our designers of dresses have taken their models from historical costumes, modifying them more or less to adapt them to our own times and conditions, but always retaining something of the characteristic of the original', and 'in a short time it became very much the *mode* among artistic people and their imitators to wear a "Liberty" gown at any special function.' The sombre yellow-amber and green tones were popular in 'artistic' households for

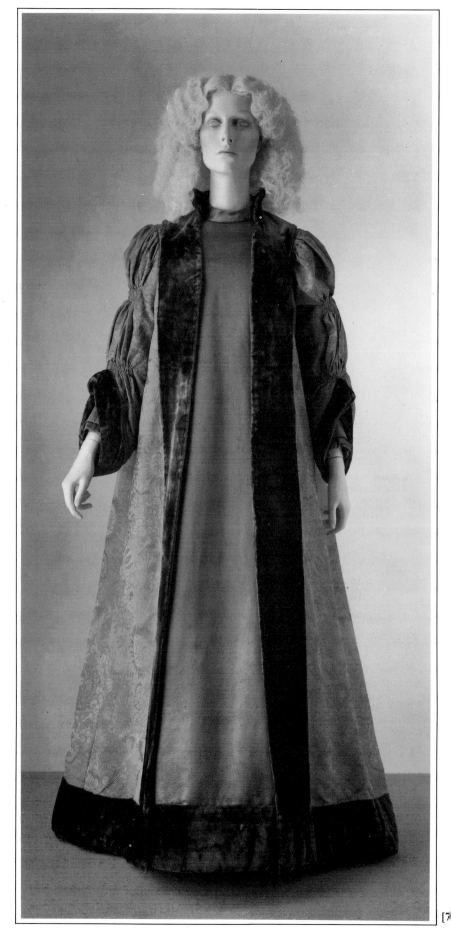

both dress and furnishing in the 1890s. The fairly large-scale woven pattern features pomegranates and sunflowers – both favoured late-19th-century decorative motifs. The gown consists of a flared front sateen panel attached to an open, flowing robe which falls from pleats at the back neck and has gathered double puffed sleeves with narrow under-sleeves. The sturdy materials combined with deep edgings of heavy plush and a stiff mid-blue taffeta lining give the robe a stately quality.
T.57-1976

74   SHIFT, fine linen
English, mid-18th century

The shift has a low, round neck and straight-cut sleeves, set with a gore beneath. They are elbow-length, gathered and pleated into an arm-band with worked eyelet holes. The shift reaches to below the knees and is flared in the front and with triangular gores inserted at each side of the back. '4 SH' is worked in red cross-stitch in the centre of the neck.
T.26-1969

CORSET, red silk damask
English, 1770s–1780s

The corset is stiffened with whalebone and lined with canvas. The cut would give the full-bosomed, small-waisted line, fashionable 1770–80.

Given by Messrs Harrods
T.909–1913

SIDE HOOP, pink striped linen
English, 1778

The hoop is probably stiffened with cane and kept in shape with tapes inside. According to the original bill it was purchased on 16 February 1778 from 'A. Schabner Riding Habit and Robe Maker at his Warehouse in Tavistock Street Covent Garden' by Miss Davis as a 'Pink Holland Hoop' for 10s 6d. It may have accompanied the Brown Silk Italian Gown and Coat, the making of which cost £1 1s 0d, listed in the same bill.

*From the family of Mrs Deborah Carter
Given by Mr & Mrs R. C. Carter*
T.120-1969   page 26

75   SHIFT, linen
English, 1835

There are cotton frills at the low, round neck and the short, gathered sleeves. The shift is cut straight and is knee-length with gores at the bust. It is inscribed '1835'. It closely resembles

the shift illustrated in Plate 6, Fig. 6. Anon, *The Workwoman's Guide*, 1836, revised and enlarged edition, 1840.
T.386-1960 *Given by Miss Blake*

DRAWERS, cotton
English, 1834

The legs are mid-calf length, trimmed with tucks. The legs are cut separately and on the cross, lapping over one another at the waistband which is adjusted with a draw-tape. According to *The Workwoman's Guide*, op.cit., 'TROUSERS or DRAWERS . . . are worn by men, women and children of all classes, and almost all ages . . . They are made in a great variety of ways. Those mentioned . . . are . . . most generally approved.' This type is closer to the kind recommended for small boys, but they are in a woman's size. They are marked '1834'.

Given by Mrs Latter Axton
T.102-1931

CORSET, white cotton
English, about 1835

The corset is stiffened with cording and whalebone. There are gores for hip and bust. In the front is a pocket for a wide busk, said to have been made from wood. The worked eyelets at the back are reinforced with tape, a process described in *The Workwoman's Guide*, op.cit., p. 82.

Given by Mrs Elizabeth Norton
T.3-1929   page 35

76   CHEMISE, white cotton
English, about 1860

The chemise has a low neckline and short sleeves edged with crochet. It is cut straight, and gathered into the neckline. The loops on the sleeves were said to be for the attachment of long day sleeves. It is marked 'M Miller'.

Given by Miss Elizabeth Morris
T.86-1951

CORSET, blue silk
English or French, 1864

The corset is stiffened with whalebone and machine-stitched with an incised swivel latch to lock the busk fastening. There is a lace fastening at the back. It is said to have been worn at a wedding in 1864.

Given by the Burrows Family
T.169-1961

CRINOLINE FRAME
English, about 1865–9

It is made from hoops of spring steel covered with braid. The hoops are

fixed to black edged tapes with stamped metal eyelets. There is a red woollen waistband and the frill is made from horsehair. An elastic stay holds the hoop in place. Unusually, there is no manufacturer's name. This may be a copy of the Thomson Crown Crinoline, 1866–8, which it closely resembles.

Given by Mr F. D. Worthington
Circ.87-1951   page 39

77   COMBINATIONS, white cotton with Bedfordshire Maltese lace trimming around the neck, sleeve and leg openings
English, about 1895

The front is trimmed with hand-made insertion and white work embroidery. The combinations are seamed to fit the body and fasten down the front with cotton washing buttons. These are used to fasten the rear flap. The label 'Robinson & Cleaver London' is stitched inside the neckline. Robinson & Cleaver advertised that they were specialists in hand-made Irish linen during the 1890s. Combinations were re-introduced in the late 1870s to give a fashionable smooth line.

Given by Mrs Raper
T.15-1958

CORSET, red sateen, the bones covered with yellow leather
English, 1883

The corset fastens with a spoon busk. There were constant attempts to improve corsets during the 1880s. The spoon busk was supposed to equalize pressure on the stomach and the leather-covered bones might have increased wear and flexibility.
T.84&A-1980

BUSTLE
English, about 1884

It is made from steel wires so constructed that it compresses if sat on. Inscribed on the waistband is 'The New Phantom Regd. No.72855 Patent Applied for'.

There is no patent but the number is in the sequence for 1884. There were many attempts to invent the ideal bustle – light, firm and flexible.

Given by Miss Mary Montefiore
T.131-1919   page 43

[78]

Men's Dress

78 DOUBLET AND TRUNK HOSE WITH CANIONS, uncut silk velvet on a voided satin ground, Italian late 16th early 17th century
English, about 1604

The doublet has a slight peascod and thickly quilted lining at the fronts and around the sides, however the centre back is not quilted. The hose (breeches) are also thickly lined with wool. They are supported by a series of laces (points) threaded to the inside waist of the doublet and the waistband of the breeches. The canions are extensions to the hose tapered to fit the leg. The suit is reputed to have belonged to James I.

Lent by the Grimsthorpe and Drummond Castle Trust Ltd
Loan 2

LACE EDGING to collar and cuffs, *Italian*, needle lace, *about 1600*, 297A,B&C-1890
HANDKERCHIEF, cutwork with detached needle lace edging, *probably Flemish, 1600–15*, 484-1903
RAPIER, the hilt of steel encrusted with silver, the blade inscribed Antonio Picino, *English, about 1600, bequeathed by Francis Mallet*, M.55-1947.

All other items are replicas.

79 DOUBLET, BREECHES AND CLOAK, yellow slashed and braided satin
English, about 1630

The breeches of this suit were originally supported by a series of large hooks (now missing) stitched to the waistband and hooked into eyelets attached to the waistband of the doublet.

T.58 to B-1910

FALLING BAND of linen edged with needle lace, *English, 1630s*, 200-1900

CUFFS, replicas edged with needle lace, *English, 1630s,* T.315-1912 and Circ. 321-1921
BOOTHOSE, replicas edged with needle lace, *English, 1630s,* 274&A-1875
BALDRICK, red velvet with silver-gilt embroidery, *English, 1630s,* 582-1897
RAPIER, *English, 1630-40, bequeathed by G. H. Ramsbottom,* M.2770-1931
PAIR OF SPURS, *English, early 17th century, bequeathed by David M. Currie,* M.187&A-1921

All other items are replicas.   page 48

80 DOUBLET AND BREECHES, stamped white satin
English, 1630s

The breeches are supported by a series of large hooks stitched to the waistband and hooked into eyelets attached to the inside waistband of the doublet. Silk ribbon bows are stitched around the waist of the doublet. They are purely decorative but represent points or laces. Formerly these were used to support the breeches as well as hooks and eyes and were threaded through the waistband of the breeches to the inside waistband of the doublet. From the 1620s they were tied in a knot above the tabs or skirts on the outside. The fronts of the doublet are slightly stiffened with 'belly-pieces', triangular pads of buckram stitched inside each front edge. These prevented the doublet from wrinkling at the waist and created the slight protuberance at the centre front. By the 1630s doublets were not as thickly padded or stiffened as they had been hitherto and from the 1630s the doublet continued to reduce not only in thickness but also in length. 348&A-1905

FALLING BAND, replica edged with bobbin lace, *Flemish, 1630s,* T.372-1912
CUFFS, replicas edged with bobbin lace *Flemish, 1620-30s,* T.325&A-1910
CANE, *English, 17th century, given by Messrs Harrods Ltd,* T.1823-1913

All other items are replicas.   page 52

81 DOUBLET AND CASSOCK, beige watered silk decorated with parchment lace
English or French, 1660

The fronts and sleeves of the doublet are paned. Lined with cream silk taffeta, the cuffs faced with beige silk taffeta.
    The cassock was a short loose coat buttoned down the front with loose or open sleeves. Originally worn as a riding coat, it was going out of fashion in the 1660s. This example was

probably intended for a formal occasion.
    Both items are reputed to have belonged to Prince Rupert (1619–82).

T.324&T.323-1980

LACE CRAVAT, *Venetian, 1660s,* raised needle lace, 1509-1888
LACE FRILLS AND RUFFLES, *Venetian, 1660s,* raised needle lace, *given by Mrs A. B. Rathbone,* 1502-1900, *and by Wing Commander H. W. Hall,* Circ. 1-1946

All other items are replicas.   page 53

82 CIRCULAR CLOAK of brown worsted embroidered with silver and silver-gilt thread
English, 1670s

Given by Mr Peter Barker-Mill
T.62-1978

COAT AND OPEN-KNEED BREECHES of brown worsted. Trimmings of black silk and silver-gilt thread braid with cuff facings of blue wool. The coat is also lined with blue wool. Worn by Sir Thomas Isham (1657–81).
English, about 1680

191&A-1900

LACE cravat ends of flat needle lace, *probably French, last quarter 17th century,* 1121-1903
LACE shirt frills of flat needle lace, *probably French, last quarter 17th century, given by the Rev. R. Brooke,* 585&A-1864
LACE ruffles of flat needle lace, *Venetian, last quarter 17th century.* 288&A-1890
CANE of malacca, ivory knob with silver piqué, *English, late 17th century, given by Messrs Harrods,* T.1821-1913

All other items are replicas.   page 51

83 DRESS COAT AND BREECHES for a boy, fine red wool embroidered in silver thread. Associated with Samuel Enys (d.1744).
English, 1700–05

T.327&A-1982.

CRAVAT, bobbin lace, *Brussels, about 1700,* 624-1904
LACE shirt frills of bobbin lace, *Brussels, about 1700,* T.397A&C-1970
LACE ruffles of bobbin lace, *Brussels, about 1700,* T.397&D-1970 and T.397B-1970
SWORD with silver hilt, *English, 1700–10,* 1733-1888

All other items are replicas.   page 54

84 DRESS COAT of very fine brown wool embroidered with silver-gilt thread.
English, 1700–20

According to family tradition the coat was worn by Thomas Severne Esq. (1644–1737), Gentleman of the Bedchamber to William III (1689–1702). The cuffs have been altered, probably between 1715–20.

T.357-1980

SMALL SWORD with silver hilt, *English, London hallmark 1720–21, maker's mark GW, given from the collection of Col. G. Stowell,* M.199-1928
CANE of malacca with an ivory knob decorated with silver piqué. The silver collar is a later addition. *English, dated 1699, given by Mr A. E. Praill,* T.21-1945

All other items are replicas.

85 DRESS SUIT of brown silk
English or French, late 1720s or early 1730s
The design is woven to shape on the coat and cuffs.
MATCHING WAISTCOAT with pattern of white silk
English, late 1720s early 1730s

This is a rare example of a decoration woven to shape for a suit and is made more interesting as the decoration on the matching waistcoat is carried out in white silk in contrast to the coat which is self-coloured brown.

938 to B-1902

CRAVAT of bobbin lace, *Brussels, 1720s, 154-1893*
RUFFLE of bobbin lace, *Brussels, 1720s, 164-1875*
RUFFLE of bobbin lace (2 lengths joined), *Brussels, 1720s, given by Mrs Cope Danby and Mrs D. J. Frost, T.98-1933 and T.261-1973*
MALACCA CANE with horn handle, *English, 18th century, given by Messrs Harrods, T.1825-1913*

All other items are replicas.   page 56

86 DRESS SUIT, green coat and breeches and red waistcoat of fine wool, trimmed with silver-gilt braid
English, 1740s

The coat is collarless, fits tightly to the body and is cut with full skirts. There are two flapped pockets at hip level. The cuffs are broad and deep, widening out towards the elbow. They are not full enough to be 'boot cuffs', nicknamed after the riding boot tops.

The waistcoat is sleeveless and has two flapped pockets. Four of the original thirteen front buttons remain. It is now fastened by modern hooks and eyes.

The breeches buckle at the knee and have a deep waistband and narrow front falls. (Front falls acted as modesty panels, introduced when the cut-away fronts of waistcoats revealed the fly opening.) There are an unusual number of pockets. Two are let into the top of the waistband either side of the opening. Each front has a horizontal slit pocket above a flapped pocket. A side-edge pocket with a single button fastening is let into each side seam with the pocket bags to the rear.

Given by Sir Charles Hope Dunbar, Bart T.250 to B-1924

All other items are replicas.   page 56

87 DRESS COAT of shot green and black silk with gilt metal buttons
English, about 1745

The buttonholes are decorative except at the neck and three at waist level. The skirts of the coat are padded and stiffened with buckram and wool. The opulent fashions of the first half of the 18th century were characterized by rich dress silks for suits and particularly for waistcoats. These were usually the most colourful item, the coat and breeches were often of plain wool, silk or velvet. These fashions proved to be the last time that men indulged in rich, colourful and extravagant clothes. For the remainder of the century men's dress was more austere.

WAISTCOAT, yellow extended tabby silk brocaded in coloured silks and silver threads. The brocaded design is woven to shape.
English, about 1745

Given by Mr F. C. Macpherson T.147&T.148-1964

LACE, needle lace, *Brussels, 1735–45 bequeathed by Edmond Dresden, 601&A-1904*

SMALL SWORD, the hilt of silver, *French, Paris hallmark 1744-5, 1718-1888*

All other items are replicas.   page 57

88 SUIT of cut and uncut yellow and purple silk velvet on a voided ground enriched with silver strip, the silk probably French, late 1750s.
English, about 1760

This is a suit of superb quality and typical of those seen in portraits of the period, such as those by John Singleton Copley.

657 to B-1898

LACE, shirt frill and ruffles of bobbin lace, *French, Valenciennes, about 1760, given by Mrs A. B. Rathbone, 1511 to D-1900*
SMALL SWORD, silver hilt, *English, London hallmark 1752-3, given by Mrs G. Stowell from the collection of Col. G. Stowell, M.198-1928*

All other items are replicas.

89 DRESS COAT AND WAISTCOAT of fine blue wool, embroidered in silver-gilt thread and sequins.
English, about 1760

The coat has a small upright collar, a style that appeared after 1760. The

buttons are decorated with silver-gilt thread and sequins in a basket weave design.

This is a suit of very good quality and would normally have been worn as formal day wear, either at home or at the local Assembly Rooms.

Given by Lt. Col. A. D. Hunter from the Gorst Collection T.73&A-1962

SMALL SWORD with pierced and chiselled hilt, *English, second half 18th century, bequeathed by G. H. Ramsbottom, M.2727-1931*

All other items are replicas.

90 SUIT of patterned cerise and cream silk, the silk probably French, about 1765.
English, late 1760s

The buttonholes from the neck to the waist are cut; the remainder are purely decorative. The skirts are stiffened either with horsehair or buckram.

This suit is of very fine quality and was probably worn in the summer for formal occasions, either at home or at public functions. The suit is only slightly stiffened and interlined, which suggests that it is intended for warmer weather.

Given by Miss Agnes Clayton East T.137 to B-1932

LACE, shirt frill and ruffles of bobbin lace, *English, Devonshire, 1760s, 532 to B-1875*
SMALL SWORD, the hilt of pierced and

chiselled silver, *English, London hallmark 1752-3, maker's mark IC, 1734-1888*
MALACCA CANE with porcelain handle, *probably German or English, mid-18th century, given by Messrs Harrods,* T.1824-1913

All other items are replicas.   page 59

91 DRESS COAT AND WAISTCOAT of sprigged red silk velvet, probably French, 1760s. Embroidered in silver-gilt thread, purl and sequins.
Probably Italian, 1760s

An elaborately decorated suit of the type worn for ceremonial or very formal occasions. These suits do not survive in large number for this period and are consequently quite rare.

Given by Mr W. R. Crawshay
T.28&A-1952

LACE shirt frills and ruffles of needle lace, *French, 1765-75, 538-1875, the ruffles given by Mrs C. M. Chambers,* Circ.9&10-1945
SMALL SWORD, the hilt of chiselled and parcel-gilt steel, *French, mid-18th century, 1738-1888*
MALACCA CANE with gilt brass knob *English, 1760s-70s, given by Messrs Harrods,* T.670D-1913
PASTE SHOE BUCKLES, *English or French, second half 18th century,* T.63&A-1982

All other items are replicas.   page 58

92 FULL DRESS COAT AND WAISTCOAT of blue watered tabby silk, embroidered with silver thread, purl, sequins and

plate. The buttons are also covered in silver plate.
English, 1760s

A typical example of the type of suit most likely to be seen at Court for the second half of the 18th century.

Given by the children of Paymaster Captain G. W. Osmond R.N.
T.26&A-1950

LACE shirt frill and ruffles of needle lace, *French, 1755-65, the shirt frill bequeathed by Mrs Bolckow, 779-1890, the ruffles bequeathed by Edmond Dresden, 612-1904, and given in memory of Mrs A. A. Gordon Clark, T.329-1975*
SMALL SWORD, the hilt of chiselled steel, *English, about 1760, 1725-1888*
SHOE BUCKLES of silver, *English, 1773–about 80, London maker's mark BM for Benjamin Mountigue. This style of buckle was introduced in the 1760s and continued until the 1780s.* T.316&A-1982

All other items are replicas.

93 SHIRT AND BREECHES
SHIRT, linen
English, second half 18th century

The full width of the linen has been used, running from front to back, without shoulder seams. Linen bands have been stitched across the shoulders for reinforcement. A 'T'-shaped cut makes the neck opening, two gussets give extra shaping at the sides. Sleeves have been made from half widths of linen, gathered at wrists and armholes, with underarm gussets. The collar is a straight band.
This is a typical example of an 18th-

century shirt. Such shirts were made from the early 18th until the early 19th century.

Given by Mrs Egland
T.246-1931

BREECHES, the silk French 1760s. The ground enriched with silver-gilt strips patterned in white and maroon silk. *English or French, 1760s*

Given by Mrs H. H. Fraser
T.435-1967

All other items are replicas.

94 PLAIN DRESS COAT AND BREECHES of red silk velvet
English, about 1772

A fine and rare example of a suit that epitomizes the professional gentleman of the late 18th century.

Given by the Rev. R. Brooke
858&B-1864

WAISTCOAT of cream ribbed silk embroidered in chenille, silver thread and sequins

English, 1770s
Given by the Rev. R. Brooke
893-1864

SMALL SWORD, the steel hilt inlaid with gold, *Northern India, 1770s–80s, made for the English market, 1737-1888*
SHOE BUCKLES OF SILVER PLATE, *English, 1770s, given by Messrs Harrods, T.572&A-1913*

All other items are replicas.

95 DRESS SUIT of cream figured cut silk velvet with a voided ground and woven to shape, the velvet French 1774–78. *Probably French, 1770s*

From the 1770s styles became more restrained and sparing in cut and design. One outfit which epitomized men's dress of the late 18th and early 19th centuries was the riding habit of long cut-away coat, short waistcoat, breeches and boots. Made popular by the increased interest in hunting and other sporting activities, it was introduced into polite society more as an act of defiance by radical young men who wished to arouse the disapproval of the 'old order'. Beau Brummel turned the riding habit into fashionably acceptable dress by insisting on a perfect fit to his coat and clean linen and boots.

Given by the Earl of Gosford
T.129 to B-1921

SMALL SWORD, *French, mid-18th century,* 164-1879
SHOE BUCKLES, *English, 1777–85, given by Messrs Harrods,* T.577&A-1913

All other items are replicas.

96 DRESS SUIT, fine quality buff wool, trimmed with silver-gilt braid and enamelled gilt metal buttons
English, late 1770s early 1780s

The overall appearance of this suit suggests the late 1770s. The coat reaches the calf. The fronts are narrow, curving away from the chest towards the hips, the skirts hang straight,

reduced to flat pleats near the centre back. The 1780s are suggested by the adoption of a frock coat for a dress suit. Frock coats of the 18th century always have a turned down collar (cape) and from the 1780s were accepted for dress suits. Other details are the tight sleeves from elbow to wrist with buttoned slit cuffs shaped to a point and stitched flat to the sleeve. The waistcoat reaches the hips with sloping cut-away fronts to the skirts. The breeches are full at the hips but fit the leg. An additional refinement is a narrow edging of green silk twill along fronts and edges of the entire suit.

Given by Lady Spickernell
T.149 to B-1937

COCKED HAT, *English 1770s, lent by The National Trust, Snowshill*
LACE, *needle lace, French 1780s,* 1236C,D,G-1888
SMALL SWORD, *English 1775, given by Mr C. Dury Fortnum,* 771-1899
SHOE BUCKLES, *English, 1770s,* T.61&A-1982

All other items are replicas.

97 DRESS COAT AND WAISTCOAT of green poplin (silk warp and woollen weft) decorated with silk braids and tassels
English, late 1770s early 1780s

This is a suit of very good quality, suitable for formal dress at home or any public occasion. It is the only example of tasselled decoration for buttons and buttonholes in the collection. This was a popular form of decoration on men's suits in the 18th century.

Given by Lt. Col. A. D. Hunter
T.71&A-1962

LACE shirt frill and ruffles of needle lace, *French, 1770s, given by Mrs A. B. Rathbone,* 1517 to B-1900

SMALL SWORD, the hilt of chiselled steel parcel-gilt in two-coloured gold. *French, about 1785, bequeathed by G. H. Ramsbottom,* M.2730-1931
SHOE BUCKLES of silver, *English, 1780s London,* T.314&A-1982

All other items are replicas.

98 DRESS SUIT, cut black silk velvet on a figured ground of purple and cream silk. The velvet English or French, 1780s.
English, 1790s

This is a very fine example of those sleek-looking suits of the late 18th century where the coat skirts have been trimmed back to fit the figure. This could have been worn on formal occasions at home or in public.

136 & 137-1880

WAISTCOAT of cream silk embroidered in coloured silks mainly in satin stitch.
English, 1780–90s
563-1896

LACE shirt frill and ruffles of needle lace, *French, 1780–90s, given by Mrs C. M. Chambers, Circ.13 to B-1945*
SHOE BUCKLES, pewter, *English, 1780s, given by Messrs Harrods, T.458B&C-1913*

All other items are replicas.

99 FULL DRESS SUIT, the coat and breeches of blue and black spotted silk with a twill ground, embroidered in coloured silks mainly in satin stitch. The waistcoat of matching white silk is similarly embroidered. Both the silk and embroidery are probably French.
Probably French, 1790s

Full dress suits of this type were worn for ceremonial events. The embroidery on this suit is of very high quality and is considered to be one of the finest in the collection. The design of the embroidery is probably earlier in date, 1780s, whereas the cut of the suit is typical of the late 1790s and early 19th century.

Given by Mr R. Brooman White
T.148 to B-1924

LACE shirt frill of needle lace, *French, 1780s, given in memory of Mrs A. A. Gordon Clark, T.328-1975*
LACE RUFFLES of needle lace, *French, 1780s, given by Mrs C. M. Chambers, Circ.14 to 17-1945*
PASTE SHOE BUCKLES, *probably French, 1780s, T.65&A-1982*

All other items are replicas.　　page 60

100 DOUBLE-BREASTED MORNING COAT (faded) shot peacock blue and purple silk twill.
English, 1790s

This is a most interesting example of the exaggerated styles of the late 1790s and possibly influenced by the fashion referred to as 'Incroyables'. Although it is not a true 'Incroyable', the broad revers and very high collar reflect this style. Coats with lapels were usually worn with waistcoats that had lapels as well, and these were turned over the coat. Most fashionable waistcoats were short and cut straight across the waist.
940-1902

WAISTCOAT, printed cotton.
Given by Messrs Harrods
T.1082-1913
SHOE BUCKLES, silver, *English, 1790s, mark probably Anderson Robert Dennison (ARD), T.64&A-1982*
CANE, the knob inlaid with tortoise-shell and finished with a silver-plated cap. The stick varnished to imitate tortoiseshell. The ferrule of brass.
Given by Col. J. L. Melville, T.233-1931

All other items are replicas.　　page 60

101 DOUBLE-BREASTED BROWN DRESS COAT, silk warp and worsted weft decorated with silk stripes. The buttons are of steel.
French, 1795–1805

The dress coat and morning riding coat of the 18th century are formal and informal styles of basically the same coat. The principal difference between them is the cut of the fronts. The dress coat is cut straight across at or above the waist and is usually double-breasted. The morning coat, usually single-breasted, is cut in a curve from the waist towards the back. There are no front skirts, only long narrow back skirts with a single flat pleat either side of the back vent. Like all 18th century coats there is no waist or underarm seam. There are three main seams, the centre back and two side seams set close to the centre back and curving towards the armholes. Both styles have continued to be worn to the present day. The dress coat has become the full evening dress tail coat and the morning riding coat is worn as formal day dress.

T.769-1919

WAISTCOAT, ribbon embroidered, *English, 1790s, given by Miss H. L. Surtees, T.14-1955*
BREECHES, machine knitted silk, *English, late 18th century, given by Messrs Harrods, T.745A-1913*
LACE, needle lace, *French, 1780s, Circ.18-1945, given by Mrs C. M. Chambers* and T.307&A-1972 *bequeathed by Miss A. C. Innes*
SWORD STICK, *French or German, about 1800, given anonymously, T.5&A-1934,*
SHOE BUCKLES, silver, *English, 1786–93, T.315&A-1982*

All other items are replicas.　　page 61

102 DOUBLE-BREASTED NIGHTGOWN, quilted blue satin
English, late 18th early 19th century

The matching waistcoat fronts are stitched to the inside of the gown. Pocket holes are let into the side seams at hip level. There is a pleat at the centre of the back.

Nightgowns of the 17th, 18th and 19th centuries were acknowledged items of informal dress worn over the shirt and breeches or trousers for comfort and warmth. Made in a variety of styles and often of exotic textiles, their cut and style was influenced by clothes and textiles brought back to Europe by traders of the English, French and Dutch East India Companies in the 17th and 18th centuries.

Given by Sir Stewart Patterson K.C.V.O., C.S.I., C.I.E.
T.113-1939

BREECHES dark green wool with embroidered knee bands and buttons
English, late 18th century
655A-1898

All other items are replicas.

103 NIGHTGOWN, cream flannel with black wool tufts imitating ermine
English, 1815–22

There are two pocket holes let into the side seams set close to the centre back pleat. The buttons are covered in linen. The edges trimmed with cream silk twill.
　　Worn by Thomas Coutts (1735–1822), founder of Coutts Bank.

Given by Mr Francis Coutts
Circ. 718/7-1912

'COSSACK' TROUSERS, unbleached linen
English, 1820s

The trousers are cut full, tapered to the ankles, and kept taut by buttoned

straps under the instep. They are attached to a deep waistband and evenly gathered at the front. 'Cossack' trousers were introduced after 1814 when the Czar came to London for the peace celebrations and brought Cossack soldiers with his entourage. Fashionable 'cossack' trousers were cut full and gathered onto a waistband; the early versions were also gathered at the ankles. Between the 1820s and 1830s they were either pleated or gathered onto the waistband and fitted over the foot. The style survived until the 1840s–50s.
Given by Mrs E. Gilvry
T.213-1962

All other items are replicas.

104 DRESS COAT, figured cut silk velvet with a spotted voided ground
French or Italian, 1800–10

Worn for evening or formal occasions. Despite the Napoleonic Wars there is little difference in cut between these clothes and those thought to be English.

WAISTCOAT, plain silk enriched throughout with silver thread and embroidered with silver-gilt wire and sequins
French or Italian, 1800–10
Coat and waistcoat given by Madame

This flannel nightgown of 1815–22 is trimmed with black wool tufts imitating ermine, and is worn here with unbleached linen 'Cossack' trousers.
Circ.718/7-1912&T.213-1962   [103]

Elsa Borgo-Baer in memory of Cesare Borgo
T.10, T.7-1972

LACE frill and ruffles, needle lace, *French, early 19th century, given by Mrs A. B. Rathbone* 1520A,B,C,E-1900
PASTE SHOE BUCKLES, *probably French, 1780s,* 223 & A-1864

All other items are replicas.

105 DOUBLE-BREASTED DRESS SUIT, consisting of coat, waistcoat and breeches, fine quality black wool
English, 1800–17

The pockets of the coat have an inner buttoned flap, and there is also an inside breast pocket.
TOP HAT, black silk plush
English, 1800–17
The suit and hat were all worn by Thomas Coutts (1735–1822), founder of Coutts Bank.

Given by Mr Francis Coutts
371 to B-1908 and 371AA-1908

All other items are replicas.   page 62

106 DOUBLE-BREASTED CAPED FROCK COAT, fine quality beige wool
English, 1820s

The coat has a cut silk velvet collar. There is a waist seam and a centre back vent with two pockets on either side. The cuffs have a two-button fly opening. The edges are trimmed with beige twilled silk.
Given by Mr Talbot Hughes
T.294-1910
WAISTCOAT, plain silk enriched with silver threads and embroidered in silver purl and spangles
French or Italian, first quarter 19th century
Given in memory of Cesare Borgo
T.6-1972
PANTALOONS, black knitted silk,
English, 1820s
Pantaloons make their appearance as day wear in the 1790s. They originate from the tightly fitted knitted breeches of the period. These were extended at first to the calf and later to the ankle. They continued to be worn for evening dress until the 1840s.

Given by Messrs Harrods
T.683A-1913

All other items are replicas.   page 64

107 DOUBLE-BREASTED DRESS COAT of fine quality blue wool.
English, 1815–20

The coat is cut with a waist seam. The waist seam was introduced in the early 19th century. Fashion required a deeper body and tight waist for the dress coat, which resulted in a crease at the waist. To eliminate this a dart was made which eventually became the waist seam.

Given by Lady Osborn
T.118-1953

WAISTCOAT, poplin
English, 1820s
Given by G. J. Lamb
T.51-1958
SLIP WAISTCOAT, silk satin facings, cotton fronts and back
English, 1820s

Slip waistcoats were worn so that only the collar and lapels showed. They were very thin so that more than one could be worn at a time.

Given by Miss E. M. Coulson
T.153-1931

TROUSERS, cotton
English, 1810–20s
Given by Messrs Harrods
T.738A-1913

All other items are replicas   page 63

108 DOUBLE-BREASTED DRESS COAT, brown wool with cut velvet shawl collar and gilt metal buttons
English, 1828–30

The original collar appears to have been altered to meet the fashionable deep roll of the shawl collar and faced with velvet. The chest and upper sleeves are thickly padded.
Given by Messrs Harrods
T.683-1913
CRAVAT, printed silk
Possibly Indian, 1820–30s
Given by Messrs Harrods
T.1738-1913

SLIP WAISTCOAT faced with blue satin, the fronts and back of cotton.
English, 1820s
Given by Miss E. M. Coulson
T.154-1931
'COSSACK' TROUSERS, silk with narrow blue satin stripes on beige tabby ground.
English, 1820s
Given by Mr Frederick Gill
T.197-1914

All other items are replicas.   page 63

109 FROCK COAT
English, 1828–30

Mixed brown silk and worsted, with cut silk velvet shawl collar and cuffs. Fastened by two hooks and eyes and silk tasselled braids and toggles. Constructed with waist and underarm

seams as well as centre back and side seams. Centre back vent and pleats with pockets. Padded shoulders. Lined throughout with umber coloured silk taffeta.

WAISTCOAT, silk plush
English, 1828–30
The waistcoat has a shawl collar, large slit pockets, and metal thread buttons.
'COSSACK' TROUSERS, printed cotton
English, 1820s
The trousers have strap fastenings under the instep to keep them taut.

This outfit is reputed to have been worn by Lord Petersham (1780–1851).

Given by Mr John Morant
T.136, T.137 and T.138-1967

All other items are replicas.   page 64

110 SHIRT AND TROUSERS

SHIRT linen, pleated front
English, dated 1844, J. Smith

Given by Mrs Beckford
T.130-1932
CRAVAT, black satin, pre-formed bow, stiffened band, buckled fastening
English, made by C. F. Sharples, Stock and Shirtmaker, 84 Deans Gate, Manchester, mid-19th century
Given by Mrs Ida Routh
T.122-1963
PAIR OF BRACES, white satin covered in silk net embroidered in coloured silks, wools and gilt metal beads. Elastic straps and white leather tips, steel buckles
Irish, about 1847
Given by the family of Major and Mrs MacKay MacKenzie
T.213&A-1915
TROUSERS, pale grey wool. They are kept taught by straps attached to trouser bottoms and fastened under insteps by brass links.
English, 1840
Given by Mr R. P. Scott
T.227 to D-1920

The shoes are replicas.   page 65

111 DRESS COAT, blue-black fine wool with velvet collar
USA, late 1840s early 1850s
TROUSERS, linen woven in twill.
USA, late 1840s early 1850s

Both items are reputed to have been worn by the donor's grandfather, William Pierson Johnes, a linen merchant of New York (d. 1853). Fashionable dress of the East Coast followed European styles.

Given by Capt. Raymond Johnes
T.176, T.177-1965

SCARF CRAVAT, black satin with pre-formed bow and buckled fastening,

English, 1840s, given by Miss C. Wigginton, T.215-1966
WAISTCOAT, figured silk damask, *English, early 1850s, given by Miss C. M. Higgs, T.121-1949*
TOP HAT, silk plush, *English, maker's label Messrs Chapman and Moore, 30 Old Bond St. London W.1, given by Mr Hubert Arthur Druce, T.19-1918*

All other items are replicas.

113   DOUBLE-BREASTED FROCK COAT, blue-black fine wool
Irish, 1871

Formal day wear of the late 19th century was of black or blue-black wool. The entire suit could be of one colour but contrasting waistcoat and trousers were worn. This style continued until the 20th century and became identified as the city business man's suit of black coat, striped trousers and bowler hat which replaced the top hat.

Given by Mr A. W. Furlong
T.47-1947

TROUSERS fine woollen twill
English, 1870s
Given by Lady Oxborn
T.118A-1953

BOW TIE, grey corded silk with pre-formed knot, *English, late 19th century, given by Miss Patten, T.35-1980*
WAISTCOAT, *English, 1870s, given by Miss W. Shaw, T.10-1951*
TOP HAT, silk plush, *English, late 19th century, given by Mrs Latter Axton, T.99-1931*

All other items are replicas.   page 67

112   DOUBLE-BREASTED MORNING COAT, cotton velveteen
English, 1873-5
TROUSERS, of wool
English, 1870s

The sharply-angled style for coat fronts was a variation of the morning coat. This was introduced in the 1870s and made in both single and double-breasted styles and known as the University coat. Two pocket flaps, without pockets, are let into the waist seam. The tails are cut straight at the bottom and have a vent and side pleats. Edges are trimmed with woollen braid. The double-breasted coats were considered to be exclusive because of the difficulty in achieving a successful cut where the fronts overlap.

T.3-1982

The trousers have no waistband and are supported by braces. Two small horizontal slit pockets are let into the fronts. The outside seams are lapped and the bottoms have $6\frac{1}{2}''$ fronts and $10\frac{1}{2}''$ backs, giving a tight bottom of $17''$. Trousers became baggier in cut from the second half of the 1870s.

Given by Dr C. W. Cunnington
T.58-1933

TIE, satin, with pre-formed knot, fastened by spring clip into back of knot, *English, 1871, given by Dame Kathleen Courtenay, DBE, T.194-1964*
WAISTCOAT, jacquard woven with aniline purple, *English, 1870s, given by Messrs Harrods, T.1093-1913*
TOP HAT, silk plush, *English, 1870s, given by Mrs Latter Axton, T.100-1931*
MALACCA CANE with ivory knob and horn ferrule, *English, late 19th century, given by Mr Peter Smith, T.53-1983*

All other items are replicas.   page 66

114   EVENING DRESS SUIT, black wool barathea
English : Morris & Co. 50 Pall Mall, probably 1880s

The jacket still has the 'button stand' around the outer edge of the lapels, a rather outdated fashion which disappeared in the 1890s. Later the entire lapel is faced with silk. Evening dress has altered very little since the 19th century. The stylistic changes which have occurred are very subtle, affecting details such as the length and width of the lapels or fullness of the trousers.

Given by Mr B. W. Owram
T.171 to B-1960

All other items are replicas.   page 66

115   DOUBLE-BREASTED SUIT, cream flannel with blue pin-stripe
English, about 1904

These light-coloured suits became popular from about the 1890s and matching coat and trousers ('dittos') were accepted dress for summer sports and holidays. The cut of the jacket is derived from the earlier 'reefer' coat, usually worn for sailing. The same style was also adopted for the bolder striped jackets or blazers which were worn with light coloured trousers.
Given by Mrs Brooks
T.159&A-1969

STRAW BOATER, *English, late 19th early 20th century, Bon Ton Ivy, Celtic Brand, bequeathed by Mr Eric Mynott, T.81-1980*

All other items are replicas.   page 68

116   DOUBLE-BREASTED DRIVING COAT, black and white wool houndstooth check.
English : Hammond & Co. Ltd. 465 Oxford St. London W.1, 1906–8
The name Paul Cocteau is inscribed on the tailor's label. He was the brother of Jean Cocteau (1889–1963) and preferred to purchase his sporting dress in England as he considered it to be the best quality.

Given by Sir Philip and Lady Joubert
T.96-1963

TROUSERS, buff wool gaberdine
Irish, late 19th century
Trouser creases date from the 1890s.
Given by Mr A. W. Furlong
T.47A-1947
BOWLER HAT, felt, *English, about 1880s, Christies, given by The Hatters Association, T.116-1937*

All other items are replicas.   page 68

117 MORNING SUIT, the coat of black wool barathea bound with silk braid. The trousers of black wool twill with fine pin-stripes.
English : Brass and Pike, 19 Savile Row, London W, 1910

A typical example of a gentleman's morning suit worn for formal occasions and for everyday dress by professional and business gentlemen. After the Great War (1914–18) the morning suit began to be superseded by the lounge suit for everyday wear, although it continued to be worn by older men.

Given by Mrs B. M. Bohener
T.57 to B-1962

SPATS *given by 'Friends of the V & A'*

All other items are replicas.

118 SINGLE-BREASTED LOUNGE SUIT, grey wool pin-stripe
English, 1918–20

The man's lounge suit first appeared during the 1870s. It originated from the lounge jacket, which was cut to fit the waist without a waist seam by means of a long dart from under the arm to the waist. By the 1870s the jacket was worn with matching waistcoat and trousers and had become popular for informal wear.

Worn by Sir Max Beerbohm and given by the Executors of Lady Beerbohm
T.215 to B-1960

CANE with silver cap and ferrule, *English, London hallmark, 1882.* The stick of honeysuckle. *Given by the Executors of Lady Beerbohm,* T.217-1960

SPATS *given by 'Friends of the V & A'.*

All other items are replicas.　　page 69

119 EVENING DRESS SUIT, black wool with black ribbed silk lapels and basket weave buttons. The waistcoat is trimmed with silk braid.
English : Charles Wallis Ltd, 9 Berkeley St. London W.1, 1923

By the 1920s the full evening dress suit had crystallized into a recognizable and apparently unchanging style. Changes of fashion did occur, but they affected details such as the width of the lapel or the cut of the trousers. In fact, these suits did follow the current fashion in men's dress, where the changes were very subtle. The width of a lapel might be altered, or the number of buttons on the cuff, or perhaps the size of trouser bottoms.
Given by Mrs E. L. Rothfield
T.232 to B-1962

BOW TIE, cotton piqué, *English, 1920–30s, given by Mrs E. Mitchell,* T.6-1983

All other items are replicas.　　page 69

120 SINGLE-BREASTED SUIT, woven wool check known as the Glen Urquhart
English, Trimmingham, London and Bermuda : 1940

Worn and given by H.R.H. The Duke of Windsor
The Cecil Beaton Collection
T.717&A-1974

SWEATER, natural coloured wools, circular knitted without seams
Fairisle, 1920s–30s
Given by Mrs Kirke
T.185-1982

TRILBY HAT, felt, *English, 1940-50s, given by Mr Gerald Cheshire,* T.104-1983

BROGUES *given by the 'Friends of the V & A'.*　　page 70

121 SINGLE-BREASTED SUIT, navy blue wool pin-stripe
English : Selfridges, Utility, 1945
TIE, red, blue and white man-made fibres
English, 1940–50s
The suit was purchased by the donor's mother at a Selfridges sale in April 1945.

The suit and tie worn and given by Mr G. Neuhofer
T.304&A and T.329-1982

SPATS *given by 'Friends of the V & A'.*

All other items are replicas.　　page 69

HAT *given by the 'Friends of the V & A'.*

All other items are replicas.　　page 70

122 SINGLE-BREASTED SUIT, charcoal grey wool twill
English, Cambridge : Carr, Sonn and Woor, 1951

This distinctive style comprising bowler hat, fitted jacket and tapered trousers with waisted overcoat and velvet collar, evolved shortly after the war in the late 1940s and early 1950s. It is attributed to a group of fashion-conscious young men, some of whom were ex-Guards officers. They were subsequently christened 'The Edwardians' and were reputed to be the inspiration of the 'Teddy Boy' fashions of the 1950s. The originators were probably influenced at first by their familiarity with the customary civilian dress for Guards officers, which consisted of a bowler hat, double-breasted overcoat known as the 'British warm', a striped shirt with white collar and pin-stripe trousers. The traditional and conservative styling of these overcoats and trousers would have blended in quite naturally

with the 'Edwardian' image. Mr MacKay took his inspiration directly from the Edwardian period by requesting his tailor to copy the suit worn by Winston Churchill in a photograph of 1911.

Given by Mr A. MacKay
T.69 to B-1976

BOWLER HAT, *English, Thomas and Stone, about 1960, given by Mr Geoffrey Squires, (The Cecil Beaton Collection)*, T.898-1974

All other items are replicas.

123 'COSMOS' SPACE AGE OUTFIT of heavy black and white wool jersey, with patent leather belt.
French, Paris : Pierre Cardin Mesures, Autumn/Winter 1967

The tunic is cut in one piece: the seams are top-stitched tucks. Monsieur Cardin regarded his 'Cosmos' outfits as *'les plus représentatifs de mon style pour les dernières années, ceux-ci ont été conçus pour la collection Automne-Hiver 1967'.*

Given by M. Pierre Cardin (The Cecil Beaton Collection)
T.703 to C-1974

The boots are replicas.   page 71

124 SINGLE-BREASTED 'NEHRU' SUIT, grey chalk-striped wool
French, Paris : Gilbert Feruch, November 1967

The style known as the 'Nehru' suit or jacket was first made fashionable in Europe by Pierre Cardin after a visit he made to India. Worn for many years by men in India, it had been made familiar to Europeans by Prime Minister Jawaharlal Nehru (1889–1964). As a European fashion it lasted for only a short time, from 1966 to 1968. A 'Nehru' jacket should be close fitting with a shaped back and short stand collar of $1\frac{1}{2}$ inches. The trousers are cut slim and tapered. For everyday wear they were made of flannel or worsted in greys or browns and in summer lighter colours and fabrics. Evening wear was transformed by the use of highly coloured silks and velvets.
Given by Mr A. Aubrey
T.318&A-1977   page 73

125 DOUBLE-BREASTED MIDI-OVERCOAT, brown herringbone tweed
English, London : Village Gate, about 1967
SINGLE-BREASTED SUIT, charcoal grey wool gaberdine
English, London : Mr Fish, about 1967

The midi and maxi coats worn by both men and women were introduced from 1966. High-waisted with broad revers, and sometimes with belts, they reached to the calf for the midi and to the ankles for the maxi-length. The style was derived from military coats at a time when the military uniforms had become fashionable. In the late 1960s there was a craze for wearing second-hand uniforms, usually Guards jackets and military greatcoats. It is these greatcoats which influenced the cut of the midi and maxi-overcoats.

KIPPER TIE, printed silk, *English, Take 6, about 1968*
HAT, olive green velours, *English, Herbert Johnson, about 1970*

Worn and given by Sir Roy Strong
T.190, T.192&A, T.201 and T.195-1979
          page 75

126 DOUBLE-BREASTED SUIT, printed corduroy
English, London : Mr Fish, about 1968

The suit was made during the period when psychedelic colours were at their most popular. The corduroy is an American furnishing fabric by Hexter, purchased by Mr Mlinaric whilst he was in the USA, with the intention of having a suit made from it.

Worn and given by Mr David Mlinaric
T.310&A-1979

The boots are replicas of those originally worn with the suit.   page 72

127 SAFARI SUIT, black cotton twill
French, Paris : Yves St Laurent Rive Gauche, about 1970

The jacket hangs straight to the hips and buttons down the front with six buttons. There are four pleated pockets with buttoned flaps. The sleeves are gathered onto a wrist band with two buttons. The shoulders are padded. The back is yoked with a centre back seam finishing with a 10-inch vent. The trousers are straight cut with two pleats at the front. The fly has a zip fastening. The waistband has six belt straps. There are two slit pockets let into the side seams and two back pockets with welted tops. The trouser bottoms measure 23 inches. All main seams are double top stitched.
  Mr Powell never wore this as a suit but alternated either the trousers or jacket with another almost identical one of beige cotton, also by Yves St Laurent. He found that worn with either a T-shirt or polo neck sweater the combination was suitable for almost any occasion. For a theatrical designer

who spends a large part of the year travelling, a suit that could be so adaptable was most useful.

Worn and given by Mr Anthony Powell
T.258&A-1978

All other items are replicas.   page 75

128 SINGLE-BREASTED SUIT, cream linen
English, Blades, 8 Burlington Gardens, Savile Row, W.1, July 1972

White suits have been popular as fashionable summer wear since the early 20th century. Although their appearance was irregular until 1960s their popularity since then has been maintained. This is a very fashionable suit; the jacket is shaped to the waist and has a waist seam, two underarm seams and side seams set close to the centre back seam, like the early 19th-century coats, and consequently this style was called 'Regency'. Instead of a back vent there is a deep pleat. The trousers are 'hipsters'—with single darts at the front and two at each back; they are cut with a slight flare, finishing with $2\frac{1}{2}$-inch turn-ups and 20-inch bottoms.

Worn and given by Mr David Mlinaric
T.353&A-1980   page 71

129 SINGLE-BREASTED SUIT, mid-grey horizontal chalk-striped wool
English, London : Tommy Nutter, 1983

With this suit Tommy Nutter has continued to maintain his belief in using classical tailoring methods and fabrics in a new and imaginative way.

SHIRT, pale grey cotton, *English, Tommy Nutter, 1983*
TIE, printed silk, *English, Tommy Nutter, 1983*

Given by Mr Tommy Nutter
T.10 to B, T.11 and T.12-1983

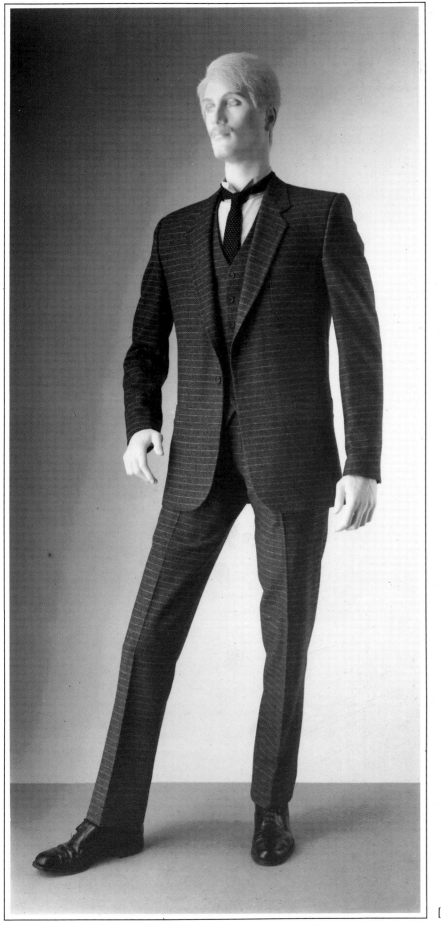

[129]

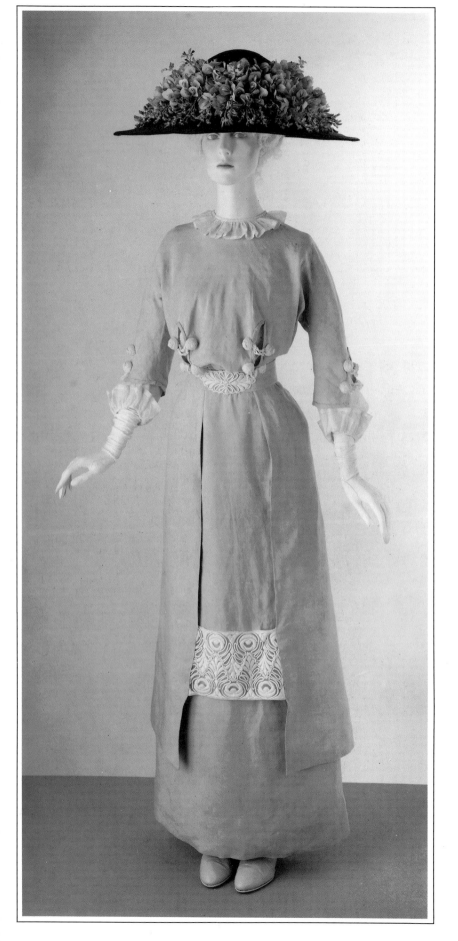

Women's Dress since 1900

130 BALL GOWN (bodice and skirt), pale peach silk velvet with diamanté trimming. The petticoat, sleeves and neck edging are modern cream crêpeline replacements in the manner of Worth.
French, Paris: Worth, 1899–1901

Evening gowns of the late 19th and early 20th centuries were both luxurious and expensive. Their more delicate trimmings have often vanished as they were usually of 'the most ethereal chiffon' (*The Lady's Realm*, May 1900). In this case they have been carefully reconstructed using original photographs of Worth designs. Flared panels form the trained skirt. The bodice's inner foundation has ten bones and laces at the centre back. The draped bodice fastens over this at the left side back with hooks and eyes.

*Worn by Princess Nicholas of Greece
Given by the Duke and Duchess of Kent
The Cecil Beaton Collection*
T.459-B-1974   page 78

131 EVENING DRESS (bodice and skirt), figured cream satin and cream net (modern) decorated with imitation pearls, diamantés and spangles
French, Paris: Maison Laferrière, about 1900

The tight-fitting bodice is mounted on a boned silk foundation with a waist

Miss Heather Firbank's wardrobe, acquired by the Museum in 1960, reflects her excellent but restrained taste. This demure pale blue-grey linen and embroidered lawn day dress of 1909–10 shows her preference for simple, uncluttered lines.
T.23&A-1960   [137]

(which would have been corseted) measuring 18 inches. It fastens at the centre back with original hooks and eyes (with positions reversed alternately to take the tension). A draped panel conceals the centre back and fastens at the right-hand side with hooks and eyes. The gored skirt has seven flared panels – the longer back two are gathered into the waistband and form the train. Its hem (under the spangled double frill) is padded to maintain the flared line and the train has a frilled petticoat of cotton gauzes and lace.

Worn by Princess Alexandra and given by Lady Lloyd
The Cecil Beaton Collection
T.282&A-1974

FAN, cream ostrich feathers set into a mother-of-pearl and silver handle with a small vanity mirror, *English, about 1900, given by Mrs G. Vickerman*, T.248-1967
CHOKER, imitation pearls and diamantés, *probably English, early 20th century, given by Mrs M. J. Wilcox*, T.98-1983   page 78

132 TEAGOWN, pale pink chiffon with écru tamboured net over pale pink satin
French, Paris : Worth, about 1900

The satin gown has two delicate over-layers of chiffon crêpe continued over the train. The bodice is pouched into the broad satin belt with falling sash. The gown is machine-stitched with hand-finishing. It has a lining with two bones which fastens at the centre front and the bodice wraps over to fasten along the left side—all with hooks and eyes. The waist stay (20-inch waist) has the 'Worth Paris' label and is inscribed with the number 63331. Its elaborate and luxurious decoration—ruching, meandering rows of puffs, rosettes and tassels characterize fashionable 'at home' wear of the late 19th and early 20th centuries.

In September 1900 *The Queen, The Lady's Newspaper* described the ideal teagown—'It is quite a perfect gown showing soft falling kilted flounces at the hem, silk muslin or silk serving to enhance the beauty of incomparable lace'.

Given by Lady Hoyer Millar and worn by her mother
T.48-1961   page 79

133 TRAVELLING GOWN (bodice and skirt), eau-de-nil woollen face cloth trimmed with braid, velvet, cream chemical lace, tapework and net
Probably English, 1905

Pastel colours combined with cream were greatly favoured by fashionable Edwardians. This costume shows how designers of the period lavishly adorned plain cloth with a variety of rich laces and trimmings. It has an alternative matching jacket, a pair of ribbon-trimmed white kid shoes and white silk stockings which are not shown.

The ensemble was worn by Viscountess Brackley, *née* Miss Violet Lambton who became the Countess of Ellesmere (1880–1976). She married the Viscount in autumn 1905 in St Margaret's Church, Westminster. This society wedding was recorded in *The Queen, The Lady's Newspaper* on 4 November 1905: 'the bride travelled in a blue cloth costume trimmed with Irish lace and braid and a hat to match'. The report was accompanied by a sketch showing the wedding gown, travelling costume and bridesmaids' dresses.

Given by Lady Alice Egerton
T.421-&B-1977

PARASOL, embroidered cream muslin trimmed with lace with a carved ivory handle, *French, about 1905*, T.205-1967

The hat is a replica.   page 76

134 DRESS AND TABARD, mauve silk crêpe (Liberty) and embroidered velvet
English, London : Forma, about 1905

This type of 'reform' dress was made for the 'advanced' woman who wished to abandon her corsets. Falling from the shoulders it does not restrict the body and it skims lightly over contours that would normally have been tightly

compressed by a boned under-garment. Loosely based on medieval attire, the dress (not especially well made) has four panels which gently flare to a trailing hem and train trimmed with velvet. It has straight, set-in, three-quarter length sleeves with velvet cuffs. The dress fastens with hooks and eyes down the centre front. The separate, long, tapering velvet tabard has fly-away shoulders and is held loosely at the waist with a crêpe band. The low round neck, cuffs and tabard ends are hand embroidered in mercerized embroidery cottons. Libertys sold a wide range of light-weight silks in soft plain colours which were ideal for artistic clothes such as this. The harmonies of muted grey, mauves and purples are typical of the period.

Given anonymously
Circ.638&A-1964

135 SUMMER DAY DRESS (bodice, skirt and belt), printed striped blue and white cotton and Broderie Anglaise
Probably English, 1905–6

Crisp-looking blue and white dresses such as this were popular for boating and beach wear. The skirt is composed of four 28-inch widths of material pleated into the narrow waistband. The bodice is pouched at the front and slightly bloused at the back—achieved by gathering the cotton into the waistband which has a flared basque that tucks into the skirt. The circular yoke consists of tucked Broderie Anglaise frills and a pin-tucked cotton infill, with a high-boned (5 bones) pin-tucked collar finished with a tape lace frill. The bodice is lined throughout in white cotton and centre back fastens with original hooks, eyes and loops. The wide, softly pleated belt has 5 bones and its centre front, hook and eye fastening is concealed by a rosette. There is evidence (at sleeve, waist and hem) that minor alterations have been made, but they have not destroyed the original form of the dress.

Worn by Miss Heather Firbank
T.21-B-1960   page 80

136 EVENING DRESS (bodice and skirt), pink satin, embroidered pink silk panels, velvet and pink net (modern replacement)
English, London : Jays Ltd, about 1908

The dress is dominated by the boldly embroidered panels imported from Turkey and made up in London. They are worked (in parts over padding) in silver-gilt strip, coil and thread with spangles, pearls and diamantés. In style this dress is transitional between the pronounced curved shapes of the early 1900s and the straighter lines (with high waists) which became current by about 1909. There is some evidence (the rather clumsy lateral overlapping of the embroidered skirt panels) that an earlier dress may have been adapted to suit the tastes of 1908. The bodice is boned and has a grosgrain waist stay with the woven label of Jays Ltd, which bears a taffeta ribbon marked 'Lady Pearson'.

Worn by Lady Pearson and given by Lord and Lady Cowdray
T.193&A-1970   page 82

137 DAY DRESS, pale blue-grey linen and embroidered lawn trimmed with bands of white embroidered net
English, 1909–10

The cut of this demure unlabelled dress is especially interesting. The bodice is bias-cut in one piece and continuously seamed under the arms and down the sides. The magyar-type sleeves have open vents secured by braid and domed, crochet-covered buttons and a similar pair of vents decorate the bodice front. An inner front panel and sleeves of lawn with open-work embroidery show through the vents. A sturdy cotton bodice lining has two bones at the centre back edges where it fastens with hooks and eyes. The linen dress fastens over this again with hooks and eyes. The skirt (cut on the straight grain) is long and pleated into the waist. A divided overskirt of four long straight panels is linked at the lower front and back by bands of boldly patterned embroidered net. The top-stitched pleated belt (decorated with embroidered motifs) conceals the waist seam and fastens at the back with hooks and eyes.

HAT, black plaited straw trimmed with white, purple and green cotton artificial flowers, *English, London: Henry, 1909–10*

Worn by Miss Heather Firbank
T.23&A-1960, T.105-1960   page 156

138 SUMMER DAY DRESS, white lacis and embroidered lawn with macramé fringe and bobble trim and black ribbon belt
French, about 1910

This type of frail whitework dress was immensely popular for wear at summer garden parties and fêtes. The

unlabelled dress has wide, inset panels of lacis patterned with a meandering leaf stem at the front, back and sleeve tops. The bodice sides and lower part of the fairly straight skirt are hand embroidered with spots, florets and borders in heavy white cotton. An inner net bodice fastens at the centre front with a row of minute lawn-covered buttons and loops. The lacis panel fastens over this along the left with similar buttons. The collar's bobbled macramé fringe matches the centre panel's fringe and the theme is echoed down the front seam and around the hem. There is evidence that the black neck trim and belt are replacements.

Given by the Hon. Mrs J. J. Astor The Cecil Beaton Collection
T.465-1974

HAT, plaited natural straw trimmed with pink, white and green cotton artificial flowers and a cream satin ribbon. *French, Paris: Magasins du Louvre, about 1910, given by Lord and Lady Cowdray*
T.185-1970

139 EVENING DRESS, pale pink silk net embroidered with silver metallic thread and crystal and silver bugle beads over satin, with a ruched fuchsia silk velvet bodice
French, Paris: Worth, 1910–11

At this time leading fashion houses such as Worth created straight-line evening dresses whose impact depended upon the juxtaposition of colours and of a variety of luxurious and richly decorated fabrics. Here, vividly

coloured velvet pile is set against light-reflecting beadwork and the triple tiered, matt net overskirt covers the sheen of the trained satin skirt until it reaches floor level. Tight, heavily boned corsets were still worn and were constructed to give the torso long, gently curved lines. Most dress foundations of the period were also boned. In this case nine bones shape the bodice. The pillar-like look exemplified by this dress replaced the exaggerated curves of the early 1900s. It shows how designers broke the strong vertical emphasis by creating overskirts with horizontal lines.

Given by Lady Hoyer Millar
T.57-1961   page 82

140 COSTUME (jacket and skirt), fine, dark grey worsted trimmed with matching bands and buttons
English, London: Lucile Ltd, about 1911
BLOUSE, white lawn with hand-made insertion
English, about 1909
HAT, plaited black straw brim and a grey chiffon-covered crown trimmed with grey and black piping and a black feather
English, London: Woolland Bros, 1910–11
BAG, black suède with a braid strap
English, about 1910

The fashion (current between about 1909 and 1912) for enormous hats which give women a top-heavy appearance was ridiculed in the popular press. However, fashionable women (even suffragettes) continued to wear these unwieldy creations. False hair pads ('transformations') were much used and the hats were anchored with excessively long hatpins stuck through the hat and the real and false hair (safety guards shielded the sharp hatpin points). The jacket has the label 'Lucile Ltd 23 Hanover Square London W' and a silk label inscribed 'Miss Firbank'. It is lined throughout with satin with bold black and white stripes. This type of understated smart costume was popular for town wear during the autumn and winter months.

Worn by Miss Heather Firbank
T.38&A-1960, T.59-1960, T.102-1960, T.73-1960   page 80

141 SIDE SADDLE RIDING HABIT (jacket, apron skirt and breeches with crop)
JACKET AND SKIRT, black wool flecked with white
BREECHES, black woollen jersey flecked with white

CROP, cane with carved horn handle and inscribed silver mount
English, London: Redfern, 1912

The construction of riding habits is a highly specialized branch of the tailor's art. In *The Cutters Practical Guide* (John Williamson c. 1910), W. D. F. Vincent suggests that 'The development of ladies' tailoring in England seems to have come about from the superiority of the tailor's skill with riding habits and other equestrienne garments'. He explains how (for the sake of safety) riding trains became shorter and close fitting and how the apron skirt eventually emerged: 'ladies cut large holes from the underpart of the train for additional safety, whilst others cleared the whole of the underpart from seat downwards away, and just left enough to fold over the leg at either side, and so still further simplified it'. Because of this structure he notes that 'it is not the most becoming garment when the lady is on the ground'.

The single-breasted jacket with cut-away fronts is lined throughout in pearl-grey satin and has the label 'PARIS NEW YORK REDFERN LONDON' plus a tape stamped with the number 57983. The matching flared apron skirt is cut away at the back and shaped at the right side to accommodate the knee (when mounted). Strong black cotton twill forms a capacious inner pocket and shaped linings. The calf-length breeches in jersey (for ease of movement) fly-fasten at the front. The seat and right knee are lined with chamois. Because these garments are subject to considerable stress the emphasis throughout is upon firm and accurate construction. Seams which take strain and might rub are lined and reinforced with black cotton and buttons are backed with cotton.

Made for and worn by Mrs James Fraser (née Miss Grace Isabelle Spencer-Smith) and given by her daughters Mrs J. G. M. Stewart and Mrs I. O'Reilly
T.333-C-1982

RIDING BOWLER, hard black felt, *English, London: A. J. White Ltd, 20th century, worn and given by Mrs Margaret Marshall*, T.29-1983

142 EVENING ENSEMBLE, 'SORBET' (skirt and tunic) cream and black satin and pink silk chiffon with glass bead embroidery in pinks, mauves, and green with a fur edging
French, Paris: Paul Poiret, 1912

In 1911 Paul Poiret held one of his 'unforgettable' fancy dress balls, 'The Thousand and Second Night'. He attired his wife in a lampshade tunic over harem trousers which subsequently inspired similar exotic creations including 'Sorbet'. The bodice is formed by large cross-over dolman-type sleeves, cut on the cross. They are softly gathered into the high waist marked by the wide sash. The tunic's skirt is gathered and its hem is wired to hold it away from the body and keep the required shape. The tunic has a deep grosgrain waist foundation. Unfortunately the delicate silks are now in a frail condition. It is probable that the embroidered design of bold stylized flowers was drawn by one of Poiret's young employees in the School of Decorative Art, 'Martine' (established in 1911). He allowed these girls a fairly free hand and was rewarded with patterns which were remarkable for their 'spontaneity and freshness'.

Publications
Paris, Musée Jacquemart-André, *Poiret le Magnifique* (an exhibition), 1974, catalogue no. 50.
Paris, *La Gazette du Bon Ton*, September 1913 (George Lepape's illustration)
White, Palmer, *Paul Poiret*, Studio Vista 1973 (portrait of Madame Poiret wearing 'Sorbet' page 88)

From Madame Poiret's collection
T.385&A-1976

The black silk skirt and the necklace are replicas.   page 83

143 EVENING DRESS, cream satin, black velvet, cream chiffon and cream machine lace
English, London, Lucile; 1912–13

In 1960 the Museum acquired a cross section of Miss Heather Firbank's wardrobe dating from the early 1900s to 1920. The particularly distinctive features are her clothes dating from about 1908 to 1916—understated pastel-coloured day dresses, immaculately tailored suits and graceful evening dresses such as this silk gown. It reveals the designer Lucile (Lady Duff Gordon) in a fairly restrained mood. The long slit skirt is especially interesting—it is cut in one panel with a single seam; the fullness of the front skirt is draped up and caught at the top of the right thigh to give the impression of an over-skirt. At the right side, the front panel is lapped over the back so the slit is not too revealing, although Lady Duff Gordon boasted that she had 'loosed upon a startled London . . . draped skirts which opened to reveal slender legs.' The layers of fine silks and lace which form the bodice (mounted on a boned grosgrain foundation) are caught by the black silk velvet cummerbund. It has a complex hook and eye fastening system and a luxurious ribbon-trimmed silk and lace petticoat.

Only the author of this romantic and impractical gown could write: 'For me there was a positive intoxication in taking yards of shimmering silks, laces airy as gossamer and lengths of ribbons, delicate and rainbow-coloured, and fashioning of them garments so lovely that they might have been worn by some princess in a fairy tale.' (*Discretions and Indiscretions*, Lady Duff Gordon, Jarrolds, 1932).

Worn by Miss Heather Firbank
T.31-1960   page 81

144 EVENING DRESS, silk chiné mainly in pastel pinks, blues and lilac and cream bobbin lace and pink silk voile brocaded with metallic threads, trimmed with mauve satin, diamantés and imitation pearls
English or French, about 1913

Before the outbreak of World War I *couturiers* created evening clothes which were complex assemblages of luxurious materials and trimmings. Lucile (Lady Duff Gordon) was the arch-exponent of the tendency, and this unlabelled confection is an extreme example of such indulgence. The layered construction is complex. The skirt has three parts—an open-fronted top with corners weighted by elaborate tassels (one is a modern replacement); a middle layer pleated from the waist and draped to the centre back and a final layer that forms the pointed train. The boned bodice is

also notable for multiple layers: over the diamanté-trimmed, lace-covered foundation, brocaded silk voile forms side panels and open-work sleeves caught with large diamanté and pearl motifs which echo the tassels. The focal point (holding the pastel-coloured concoction together) is the wide, softly-pleated satin sash which back-fastens with an enormous floppy bow.

Given anonymously
T.33-1947

145   DAY DRESS, heavy ribbed pink silk and pink silk chiffon trimmed with matching buttons and cream machine lace
English, about 1913

This garment reveals the fashionable

elements of dress immediately before World War I. The line is straight and the cut (especially of the cross-over draped bodice) is intricate. Rows of non-functional, tiny buttons were frequently used as decorative motifs at this period. The bodice is lined with white cotton (with ruffles attached to give fullness at the bust) and has a stiff, silk-faced waistband. It was not made by one of the top houses but is probably a copy of a Paris model produced by a good dressmaker.

Given by Mr J. R. H. Cook
T.288-1973

The hat is a replica.

146   EVENING DRESS, black taffeta brocaded with magenta and bright green silks, gilt lace and black net
Probably French, 1916–17

This dress demonstrates the fashion for exotic shapes and for bright colours (on black backgrounds)—trends which were established by Paul Poiret's brilliantly coloured clothes and by Leon Bakst's vivid designs for the Russian Ballet. The skirt is seamed at the centre front and pleated into a high waist to form exaggerated drapes over the hips. It overlaps to fasten at the centre back. The hobble skirt narrows to the hem and the wearer's stride is further restricted by an elastic strap at the ankles (attached to the centre back and front of the hem). The wide, loosely ruched cummerbund is a feature retained from the 1910s. The dress brings to mind the fashion illustrations of artists such as Georges Lepape and Charles Martin for the *Gazette du Bon Ton*.

Given by Mr B. W. Owram
T.165-1960

147   COSTUME (jacket and skirt), dark blue silk taffeta trimmed with matching braid and tassels
English, London: Marshall and Snelgrove, about 1917

The flared skirt and waisted jacket (with a gathered basque) of this civilian costume echo the lines of many female World War I uniforms which were, of course, made of more durable and practical fabrics. The braid and tassels add a further military touch and the shorter freedom-giving skirt is of particular interest. The deep navy is typical of the plain dark, dull colours which were worn during these sombre times. The jacket is lined with white silk and has the label 'Marshall and Snelgrove Oxford St W'. The costume has a matching blouse of silk chiffon which is not shown.

Given anonymously
T.172&A-1964

UMBRELLA, blue-black silk cover and grained cane handle with silver, enamel and quartz
English, about 1911

Although this is earlier than the costume such long, elegant tightly-furled umbrellas continued to be fashionable until the early 1920s, when a shorter 'dumpy' shape became popular.

Given by Major and Mrs Broughton
T.221-1972   page 83

148   EVENING JACKET, black silk velvet, hand-printed with metallic pigment bound with printed green velvet and with a red silk and wool *faille* lining
EVENING DRESS, pleated black satin
Italian, Venice: Mariano Fortuny, about 1920

Fortuny's distinctive creations were worn by *avant-garde* beauties in Europe and America from the 1910s to the 1930s and there has been a recent revival of interest in his work. This 'Delphos' dress (inspired by the Ionic chiton) hangs in minute pleats from a neck with a drawstring adjustment decorated with Venetian glass beads (not visible). The kimono-type jacket is cut in three sections which are seamed at the shoulders and sides. It is printed in metallic pigment—probably based on bronze or copper powder. The edges are bound with green velvet printed with a different design. Fortuny based his textile patterns on historical designs—he was especially fond of Renaissance motifs. By 1920 he had established a factory on the Guidecca (still in production) as well as his original Palazzo Orfei (now the Palazzo Fortuny) workshops.

Given by Mrs Hollond
T.423 and T.424-1976

The turban and necklace are replicas.

page 81

149 EVENING DRESS AND BELT, printed silk voile (pinks and greens on pale yellow) embroidered with pearlized sequins and gold glass bugle beads, inset and trimmed with gold lace.
French, Paris: Callot Soeurs, about 1922

Superb materials and top quality workmanship combine to make this dress totally successful. Light-reflecting beads and sequins had long been favoured adornments for evening fabrics but in the 1920s the fashion reached its peak. The embroidered sequins and beads follow the lines of the printed floral design. The sleeveless dress has a straight bodice with a dropped waistline marked by a wide, matching belt with a bold paste buckle. The slightly flared skirt of pointed panels with scalloped hems has inset flounces of gold lace which echo the bodice's inset decorative panel.

Worn by Winifred, Duchess of Portland and given by Lady Victoria Wemyss
The Cecil Beaton Collection
T.74&A-1974

The shoes are replicas.

150 DAY DRESS, 'BRIQUE', fine orange worsted flecked with cream, trimmed with black and white rayon braid and tassels
French, Paris: Paul Poiret, 1924

The dress is narrow but the impression of a full front skirt is created by two gathered 'pocket' panels overlaid at the sides. The garment is machine-stitched and rather crudely hand-finished. The sleeves are set in low—almost to waist level—and are extremely narrow in the arms. The dress is deftly trimmed with wide rayon braid. In spite of the rapid development of man-made fibres *couturiers* remained faithful to costly natural fabrics with the exception of trimmings such as this braid. Braid manufacturers were among the first bulk buyers of artificial silk and were then joined by hosiery and underwear manufacturers. Only in the 1930s were *couturiers* attracted to newly available sophisticated rayon dress goods.

The Musée des Arts de la Mode in Paris has a photograph of this dress from the house of Poiret. It is inscribed 'No5521, Fev 1924' Model no. 164.

Worn and given by an anonymous lady
The Cecil Beaton Collection
T.339-1974   page 85

151 EVENING DRESS, 'Byzance' matt ivory silk embroidered with bronze, pink and gold glass bugle beads and imitation baroque pearls
French, Paris: Patou Spring – Summer 1924

1920s dresses with beaded all-over patterns presented their owners with various problems. For example sitting down was hazardous and the weight of so many beads often strained the usually frail silk grounds to which they were sewn.

This sleeveless dress has a low square neckline which was much favoured in the mid-1920s. Its straight bodice is embroidered with a design which reveals the influence of Egyptian patterns. The dress is lined with georgette and fastens with hooks and eyes at the left shoulder and side. Unfortunately the under-dress has not survived and a replacement has been made in a matching ivory silk crêpe de Chine.

Given by Lord and Lady Cowdray
T.198-1970

The shoes are replicas.   page 84

152 EVENING ENSEMBLE (sleeveless dress, jacket and sash), mustard yellow silk georgette with metallic thread

embroidery and orange and grey silk piping
English, London: Nabob, 1927–28

Skirts with handkerchief points were especially fashionable in the later 1920s. They were forerunners of the longer skirts which became generally accepted by 1929. Soft, light silk fabrics were ideal for this bias-cut flowing style. Such diaphanous silks presented designers with a problem which they solved by making matching petticoats to accompany the garments. The dull mustard yellow is trimmed with sharply coloured piping and enlivened by the sparkle of the embroidery which is probably Indian. The few Nabob '20s clothes in the collection are made from imported 'exotic' materials.

The owner of this dress, Miss Emilie Grigsby, was 'a slightly mysterious name' (*Long Shadows*, Shane Leslie, John Murray, 1966), but she lived a full and well-dressed life and when she died in 1964 Shane Leslie estimated that she was a hundred years old.

Worn by Miss Emilie Grigsby
T.144-C-1967

The shoes are replicas.   page 84

153 ENSEMBLE (coat, dress and cloche), fine mid-blue woollen face cloth, block printed satin (creams, blues and red), mid-blue ostrich feather, trimmed felt
English, London: Liberty & Co Ltd, 1928

The dress has a cross-over bodice with a low waist and long set-in sleeves gathered and pleated into cuffs. It is collarless with two scarf ties. The skirt front has a double tier of accordion-pleated frills. The coat sleeves flare from seams below the elbows. At the front it is long-waisted and bias-cut panels flare from the hip whereas the back is cut straight and in one panel. The coat fastens on the left hand side with two self-covered buttons, one at the neck, the other at the low waist. It has a half collar with attached scarf ties. The coat's satin lining matches the dress. The outfit was especially designed and made for Mrs Hazel Moorcroft. The printed design first appeared in about 1912 and was constantly re-issued—most recently in the 1970s.

Publication
London, Victoria and Albert Museum, *Liberty's 1875–1975* (an exhibition), catalogue no. E11.
T.71-B-1982

The shoes are replicas.

154 AFTERNOON DRESS, printed silk georgette (peach, red, blue-grey and black)
French, Paris : La Samaritaine, 1930

The printed pattern of waved bands of massed flower heads is carefully disposed in all pieces of the dress. On the bodice, sleeves and skirt yoke the bands run diagonally, while on the skirt's bias-cut gores they run horizontally. The minute pin-tucks on bodice, sleeves and skirt are hand sewn. The light dress is typical of 1930s flowing summer dresses in gossamer fabrics with floral prints. Such delicate

silks are extremely difficult to handle and sew, demanding a great deal of time, skill and patience.

Given anonymously
T.171-1964

The shoes are replicas.

155 DAY DRESS AND CAPE, mid-grey heavy woollen jersey, chrome clips and black leather belt
French, Paris : Madeleine Vionnet, about 1933

The streamlined dress and cape are both bias-cut and machine-stitched with hand finishing. The slenderly flared, wide-necked dress has no fastenings and simply slips over the head. It has set-in, tight-fitting long sleeves with under-arm gussets for ease of movement. The triangular insertion at the front of the neck is counter-balanced by the angles formed by the overlapped cape top. The outfit is an understated masterpiece with every tiny detail resolved by Madame Vionnet. To achieve the correct hang and to avoid unnecessary bulk the hems are turned once. The skirt was originally longer and the hem has been professionally altered, which slightly impairs its line. The severe ensemble has an alternative grey jersey belt, matching handbag and shoes (not shown).
T.302-B-1971

HAT, lacquered straw, *English, early 1930s,* T.103-1983

156 EVENING DRESS, pale flesh pink satin with paste clasps
French, Paris : probably Madeleine Vionnet, about 1933

In this dress the fashionable low back is taken to the extreme—it almost reaches the waist; whereas at the front the cowl neckline is high and almost demure. The bias-cut garment appears simple but the cut and construction are complex and immaculately executed. The box-shaped sleeves are cut in one with the front piece of the dress—the shape is retained by interlinings of cream grosgrain. The sleeves are cut away around the under-arms, meet at the top of the spine behind and fasten with a hook and loop. Two thin shoulder straps support the dress and they are concealed under the sleeves. The back piece is cut to include waist level half-belts at the side seams which pass to the front and fasten with paste clasps. The main seams are machine-stitched but the garment is hand-finished—all the raw edges are hand-whipped.

Given by Miss Amy Bird
T.203-1973   page 86

157 EVENING DRESS, ivory satin, jade green silk velvet ribbons and diamanté buckles
London : Paul Poiret for Liberty & Co Ltd, March 1933

In 1933 Paul Poiret (who was bankrupt and no longer in the vanguard of fashion) was commissioned by Liberty's to create a number of designs for their Model Gown Salon in London. This elegant gown (one of the few from that collection to survive) is typical of 1930s evening attire, in bias-cut ivory satin which plunges at the back, clings to the torso and gently flares below the thigh. The front has a cowl neckline (with a small inner covered weight to hold the drape). It is fitted by a panel of vertical gathers at the midriff and fullness is achieved below thigh level by a group of pleats centrally positioned. Interest is focused on the back with its cascade of velvet ribbons and diamanté buckles.

Given anonymously
T.173-1964

158 EVENING DRESS, matt pale peach silk crêpe and matching silk velvet
English, London: Norman Hartnell, 1933–34

By 1934 Norman Hartnell was well established in his Bruton Street premises. In his autobiography *Silver and Gold* (Evans Brothers Ltd, 1955), he sums up his position in that year: 'The well-dressed women of society flocked to my dress parades and had bought generously, and the Press was proving both amiable and encouraging.' Throughout the 1930s he designed stage clothes for leading actresses including Gertrude Lawrence, Evelyn Laye and Gladys Cooper. The turning point in his career came in 1935 when Lady Alice Montague Douglas-Scott asked him to design her wedding dress for her marriage to the Duke of Gloucester. Royalty was then added to his already impressive list of customers and his business flourished. A house press release pointed out that he was 'equally at home when creating costumes of dazzling brilliance that will be the focal point of a great occasion, or when designing a discreet shopping outfit of a well-groomed woman.' He is best known for these intricately embroidered dresses for grand occasions, especially those made for the Queen and the Queen Mother in the 1950s. This earlier and more modest evening dress is bias-cut and the designer skilfully contrasts ruffled sleeves and knife-pleated godets with the perfectly plain bodice. The drape of the cowl neckline is retained by a small inner weight.

Given by Mrs V. Fisher
T.190-1973   page 88

Charles James's pneumatic white satin evening jacket, created in 1937, has a contemporary appeal, and in the 1970s became a cult object linked with the fashion for voluminous padded coats. It was constructed in the same way as eiderdown bed quilts.
T.385-1977   [161]

159 EVENING DRESS, gold satin
English, London : Charles James, 1934

The slinky dress is bias-cut and the
bodice is constructed to emphasize the
body's curves. It is sleeveless with a
plunging back neckline and fastens on
the left side with hooks and eyes. There
is evidence that the shoulder straps
have been altered.

Worn and given by an anonymous lady
The Cecil Beaton Collection
T.272-1974

EVENING COAT, white ermine lined
with satin
French, Paris : Madeleine Vionnet,
1935–1937

The luxurious coat is composed of
narrow ermine strips. The front
sections are continued to form the
large falling collar. The ensemble—
gold satin combined with supple white
ermine—is typical of the 1930s
'Hollywood' look.

Given by Ottilie, Viscountess Scarsdale
T.441-1980

NECKLACE, diamanté, *probably French,*
mid-1930s, given by Miss Wendy
Hefford, T.67-1983   page 86

160 EVENING ENSEMBLE (DRESS AND CAPE),
satin embroidered with black sequins
with plain scarlet satin panels and
sashes
French, Paris : Chanel, 1937–38

Chanel's name is usually associated
with her classic cardigan suits (which
first appeared in about 1917), but as
well as these practical garments she
also created extravagant evening wear

such as this sequinned ensemble. The
combination of glistening black sequins
(applied in the 'fish scale' manner) and
vivid scarlet satin panels is particularly
dramatic. The bodice is sleeveless with
a low *décolletage* and is supported by
narrow straps. The short, semi-
circular cape falls in soft folds over the
shoulders and is lined in scarlet satin.
It can be caught at the neck with a
hook fastening.

Worn and given by Mrs Leo d'Erlanger
The Cecil Beaton Collection
T.87&A-1974

161 EVENING JACKET, quilted white satin
with eiderdown filling
French, Paris : Charles James, 1937

Charles James created this jacket for
Mrs Oliver Burr Jennings. In 1975 he
wrote a full description of its
development. It was constructed in the
same manner that eiderdown bed
quilts are worked: 'The stitching
which held the shaped masses of
eiderdown in place, being treated as
scrolls, or, as in the case of my coat as
tapered arabesques one within another.
The stitching however had to be
worked out with the cut . . . This is
done while the pattern lies in pieces
after it has been first planned . . . The
great problem in the development of
this concept was that it concerned the
expansion of the silhouette by inflation
with eiderdown which in some areas
would be three inches thick at least.'
In certain parts this thickness would
impede movement but Charles James
resolved the question by diminishing
the depth of padding around the
neckline and armhole. The sleeves are
cut in one with the front panels and
underarm gussets allow free
movement. This garment became a cult
object in the 1970s and Charles James
longed for it to be translated into other
materials—an expensive version in
glove leather or a mass market example
in 'NYLON stuffed with foam rubber
or better kapok or whatever has taken
the place of KAPOK and "marketed"
for ski wear, use on motor bicycles etc.
at a low price.'

Publications
Harper's Bazaar October 1938 p. 67
(photographed by Hoyningen-Huene)
and numerous magazines in the 1970s
including *Esquire, American Fabrics and*
Nova
Purchased with the aid of the Art
Students League of New York
T.385-1977

EVENING DRESS, black wool crêpe and
black silk chiffon
French, Paris : Jeanne Lanvin, about
1935

This sleeveless dress is part of an
evening ensemble which is normally
completed by a sequinned black wool
crêpe jacket. It is bias-cut to cling to
the figure and flares out at the hem
which has a double looped construction.
The top back and side fronts are of
double layers of black chiffon.

Given by Mrs Thompson
T.4-1973   page 163

162 EVENING JACKET, heavy cream silk
crêpe embroidered all-over with bright
blue, dark blue and white sequins
French, Paris : Mainbocher, 1937

The straight-cut jacket is similar to one
worn by the Duchess of Windsor in her
portraits (1937) by Cecil Beaton. She
wore it over a long, bias-cut white
crêpe dress with a wide sequinned sash
to match the jacket. The jacket's back
and sides are in one piece and seamed
only at the shoulders. The sequins
(applied in the 'fish scale' manner) form
bold diagonal stripes—the white
sequins are impressed with a ray
pattern. The collarless garment fastens
at the neck with a hook and eye. The
diagonal stripes are continued around
the long, straight sleeves. It is lined
throughout with cream crêpe de Chine
and has the label 'MAINBOCHER 12
AVENUE GEORGE V A PARIS' and a white
tape inscribed with the number 75361.
Beaton's photographs of Mrs Wallis
Simpson in her Mainbocher ensemble
were particularly successful. Its stark,
simple lines suited her elegant,
uncluttered style.

Given by Mr Vern Lambert
The Cecil Beaton Collection
T.306-1974

EVENING DRESS, white silk chiffon
French, Paris : probably Madeleine
Vionnet, about 1934

The dress is mounted on a bias-cut silk
crêpe foundation. The layered chiffon
(also bias-cut) forms a draped, bloused
bodice over a flared skirt. The bodice
has a low *décolletage* supported by thin
shoulder straps.

Given by Miss Amy Bird
T.204-1973

NECKLACE, pastes set in silver, *French,*
Paris : Adora, about 1935, given by Mrs
Thompson, T.3-B-1973   page 87

163   EVENING ENSEMBLE
DRESS, pleated pale pink, matt crêpe
with bead and diamanté embroidery
COAT, tan silk *faille*
English, London : Peter Russell, 1937

The sleeveless trained dress is
accordion pleated—horizontally in the
bodice and vertically in the skirt. The
skirt falls from a high waist marked by
an embroidered inverted Y-shaped
band. The back neckline is low and
V-shaped and the embroidered band
continues across the back, just above
waist level. The right-hand seam
fastens with hooks and eyes and press-
studs. For protection against evening
chills the coat is interlined with
warmth-giving, plain weave undyed
wool and lined with pale pink silk *faille*.
It is constructed in seven main flared
panels and the cut around the sleeves is
extremely complex. The shoulders are
square—forerunners of the line which
was to dominate fashionable dress at
the end of the 1930s and for most of
the 1940s. Both garments have the
label 'PETER RUSSELL 2 CARLOS PLACE

BERKELEY SQUARE W1'. An almost
identical version in lamé was shown in
Vogue and described as an ideal
presentation dress.

*Worn by Mrs John Fraser (Ruth
Vincent) and given by her son Mr John
Fraser*
The Cecil Beaton Collection
T.362 and T.363-1974

164   EVENING ENSEMBLE (dress and jacket),
black, satin-backed rayon marocain
embroidered with various gilt threads
pink glass beads and diamantés
London : Schiaparelli, 1938

Schiaparelli was famed for her
attractive and wittily designed evening
jackets of this period. Here one with
bold embroidered leaves (motifs which
are repeated in the moulded buttons)
and 'leg-of-mutton' sleeves is worn
over a bias-cut sleeveless dress which
fastens at the side with a bold plastic
'Lightning' zip made by ICI. The dress
is slim-fitting and cut to flare at the
bottom. The front has two raised darts
under the bust and a low V-neck
decorated with a frill. The back has a
low square neckline and a shirred
bodice. The jacket is fitted by means of
darts and curved side seams. Large
crescent-shaped pads shape the
shoulders. Both garments have the
label 'Schiaparelli London', and tapes
inscribed with the number 6313. The
ensemble was worn by Lady Alexandra
Dacre (then Lady Alexandra Haig) at a
masked carol party in December 1938.

*Worn and given by Lady Alexandra
Dacre of Glanton*
The Cecil Beaton Collection
T.399&A-1974   page 87

165   EVENING DRESS, pale pink ribbed silk
French, Paris: Molyneux, 1939

At the end of the 1930s designers
offered a wide variety of styles
including wide-skirted dresses as
alternatives to the ubiquitous clinging,
bias-cut dresses. In August 1939 *Vogue*
described the scope of the Paris
collections: 'Molyneux's hoop-flared
day skirts walk beside Lanvin's
modern peg-topped hobble skirts;
Balenciaga's wide Velasquez paniers
dance past Paquin's tightly wrapped
mummy skirts . . .' Indeed Balenciaga
took the look to the extreme with his
'Infanta' dresses inspired by the 17th-
century court portraits by Velasquez.
This Molyneux creation has its double-
tiered, full skirt held out by four bone
hoops. The bodice (with a slightly
dropped waistline) is softly ruched into
the side seams—the left side fastens
with a pink metal zip. The bodice is

supported by a wide halter strap which
is attached to the straight, low neckline.

Illus.: *Vogue* January 1939
Worn and given by Stella, Lady Ednam
The Cecil Beaton Collection
T.320-1974   page 89

166   DAY DRESS, red rayon crêpe
*British, London : possibly Edward
Molyneux, 1942*
From the Utility Collection by the
Incorporated Society of London
Fashion Designers for the Board of
Trade.

The dress, (Board of Trade pattern
no. 4) has square padded shoulders and
its maximum selling price (in the rayon
crêpe) was set at 53s 6d. The bodice is
slightly bloused into the waist, fastens
at the front with matching composition
buttons and has a small collar. The
three-quarter length sleeves fasten
with matching buttons. The skirt has
soft pleats and a pair of flap pockets.
All the designs for the Utility
Collection had to meet the Board's
strict rules governing factors such as
amounts of material and numbers of
buttons to be used. When offering the
clothes to the Museum in August 1942,
Sir Thomas Barlow explained that
'They conform in simplification and
economy of material to the conditions
laid down by the Board of Trade in
relation to the manufacture of civilian
clothing.' *Vogue* (October 1942) hailed
them as 'some of the most entirely
wearable clothes we have ever seen'.

*Given by the Board of Trade via Sir
Thomas Barlow (Director-General of
Civilian Clothing)*
T.57-1942

167 SUIT (jacket and skirt) brown, yellow, maroon Scottish woollen tweed
BLOUSE, yellow rayon crêpe
COAT, heavily milled yellow wool (possibly designed by Worth)
British, London : 1942. From the Utility Collection by the Incorporated Society of London Fashion Designers for the Board of Trade.

The long, fitted jacket (lined with fawn rayon) has wide padded shoulders which make the waist look small in contrast. It has two deep and wide patch pockets. The skirt consists of four flared panels. The blouse also has padded shoulders and long, full sleeves gathered into cuffs. It has a yoke at the front and back and a Peter Pan collar. It fastens at the front with a row of yellow composition buttons threaded with red ribbon. The coat is partially lined with yellow rayon and fastens with a single button at the neck and a tie belt. The maximum retail selling price for the entire outfit (in the materials listed above) was £8 16s 5d.

Publication
Vogue, October 1942 p. 27 (the suit and blouse)
Given by the Board of Trade via Sir Thomas Barlow (Director-General of Civilian Clothing)
T.42&A-1942, T.63-1942, T.50-1942

The hat and shoes are replicas. page 89

168 SUIT (jacket and skirt), flecked pale blue and navy wool.
British, London : possibly Victor Stiebel, 1942. From the Utility Collection by the Incorporated Society of London Fashion Designers for the Board of Trade.

This bloused jacket with square padded shoulders closely resembles the battle-dress top of army uniform. It is single-breasted with a collar with deep revers and two flap pockets. It is gathered into a shaped wide belt which fastens with a buckle at the left side. The slender skirt has gently flared panels set into a yoke. It is Board of Trade pattern no. 33 and the retailers' maximum selling price for the suit in 13/13½ oz woollen frieze was 82s 2d.

Given by the Board of Trade via Sir Thomas Barlow (Director-General of Civilian Clothing)
T.46&A-1942

HAT, dark red leather with matching ribbon, *English, Harrogate : Marshall and Snelgrove 1937-9*, worn by Mrs Doris Langley Moore, T.105-1980

GAS MASK BAG, dark blue leather
English, early 1940s

Gas mask bags came in the familiar regulation brown but slightly smaller versions in different colours were available for fashion-conscious women.

Given by Valerie D. Mendes
T.331-1982

The shoes are replicas. page 88

169 SUIT, 'BAR' (the New Look), jacket and skirt, cream silk tussore (plain weave) and fine black wool crêpe
HAT, coarse natural straw plait with black silk grosgrain band
French, Paris : Christian Dior, Spring 1947

The construction and finishing is complex and highly skilled. The jacket is cut to fit tightly above the narrow (18-inch) waist, while below it has a deep basque (with pockets) which is stiffened, padded and weighted to create exaggerated 'teacup' curves over the hips. It is lined throughout in cream poult. The skirt is long (2′ 9″) and very full (8 yards around the hem). An elaborate, many-layered petticoat of black poult and net ensures that the knife-pleated skirt maintains its line. The weighty skirt and petticoat are attached to a sturdy quilted waist yoke which fastens with hooks and eyes at the back. This was one of the most popular models in Dior's first collection which he called '*La Ligne Corolle*'— the press dubbed it 'the New Look' and the name endured. He took the softer feminine shape—round sloping shoulder line, narrow waist and spreading skirts—to the extreme, and despite official complaints it was a resounding success.
Harper's Bazaar published detailed line drawings of the New Look's construction, and 'Bar' was also illustrated in *Vogue* and *L'Officiel*.

Given by Christian Dior, Paris
T.376&A and T.377-1960 page 90

170 SUMMER DAY DRESS, heavyweight yellow cotton
SASH AND PICTURE HAT, printed plain weave cotton (orange, yellow, green, black etc., on a red background)
French, Paris : Jacques Fath, Summer 1949

The dress has padded, rounded shoulders and a wrap-around slim skirt which buttons at the back on the left. The stiffened sash also fastens on these buttons. The bodice has a complex double construction with the outer fronts forming a stand-away V-shaped neckline. This dress has many features which became current in the 1950s such as the sheath skirt, the pointed

fly-away cuffs and the sharp yellow colour set against predominantly red accessories. The stiff cotton is ideal to hold the angular details and keep the line of the straight skirt. Until the mid-1950s the alternative to this shape was the silhouette with a similar neat corsage and small waist but with a full, *bouffant* skirt.

Worn and given by Lady Alexandra Dacre of Glanton
The Cecil Beaton Collection
T.175-D-1974 page 93

171 DANCE DRESS (bodice and skirt), black and white printed silk organza (Ducharne)
French, Paris : Christian Dior, Spring/Summer 1953

The bodice is mounted on a long, boned, net foundation and fastens at the centre back with a row of small covered buttons. The neckline is low and off-the-shoulder and the construction around the armholes is intricate, involving matching tiny bias bands and triangular gussets. It has the label 'PRINTEMPS-ETE Christian Dior PARIS MADE IN FRANCE' stamped with the number 34377. The tiered, full skirt has many yards of hem which are hand rolled. The skirt fastens at the back with hooks and eyes, covered buttons and press studs. It has a straight ivory crêpe de Chine petticoat and over this a full layered petticoat of stiffened net and organza. In the summer of 1953, the Duchess of Windsor chose a different Dior dress made in satin printed with the same scallop and dot pattern to wear at the Circus Ball in Paris (American *Vogue*, 15 August 1953).

Publications
French *Vogue*, March 1953
L'Officiel, April 1953
Keenan, Brigid, *Dior in Vogue*, Octopus Books, 1981

T.264&A-1981

CHRISTIAN DIOR ADVERTISING FAN, printed paper with wooden sticks, *French, Paris : Évantails Gané for Christian Dior, early 1950s, given by Mrs Margaret Marshall*
T.31-1983 page 91

172 EVENING DRESS, white silk organza with cotton machine embroidery and velvet appliqué in pink, green, yellow and white (probably Swiss) on an under-dress of shocking pink Thai silk
French, Paris : Schiaparelli, Summer 1953

The long, circular skirt is cut on the cross and flares from the side-dropped waist. Schiaparelli remains faithful to one of her favourite colours—shocking pink—but here tones it down with an overlay of semi-transparent white organza. Attention centres on the dramatic neckline where the organza forms a deep inverted, rippling frill which encircles the body at bust level and occasionally allows the pleated neckline and short sleeves of the under-dress to peep through. The dress has a full-length stiffened white holland circular petticoat and a grosgrain waist stay.

Publications
Paris, Centre de Documentation du Costume, (now part of the Musée des Arts de la Mode) Schiaparelli Album no. 52, 1953, p. 217
L'Officiel, June 1953

Worn and given by The Duchess of Devonshire
The Cecil Beaton Collection
T.397-1974   page 94

173 DAY DRESS, grey woollen tweed
French, Paris : Jean Dessès, about 1953

Sheath dresses were popular throughout the 1950s. This example appears simple but its clean lines are achieved by skilled cutting and intricate diagonal seaming. The bodice is cut in four sections with the centre front seam slit to form a long, stand-away V-neck. Triangular panels overlap at the midriff and a raised seam defining the waistline is pin-pointed by two large metallic grey leather buttons. Similar buttons secure the darts at the cuffs of the straight, elbow-length sleeves. The triangular seaming and darting at the midriff and sleeves is reinforced inside by white cotton and the bodice front has a crêpe de Chine lining. The grosgrain waist stay bears the label 'Jean Dessès 17 Avenue Matignon PARIS'.

HAT, black silk velvet, *American, New York : Hattie Carnegie, 1952–53, worn by Mrs Opal Holt and given by Mrs D. M. Haynes and Mrs M. Clark,*
T.102 and T.146-1982   page 92

174 'CHESTERFIELD' SUIT (jacket and skirt), black and white Donegal tweed and black silk velvet
English, London : Digby Morton, about 1954

The mid-calf length narrow skirt is straight-cut with four panels and has a pair of pockets let into the top front. It has a long, centre-back kick pleat, a half-lining of black crêpe de Chine and a side-fastening of a zip and hooks and eyes. It is labelled 'DIGBY MORTON GROSVENOR HILL LONDON W I'. The single-breasted jacket is waisted and tailored to the body. Two wide, deep, cuffed pockets are sloped to emphasize the curve of the hips. The collar has deep revers and the top lapels are of black silk velvet. The hem is interlined, weighted and padded to hold the line. The jacket is lined throughout in black crêpe de Chine and has the label 'DIGBY MORTON COUTURE'. A small matching, fringed bow-shaped scarf is not shown. Black and white tweed was popular throughout the 1950s—*Vogue* (USA) in August 1954 stated: 'this Autumn without question the smart woman's place is in tweed'.

HAT, black velours, *French, Paris : Christian Dior, 1953–4, worn by Mrs Opal Holt and given by Mrs D. M. Haynes and Mrs M. Clark,*
T.101&A-1982 and T.158-1982

UMBRELLA, with silver finish swan's neck handle, *English, London : Peter Todd Mitchell for John Cavanagh, 1953*
T.38-1983   page 92

175 EVENING DRESS AND ROULEAU BELT, pleated fine white jersey
French, Paris : Madame Grès. A replica of a 1955 design made especially for the Museum in 1971.

Thirteen straight panels are joined and minutely pleated to form the dress. There is no seam join at the waist—the skirt and bodice are in one. The pleats are top-stitched at the waist and then carried on in a diagonal manner in the form-fitting bodice. Finally they are twisted and stitched at the neck to form a plaited edge. The dress has one strap over the left shoulder and the other is left bare. The bodice pleats are couched onto a cream silk crêpeline foundation which is boned and has a wired brassière. A straight, heavy, white silk crêpe petticoat is attached to a white grosgrain waist-stay which has the label 'GRES I rue de la Paix Paris'. The dress fastens at the left seam with small hooks and eyes. The main seams and hem are machine-stitched but the rest of the garment is hand-sewn. A house press release described Madame Grès' personal manner of handling materials 'almost without seams', and how she 'induced manufacturers to produce jersey in large widths and took part in their researches to apply these techniques'.

Given by Madame Grès
The Cecil Beaton Collection
T.246&A-1974

176 EVENING DRESS, mid-blue silk taffeta
American, New York : Charles James, 1955

The construction is highly complex but, briefly, consists of an outer taffeta 'shell' of bodice, two form-hugging ruched skirts over a full lower skirt which are attached to and depend on a shape-forming foundation. This is intricate and heavy with a boned corset and 12 layers of under-skirts ranging from stiffened cotton webbing to fine net. 1870s dress (especially the

cuirasse bodice) was probably the initial inspiration for this creation. It fastens at the centre back with two zips. Some seams are machine-stitched but the garment is mainly hand sewn. The hem has a deep facing of bright peacock blue silk taffeta which would have been seen occasionally when the dress was in movement. Full details are given in the excellent exhibition catalogue *The Genius of Charles James* by Elizabeth Ann Coleman (The Brooklyn Museum, 1982) no. 123 p. 127.

Worn and given by Mrs Ronald Tree
The Cecil Beaton Collection
T.277-1974

NECKLACE, white and amethyst coloured pastes set in black enamelled metal, *French or American, early 1950s*, T.135-1970

177 EVENING DRESS, fuchsia silk taffeta
French, Paris: Balenciaga, about 1955

Throughout the 1950s Balenciaga designed a series of extravagant and inventive evening dresses (mainly in fine silk taffeta) which were based upon immense drapes and flounces. In this dress he confines the *bouffant* drapes to the back and in contrast the front has a simple appearance with a V-neck and a straight, very narrow skirt, slit at the centre front hem to allow movement. The bodice back has a plunging V-neckline and the construction of the skirt back is highly involved. Basically it consists of a swathed, drawn back skirt with a double tier of enormous triangular flounces (formed by looping and gathering) topped by a large bow. The flounces are wired to keep their *bouffant* shape. The dress is mounted on a boned and padded foundation which fastens at the centre back with a zip. The dress fastens over this with a row of covered buttons. It is labelled 'BALENCIAGA AVENUE GEORGE V PARIS'. The dress is machine sewn and hand finished.

Given by Miss Caroline Combe
T.427-1967   page 95

178 EVENING GOWN, yellow satin Duchesse
French, Paris: Pierre Balmain, 1956

Balmain maintained that 'the basic job of a *couturier* . . . is to dress women for everyday living' (*My years and Seasons*, Cassell 1964). For his clientèle normal life involved numerous grand evening occasions and Balmain is perhaps best known for the lavish ball gowns he created for these events. The vertically looped ribbon decoration and the full, long skirt of this special

occasion dress were inspired by 18th and 19th-century dress. The shape—a tightly fitted strapless bodice and 'crinoline' skirt—depends upon an immaculately constructed foundation of a boned corset and a many-tiered, stiffened net petticoat. The satin is underlined throughout in silk crêpeline and the dress fastens at the left side with a zip.

Worn and given by Lady Elizabeth von Hofmannsthal
The Cecil Beaton Collection
T.49-1974   page 95

179 EVENING DRESS, bright pink silk organza
French, Paris: Jacques Heim, Jeunes Filles, 1959

The dress consists of a double layer of organza and overlays a strapless under-dress of silk taffeta and organza. The

front panel is cut in the Princess manner but the sides and back have a waistline seam. The under-dress follows the lines of the over-dress but attached to the back are horizontal rows of stiffened net and organza frills. The *bouffant* dipping skirt is petal-pleated into the bodice and is supported by a petticoat of eleven layers of bright pink stiffened net. The two dresses are attached to a long, boned foundation. The under-dress fastens with a metal zip at the centre back and the dress fastens over this with press studs. The garment is machine-stitched and hand-finished.

Worn and given by Mrs Rory McEwen
The Cecil Beaton Collection
T.266-1974

180 SUIT (jacket and skirt), woven wool and silk
French, Paris: Balenciaga, about 1964
HAT, velvet trimmed straw
English, London: Elfriede Ltd, early 1960s

This understated ensemble reveals Balenciaga's supreme talents. The cut is impeccable and is matched by the finishing. The seams are machine-stitched but other details are completed by hand. To avoid unsightly bulges, the hems are turned once; the raw edges are minutely bound with silk chiffon and then blind-stitched into place in the usual *couture* manner. The jacket has magyar sleeves cut in one with the fronts. The back is cross-cut and flared. The slightly flared skirt has four panels which are gently gathered into the waistband. It fastens at the side with a zip. Both garments are lined throughout in fine silk.

The refinement manifested in Balenciaga's clothes pervaded his entire establishment. In 1972 Jose Maria Arielza described it: 'this fashion house had a curious monastic seal, in which there was no room for loud and outspoken people, nor for laughter and disorder. Everything was done in an atmosphere of silence and efficiency: fashion shows, work rehearsals. Even among his models there was a sign of restraint, no airs or graces. To see his show was to be present at a pure aesthetic spectacle, reverent and organized.' (*El Diario Vasco*, August 1972)

Worn by Mrs Opal Holt and given by Mrs D. M. Haynes and Mrs M. Clark
T.127&A-1982, T.154-1982

181 Suit (jacket, belted dress and hat),
black worsted crêpe
French, Paris: Chanel, mid-1960s

For fifteen years Chanel's salon was
closed and the re-opening in 1954 was
greeted with lukewarm reviews. She
revived her classic suits with the lines
pared down to bare essentials but only
American *Vogue* acknowledged their
significance. As well as her familiar
braid-trimmed, soft tweeds, she showed
stark black two-pieces which were the
forerunners of this streamlined
ensemble. Here, the components are
stripped down to a bare minimum.
The garments are totally functional and
without decoration; this is provided by
the highlights of the white blouse and
the costume jewellery. The neat
sleeveless dress is slightly flared,
fastens with covered buttons and is
lined throughout with black silk. The
threequarter-length jacket echoes the
same lines. Chanel was a rigorous and
uncompromising designer—to her the
total look was vital.

*Said to have been made by Mademoiselle
Chanel for herself and worn in Italy and
Switzerland*
T.22-c-1979, T.37-1983

All other accessories by courtesy of the
Chanel Ltd Boutique, London.

182 Cocktail Dress, white, black, yellow
and red silk crêpe (Abraham and
Bianchini Ferier)
*French, Paris: Yves St Laurent,
Autumn/Winter 1965*

The dress is sleeveless, short (just
above the knees) and straight cut. It is
pieced together in heavy silk crêpe and
is mainly white with a 'window pane'
design carried out in horizontal and
vertical bands of black with an inset
panel of sharp yellow at the lower right
front and another of bright red on the
left shoulder. Inspired by the abstract
paintings of the Dutch De Stijl artist
Piet Mondrian (1872–1944), Yves St
Laurent designed a group of bold
dresses based on intersecting black
stripes and blocks of primary colours.
It became known as the Mondrian
Collection and was featured on the front
of French *Vogue* in September 1965
and in many other fashion magazines.
The designs were immediately taken up
by manufacturers who made cheap
copies for a mass market.

*Given by M. Yves St Laurent
The Cecil Beaton Collection*
T.369-1974   page 96

[181]

183 DAY DRESS AND JACKET, lime green with magenta, orange and turquoise striped wool gaberdine (Nattier)
French, Paris: Ungaro, Spring 1966

The short, sleeveless 'A' line shift dress has a square neck and broad shoulder straps formed by applied striped vertical bands which are continued along the front and back. The bodice top is horizontally striped whereas the lower dress is plain lime green. It is lined throughout in lime green surah and fastens at the back with a concealed zip and at the top, left shoulder with hooks and eyes. The short, double-breasted, horizontally striped jacket is worn with one deep rever and the left rever is worn flat against the chest. It is unlined and has the label 'Emanuel Ungaro 6 BIS AV MAC MAHON PARIS'. The buttons with red centres circled by orange are custom-made to echo colours in the stripes.

Publications
French *Vogue*, March 1966
French *Vogue*, March 1967

Worn and given by Mrs Brenda Azario
T.320&A-1978   page 96

184 MINI-DRESS, black and cream bonded wool and nylon jersey
English, London: Mary Quant (Ginger Group), 1967

A similar Ginger Group 'vest buttoned jersey dress' was illustrated in *Honey* (March 1967) when it cost 8½ guineas—the approximate equivalent in 1983 is £50. The short skirt is gently gathered into the low waist. The short sleeves and neck facing are cream and the front fastens with a row of cream buttons. The sleeve edges are top-stitched in black and the hem is top-stitched in cream. It has the label 'MARY QUANT'S GINGER GROUP MADE IN ENGLAND'. This and similar jersey dresses from the same collection were worn with dense black or white tights (Mary Quant designed her first tights in 1965), and big-brimmed felt hats or berets in matching Ginger Group colours. A long-sleeved version of this dress was shown in the London Museum's exhibition held in 1973–74, *Mary Quant's London*, catalogue number 44.

Given by Miss Mary Quant
The Cecil Beaton Collection
T.351-1974   page 97

185 MINI-DRESS, cotton and machine-embroidered organza
French, Paris: Courrèges, Spring, 1967

In 1964 the fashion press widely acclaimed Courrèges' Spring collection.

He showed clean-cut clothes including trouser suits with immaculately cut straight legs and streamlined jackets. The look was dubbed 'Space Age' and was created by using heavyweight gaberdines by Nattier and other solid fabrics that maintained the rigid lines. The Museum does not have a Courrèges trouser suit nor an outfit from the famous Spring 1964 collection but, fortunately, it does have a summary of the mid-60s Courrèges look in this flared, daisy-patterned shift.

The round-necked, sleeveless dress fastens with a zip at the centre back. The semi-transparent embroidered organza panels are backed with flesh-coloured silk and the garment is lined in white silk. It has the label 'COURREGES PARIS'. A Courrèges house photograph shows a bronzed young model with a geometric haircut wearing an almost identical dress (model number 54). The mannequin wears short white gloves, long white socks and white, flat, wide-toed bar shoes.

Worn and given by Princess Stanislaus Radziwill
The Cecil Beaton Collection
T.100-1974

186 DAY OUTFIT, 'COSMOS'
TABARD, woollen jersey with applied vinyl motif
JUMPER, knitted ribbed wool
SKULL CAP, woollen jersey
SUN VISOR, shaped smoked plastic
BOOTS, zip-fastened vinyl
French, Paris: Pierre Cardin, 1967

In 1966 *The Observer* said of Cardin's functional clothes: 'His contribution to

modern living may be practical but it's rather a shock.' From the mid-1960s until about 1971 for his futuristic garments Cardin favoured heavyweight woollen jersey which allowed free bodily movement but at the same time was sufficiently rigid to maintain clean-cut shapes. He made frequent use of top-stitching and curved hems. These bold clothes were designed for active young women.

Given by M. Pierre Cardin
The Cecil Beaton Collection
T.75-F-1974   frontispiece

187 EVENING COAT, yellow felt screen-printed in orange and black and trimmed with bead-decorated streamers
English, London: Zandra Rhodes 1969

In 1969 and in the early 1970s Zandra Rhodes made a number of screen-printed felt coats and capes with immense flared or circular panels which were ideal for her bright painterly patterns. This circular coat falls from a high yoke and has a collar of inverted top-stitched scallops decorated with beaded streamers. The large sleeves are elasticated at the wrists. The coat was originally worn over a screen-printed chiffon hooded dress in matching colours, and with a pair of yellow patent shoes by Charles Jourdain.

Publication
Vogue, Oct–Dec, 1969

Given and worn by Miss Irene Worth in the Royal Shakespeare Company's production of Edward Albee's 'Tiny Alice' at the Aldwych Theatre 1970
The Cecil Beaton Collection
T.356-1974   page 98

188 EVENING DRESS AND HAT, grey-green moiré rayon jersey
English, London: Jean Muir, Autumn/Winter 1971

In August 1971 *Vogue* illustrated six designs from Jean Muir's latest collection including this classic dress. The description ran: 'isn't it romantic? tucked or gathered bodices springing great or greater sleeves'. With its top-stitching, carefully tucked bodice and softly pleated skirt the fluid dress characterizes the designer's meticulous attention to the dictates of cloth and methods of construction. The bodice is given additional weight by a crêpe de Chine lining and the voluminous, bat-wing sleeves are elasticated at the wrists. The matching domed hat, designed for Jean Muir by Graham Smith has a shape-forming interlining of foam and the deep plaited band is padded.

Given by Miss Jean Muir
The Cecil Beaton Collection
T.321&A-1974   page 98

89 DAY ENSEMBLE
MAXI-DRESS, black and white tweed
with woven stripes
BLOUSE, cream plain weave rayon
SKULL CAP, black woollen jersey knit
English, London: John Bates at Jean
Varon; Autumn/Winter 1971

In the later 1960s and early 1970s such
high waistlines were popular, especially
for the young. This outfit was part of a
collection for winter wear which ranged
in bold looks from the puritan to the
choirboy. One dress in particular was
an instant success and within a week of
its appearance cheap copies (with slight
adaptations) were available in certain
chain stores. The turned down circular
collar and cuffs of the blouse are
stiffened to hold their shape. The dress
fastens with a zip at the centre back
and was originally worn with knee-
length, square-toed, zip-fastening
black suède boots.

Given by Mr John Bates
The Cecil Beaton Collection
T.53-B-1974

90 DRESS, printed Liberty cottons—*Tana*
lawn, *Nimbus* voile and *Country* cotton
—trimmed with leather mainly in tones
of blue, brown and cream
English, London: Bill Gibb, 1972

At the end of the 1960s clothes with

geometric lines dependent upon firm
fabrics were abandoned in favour of
flowing styles in soft materials. For a
period different patterns (usually of the
same scale) in toning colours were put
together either in one garment or in
interchangeable outfits. Here Bill Gibb
assembled cottons designed by Susan
Collier and Sarah Campbell for
Liberty's to create a romantic, full-
skirted dress with peplum and
enormous double sleeves. The printed
designs sit happily next to each other
and are further embellished by floral
leather motifs and streamers.

Worn by Miss Sandie Shaw
T.94-1981   page 99

191 EVENING CLOAK, white rayon jersey
with pleated organdie frills
English, London: Yuki, 1977

The long, trailing cloak is cut in a
T-shape from two enormous panels of
the supple knitted fabric. It has just
three seams—two along the sleeves and
one down the centre back. It drapes
and flows around the body from tight
gathers at the high round neck which
has a deep double 'ruffle' collar in
pleated organdie. Frills in the same
organdie decorate the hem and sleeve
edges. The crisp, stiff pleats are set
against the soft and clinging jersey.
The cloak fastens at the neck with a

hook and eye and falls open at the
front. It has the label 'Yuki London'.

Publication
Carter, Ernestine, *The Changing World*
of Fashion, Weidenfeld and Nicolson,
1972, p. 102.

Given by Yuki
T.1-1979

192 DAY OUTFIT
COAT, black and white woven woollen
shepherd-check
SHIRT, black plain weave wool
SKIRT, black woven worsted
English, London: Wendy Dagworthy,
1979
HAT, felt
English, London: Herbert Johnson, 1979
BELT, suède
English, London: Christopher Trill, 1979

In 1979 Simpson (Piccadilly) Ltd held
an exhibition of designs for day and
evening dress by 25 leading British
designers. Simpson's decided to offer
the entire show as a gift to the V&A.
All the designers agreed to give their
exhibits and Adel Rootstein and
Richard Hopkins gave the entire
collection of mannequins. The outfits
will be shown in rotation to reveal
British design for Winter 1979. This
ensemble by Wendy Dagworthy uses a
variety of top-quality wools. The chic
black and white is punctuated by the
red of the soft suède belt. The skirt is
narrow and straight cut and the simple
black shirt has contrasting white
buttons. The slim, threequarter-length
coat has deep pockets, but particular
interest lies in the cut of the sleeves
(full at the top and narrowing to the
wrists), and in the broad padded
shoulders which are reminiscent of the
1940s.

Outfit given by Wendy Dagworthy;
mannequin given by Miss Adel
Rootstein; via Simpson (Piccadilly) Ltd
T.225 to T.236-1980

193 PIRATE OUTFIT

TUNIC TOP AND SASH, printed yellow and orange plain weave cotton
WAISTCOAT, figured black and yellow cotton and rayon
JACKET AND TROUSERS, figured yellow cotton and rayon
BICORNE, stiffened black felt with red leather and gold braid
STOCKINGS, yellow muslin
BOOTS, black leather and suède
*English, London: (World's End)
Vivienne Westwood, 1980*

The recent wave of nostalgia, labelled 'neo-romantic', led to a colourful masquerade of highwaymen, pirates and others, and Vivienne Westwood's clothes were in the forefront. Some adopted the entire bold pirate's outfit, but many took elements from the collection (the tunic with its powerful meandering print, the waistcoat and the fall-down stockings were especially popular) and wore them in a free manner. Vivienne Westwood, in the vanguard of contemporary young fashion, expressed her philosophy in an interview in *Harpers and Queen* (April 1983): 'I'm very anarchical and perverse about what I do with clothes but what I drive at is simplicity . . . The great thing about my clothes—the way they make you feel grand and strong—is to do with the sexy way that they emphasize your body and make you aware of it.'

Given by Mrs Vivienne Westwood
T.334-1-1982   page 100

194 EVENING ENSEMBLE 'Renaissance, Cloth of Gold Crinoline' (bodice, skirt, and over-skirt over hoops), printed quilted black satin, printed black silk net and knife-pleated 'cloth of gold and silver' —a mixture of polyamide, polyester and lamé
English, London: Zandra Rhodes, the Elizabethan Collection, Autumn/Winter 1981
DIADEM, multi-coloured glass and mirror glass in resin on metal
English, London: Andrew Logan for Zandra Rhodes, Autumn/Winter 1981

Zandra Rhodes is renowned for her romantic and highly decorative evening

clothes. Here is one of her most luxuriant early 1980s dresses. It can be worn in two ways—as it is displayed with hooped calico under-panniers to support both the skirt and the separate swirled hip decoration, or the over-skirt and under-panniers can be removed and the bodice, which has a peplum, can be worn outside the skirt. She studied panniers in the V & A collection before completing this 'Renaissance crinoline', so it is only right that the garments are now united in the Museum. In the *Observer* (9 October 1977) Zandra Rhodes was described as 'The most original and fearless of British designers, admired for her dedication to doing what she feels . . .'; and in *The Times* (19 September 1981) Suzy Menkes might have had this ensemble in mind when she wrote: 'She is best known in her native Britain for her extravagant Cinderella chiffon ball gowns and pre-punk use of extraordinary make-up and colour for visual effect.'

*The ensemble given by Miss Zandra Rhodes
The diadem given by Mr Andrew Logan*
T.124-C-1983, T.125-1983

195 DAY OUTFIT

T SHIRT, dark brown Sea Island cotton jersey
SINGLET, black linen shirting
SKIRT, dark brown linen
English, London: Margaret Howell, Summer 1983

Margaret Howell's clothes are modern classics in natural fabrics. She takes many of her themes from traditional British attire including tailored jackets and pleated skirts, but her interpretation is fresh and contemporary. She skilfully adapts conventional features— deepening pleats or lengthening the line so that her clothes are in tune with the moment. They are both comfortable and elegant, appealing to a wide age range. For her Summer 1983 collection she used dark colours in layered light-weight fabrics, juxtaposing the subtle textures of cottons and linens.

Given by Miss Margaret Howell
T.136-C-1983

GLOSSARY

The minimum of technical terms have been used in the text and ephemeral trade names for materials avoided unless the authors are quite certain that designers used them. This glossary explains the words used in this book which may be obscure to the reader. It is not intended to be a universal guide. Glossaries will be found also in other books cited by the authors. Dorothy K. Burnham's *Warp and Weft: a textile terminology*, Royal Ontario Museum, Toronto, 1980, will also be found useful; it is based on the internationally accepted terminology of CIETA (Centre Internationale d'Etude des Textiles Anciens).

ANILINE DYES These were first extracted from a by-product of the new gas industry, coal tar, by Sir William Perkin in 1856. Mauve was the first colour invented, followed quickly by a vibrant purple, green, magenta, and pink. Although very bright, aniline dyes are also very fugitive both in light and in water.

BANYAN (Indian nightgown) A loose coat ending just above or below the knees. It wrapped over in front and was fastened in various ways (see also nightgown). The terms have been used interchangeably both at the time and by costume historians. The coat was fashionable in the 17th–18th centuries as informal wear.

BAR SHOE Shoe with one or more bars over instep, fastening with button or buckle at side.

BASQUE A short addition (gathered or flared) attached to a bodice at the waist seam. In the 20th century the term has become synonymous with PEPLUM.

BICORNE A two-cornered hat.

BISQUE Porcelain with a matt unglazed surface. It was first used for making dolls by the French toy industry in the 19th century.

BOBBIN LACE A technique whereby a number of threads wound on bobbins and secured at their upper ends to a hard pillow are woven, plaited and twisted together to form an openwork fabric. Bobbin lace can be made in a single, continuous length (Valenciennes, Mechlin and Buckinghamshire lace), or it can be made in a number of small pieces that are subsequently joined together (Brussels and Honiton lace).

'BOOT' CUFFS Deep, wide cuff, open under the forearm. The name derived from the wide wing-shaped tops of riding boots. These cuffs were current on men's dress in the 1730s and 1740s. (See catalogue no. 86)

BOX PLEATS & DOUBLE BOX PLEATS A method of accommodating a greater breadth of fabric in a smaller space by folding under the sides of the pleat to a depth of less than half the size of the top. In a DOUBLE BOX PLEAT the material turned under is longer. It is then re-folded so that another, narrow pleat shows on each side of the main one.

BRANDENBURG A large, loose overcoat reaching to the calf and similar in style to the CASSOCK. It was named after the Prussian city famous in the 17th century for its woollens. (19th century)

BRITISH WARM A double-breasted overcoat with a shaped body and a slight flare to the skirts, knee-length or shorter. It had leather buttons. Influenced by the coats worn by Guards officers of foot regiments, it was made in camel-coloured fabric in melton, camel or cashmere. (20th century)

BROCADED A pattern is brocaded when a supplementary weft is introduced into the ground weave only for the width of the motif and not from selvage to selvage. Brocading saved expensive silk.

BRODERIE ANGLAISE All-white cotton embroidery, usually of a floral design, incorporating small holes mainly worked in satin and buttonhole stitches.

BUGLE BEAD A small long bead (glass, metal, jet or plastics) which can be a smooth cylinder or faceted.

BUSK, also SPOON BUSK The piece of stiffening material, usually whalebone, wood or metal, inserted into the front of the corset to keep it braced against the curves of the figure. (16th–19th century). The SPOON BUSK introduced in the late 1870s, was rounded, broadened and curved at the bottom so that this portion resembled the underside of the curved bowl of a spoon. This shape was introduced to prevent the busk from unduly compressing or digging into the belly.

CANIONS Extensions to the hose (breeches) which fit the thigh. (16th–17th century; see catalogue no. 78)

CARTRIDGE PLEATS   Pleats which are drawn so tightly together that they have a greater depth than width. On the face of the fabric they have the appearance of cartridges in a belt, hence the term.

CASSOCK   See catalogue no. 81.

CASTOR   A hat made from beaver fur (Latin, from Greek kastor = beaver). The highest quality, and very expensive, and therefore often adulterated with other materials, such as coney fur. (17th–19th century)

CHATELEINE BAG   A bag suspended from a waistband by a cord or chain, very popular from the 1860s until the end of that century.

CHENILLE   A furry thread like a caterpillar—hence the name. A fabric is woven with the warp threads in groups. It is then cut along the length between the groups (CIETA). The thread thus formed is used in both woven textiles and embroidery. The earliest samples date from the late 17th century.

CHESTERFIELD   Named after the 6th Earl of Chesterfield, a leader of fashion in the 1830s and 40s. Originally referring to a man's overcoat but towards the end of the 19th century for women also. The woman's coat was slightly waisted, single-breasted with a short back vent, hip-level pockets and outside breast pocket. The collar was generally velvet. These features became modified in the 20th century, the coat became more fitted and was often double-breasted.

CHINÉ   A method of printing the warp before weaving. The weft is not printed so the pattern has a misty appearance when woven—hence the English 18th-century term 'clouds' for materials printed in this way. The technique continued to be used into the present century.

COIF   Close-fitting cap, shaped like a baby's bonnet. From 12th to mid-15th century, made of plain linen. In the 16th century often worn by the learned professions or the aged as under-caps. During the late 16th and early 17th centuries frequently embroidered with the sides curved forward to keep the ears warm. Up to about the middle of the 17th century often worn with a forehead cloth.

COSSACK TROUSERS   See catalogue no. 103

COUCHED WORK   A means by which laid threads are stitched down on a ground fabric either by an extension of the same thread or by others.

COWL NECKLINE   A neckline with soft horizontal drapes achieved by a cross-cut bodice with an extra amount of material at the neck.

CREPELINE (silk lisse)   A silk fabric very finely woven in tabby which is much used for the conservation of textiles. (20th century)

CROMWELL SHOES   A term which occurs first in 1868 to describe a shoe made of leather, with large buckle and tongue over the instep. It reappears in 1888 describing a day shoe with high-cut front and large bow.

CUTWORK   A technique whereby small holes are cut in a piece of fabric. When taken to its extreme, only widely-spaced groups of warp and weft threads are left. These are oversewn in buttonhole stitch and the holes are partially filled with decorative stitches. The earliest form of needle lace was made in this way.

DITTOS   A man's suit of matching material. (19th century)

DOLMAN SLEEVE   A sleeve which is cut in one piece with the bodice and thus has no seam around the arm socket. It is wide and creates a deep armhole which almost reaches the waist. (20th century)

DUCHESSE   A firm satin with a high sheen. (20th century)

EPAULET(TE)S   A trimming mounted on the shoulder. The term is taken from military usage but the decoration need not resemble that on a uniform.

THE EDWARDIANS   See catalogue no. 122

FACE CLOTH   High quality medium-weight wool with a slightly raised, lustrous dense surface. (19th–20th century)

FAILLE   A silk with a ribbed weave which is mid-way between the delicate rib of a POULT and the pronounced rib of a GROSGRAIN. (19th–20th century)

FAN LEAF   In folding fans, the semi-circular mount made of various materials, such as vellum, silk or paper. This generally bears the main decorative burden of the fan and, until the 19th century, was more usually painted; but printed leaves and applied decoration are also common.

FAN STICKS   The framework of spines onto which the fan leaf is mounted, or, in the case of brisé fans, which constitute the entire fan. Typically of ivory, tortoiseshell or mother-of-pearl, the section beneath the leaf (the shoulder) is often carved or decorated with gilt, or painted.

FLY BRAID   A trimming, usually of silk floss, knotted so that it has short lateral extensions and looks like a series of winged insects. (18th–19th century)

FRIEZE   A heavily milled woollen fabric with a dense surface which conceals the weave's structure. (20th century)

FROCK COAT   In the 18th century worn as informal dress until about 1780, distinguished by its turn-down collar. In the 19th century it became formal dress, introduced between 1810–20, probably influenced by military dress and distinguished by its fitted body and rather full skirts; early versions had standing or upright collars with decorative braided fronts. By the 2nd half of the 19th century it had become standard formal dress.

FRONT FALLS   See catalogue no. 86

GAUGING   A method of gathering up material with aligned rows of stitching so that a greater breadth of stuff is drawn into a smaller span.

GAUGED HEADING   Gauging used to give a three-dimensional effect to the top of a flounce or other piece of fabric applied to another.

GAUNTLET   The cuff of a glove which spreads out to cover the wrist.

GUARD STICKS   The outer sticks of a folding fan which, when the fan is closed, protect the fan leaf. These are often richly decorated with carving, precious metals and jewels.

GAUZE   A woven fabric in which a certain proportion of the warp threads (forming the 'doup' warp) are twisted around the rest after each passage of the weft. This weave can be used to produce an open but still very strong fabric.

GLAZED   A glossy surface may be produced on a cotton or wool textile by the application of heat, pressure, chemical action or a starch—or by a combination of these. Apart from its smart appearance a glazed fabric repels dirt.

GODET   A triangular or gathered or pleated section of material inserted (usually at the hem) to give a garment fullness and assist movement. (19th–20th century)

GORE   A flared panel normally used in skirts.

GOWN   An overdress. Also used indifferently for a woman's main garment. (17th–19th century)

GROSGRAIN   A non-technical term for a heavily ribbed silk. (See also FAILLE.)

GUSSET   A small triangular or diamond-shaped piece of material inserted under the arms or crotch to aid movement and facilitate the garment's fit.

KIPPER TIE   Term applied generally to broad-bladed neckties worn between about 1968 and 1976–7. Said to have been coined by Michael Fish (Mr Fish) in 1969, the term lost favour after 1972. An attempt to name the ultra-wide ties of this period 'Bloaters' failed to catch on.

LEG OF MUTTON SLEEVES   They were cut narrow on the forearm and wider at the upper arm so that when gathered into the shoulder they resembled a leg of mutton. Sometimes called 'gigot' sleeves. (19th–20th century)

LODEN   A sturdy fabric traditionally woven in the Tyrol mountain area of Austria, and made in the same way for centuries. At one time, only sheep's wool was used but now a blend of wool, alpaca, mohair and camel hair is used. Once woven, the fabric is shrunk by a third and then raised, sheared and brushed. Traditionally black, red and white, green has now become the most popular colour for the well-known Loden coats.

LUSTRING (lutestring)   A lightweight, shining silk used between the late 17th and the early 19th century. It could be plain or patterned. It was woven in tabby and the glossy effect was produced by heating and stretching the silk, adding a suitable glaze in the process.

MALACCA   A woody cane belonging to the group of rattan palms. Named after a district of the Malay peninsular, though grown throughout S.E. Asia.

MAGYAR SLEEVE   A sleeve which is cut in one piece with the bodice and thus has no seam around the arm socket. It is narrower than the dolman sleeve. (20th century)

MANTUA The late 17th and early 18th-century term for a woman's gown. By the second quarter of the 18th century it was more often used specifically for a gown with the skirt opening draped back with loops and buttons. (The same term was used in the 18th and early 19th century for a material, a type of plain silk tabby.)

MAROCAIN A heavy crêpe fabric which can be of silk, wool or rayon or mixtures of these yarns. (19th–20th century)

MOIRÉ (watered) Textiles in which a rippled or watered effect is produced by pressing a ribbed fabric in such a way as to flatten parts of the ribs and leave the rest in relief. The flattened and unflattened parts reflect the light differently (CIETA). The effect is generally produced by passing the textile through heated, engraved, copper rollers.

NEEDLE LACE This type of lace is built up stitch by stitch with a single needle and thread. Thicker outlining threads are tacked along the outlines of the design drawn on a parchment pattern and the lace is built up by stringing rows of stitches across the space between them. In some laces (17th century Venetian lace) additional pieces are added to the surface of the basic lace to form three-dimensional effects.

OPENWORK (of embroidery) Any technique whereby the ground fabric is decorated with holes. These can be made by pulling out some of the woven threads (drawn-thread work) or by pulling together groups of threads with embroidery stitches (pulled fabric work) or by cutting small holes (cut-work).

ORGAN PLEATING Similar to cartridge pleating (see above), but an extra lower row of stitching on the face or reverse holds the pleats together so that they resemble the pipes of an organ.

OXFORD Low-heeled shoes lacing over the instep with closed tabs stitched under the vamp.

PAGODA SLEEVES Half or three-quarter length sleeves which widened towards the hand. The seam was sometimes curved and, or, tucked so that in outline the outside edge of the sleeve was curved rather like the roof of a Chinese temple or pagoda. They were fashionable in the third quarter of the 19th century.

PANES Panels of varying length and number along the sleeves and body of a doublet and the legs of hose. They could be so numerous that the fabric appears to be a series of stripes. (16th–17th century). The term is also used in furnishings.

PANIERS In the later 19th century this was dressmaker's French for a drapery attached around the hips of a dress. The term derived from the 18th-century French word for the hooped petticoat which supported the skirt.

PASTE Hard vitreous composition used in making imitation gems.

PELISSE A late 18th and 19th-century term for a lady's mantle or overcoat.

PEPLUM An extension (almost of over-skirt dimensions) attached to the bodice at the waist seam. In the late 20th century the terms BASQUE and PEPLUM have become interchangeable.

PIQUÉ WORK Tortoiseshell or ivory inlaid with small studs or strips of metal.

PLEATS See BOX and DOUBLE-BOX PLEATS
CARTRIDGE PLEATS
ORGAN PLEATS

POINTS Laces or ribbons with pointed metal tags at each end. Used to support breeches. (15th–17th century)

POLONAISE An overdress with a decoratively looped skirt shorter than the petticoat or underskirt. The term was of French origin and used from the 1770s. It was used again from the later 1860s as dressmaker's French for almost any form of draped overskirt.

POULT Originally '*poult de soie*' from 'paduasoy', a type of silk well known in the 18th century but of a rather different character. The 19th–20th century 'poult' is a fabric woven in tabby with fine ribs in the weft direction, belonging to a group which includes faille and grosgrain, although it is finer. The name derived originally from Padua in Northern Italy.

PURL Silver, silver-gilt or gold wire twisted in a series of continuous rings like a corkscrew.

PURL EDGED Instead of a plain selvage ribbons were frequently edged with rounded loops (as well as more elaborate borders). The term is also used to describe the looped edgings in lace.

QUILTING A technique used originally to join together layers of fabric including, for warmth, a middle layer of woven wool or teased-out woollen or cotton fibres. Decorative quilting was often worked through only two layers, although parts of the pattern were padded. False quilting, in which lines of back-stitch were worked through a single layer or two thin layers of fabric, was common during the first half of the 18th century.

REDINGOTE A man's or woman's travelling coat. By the later 18th century it was used for a woman's informal gown which was modelled on a man's coat or riding coat and which had a turn-down collar and long sleeves. The term originated with the French form of the English words 'riding coat'.

REEFER JACKET A short double-breasted jacket introduced in the 1860s. It was cut without a back seam and was one of the many variants of the lounge jacket.

ROBING(S) An 18th-century term for the front edges of the robe which were pleated back over the face of the garment.

ROULEAU(X) A piece of material usually cut on the cross, which has been folded and stitched into a tube. It is used for an applied decoration and a cord is sometimes inserted to provide extra stiffness. It is similar to piping except that it is not used to strengthen a join between two portions of a garment.

RUN AND FELL SEAM A method of joining two pieces of material. The two pieces of fabric are seamed together with running stitch. The heading of one of the pieces is then cut down to half length and the longer heading is turned over it and hemmed.

SACK A gown, the back of which was full, pleated and did not have either shaping or a seam at the waist. (18th century)

SATIN STITCH A double-sided embroidery stitch whereby the ground is covered with lines of closely-laid thread to achieve a smooth, satin-like finish.

SHEATH DRESS A figure-hugging garment with a tight, straight skirt. (20th century)

SHOT Textile in which the warp and weft are of different colours, producing variations in tone owing to the reflection of light (CIETA). The different colours are most apparent in folds or drapes or when the textile is viewed from different angles in which one element predominates over the other.

SIDEBODY The panel which was inserted at the side, under the arm and between the front and back panels of the bodice. (17th–19th century)

SIDE-EDGE A scalloped shaped pocket flap or decorative pleat used in men's dress. (18th–19th century)

SLASHES Small decorative cuts arranged in an orderly manner all over a garment. The cuts were made before the garment was made up. (16th–17th century)

SLEEVES See LEG OF MUTTON SLEEVES
PAGODA SLEEVES

SLEEVE-HEAD The upper portion of a sleeve, where it is stitched into the armhole.

SLIP WAISTCOAT Half silk, lightweight waistcoats with colourful fronts which were the only part to be seen. They were worn under a full waistcoat. (19th century; see catalogue no. 108)

SMOCKING Method of controlling a tightly-gathered panel of material; the tiny 'tubes' formed by the gathers are held in place by decorative surface stitching.

STOCK A ready-made high neckcloth, usually of linen or cambric, which fastens at the back, usually with buckles. In the 18th century they were typically white and pleated, but from about 1835 to the end of century a stiffened black military stock became fashionable.

STOCKING PURSE Popular in the 18th and 19th centuries, they were closed tubes of knitted or netted fibres. Coins were put through a vertical slit in the middle and allowed to fall to either end. Two metal rings slid towards the ends to secure the contents.

STOMACHER An additional panel of material, usually triangular in shape, inserted within an open bodice to cover the front of the corset. It was often embroidered or decoratively trimmed. (Late 15th–late 18th century)

STUD BUTTON A button with a metal loop or stem at the back intended to be inserted through an eyelet in the garment and then fixed on the reverse with a thread or metal tag. This made the button easier to remove when the garment was cleaned. Especially expensive or attractive buttons were often made in this form so that they could be easily transferred from one garment to another.

SUPPORTASSE A 16th and early 17th-century term for the support for the large collars then fashionable. The shapes varied according to the designs of the collars. Some were stiffened, padded and covered with material, others were made from covered wire.

SURAH A soft, lightweight silk. (20th century)

SUGARLOAF A hat with a high conical crown shaped like a sugar loaf, and a wide brim. This is a revival of the 16th-century 'copotain', differing mainly in the width of the brim. (mid-17th century)

TABBY Basic weave based on a unit of two warp threads and two shoots of the weft in which each warp thread passes over one and under one weft or pick (CIETA). The threads alternate in each row—as in darning. Synonyms: cloth weave, plain weave. In *extended* tabby the warp threads or wefts or both move not singly but two threads or more together.

TAIL A piece of fabric attached at the back of the garment and hanging down from the waist.

TAMBOUR Embroidery worked to shape with a special hooked needle (which makes a chain stitch) on fabric stretched over a frame. (used since the 2nd half of the 18th century)

THAI SILK A wild, spun silk from Thailand often in bright or 'shot' colours. (20th century)

TOBINE English 18th-century term for a silk with an additional flushing warp. The ground may be entirely covered by its floats, regularly bound at intervals, or the pattern may be made by the flushing warp, or the tobine may be combined with a brocaded weft pattern.

'TREE OF LIFE' DESIGN A name given to the branching, flowering tree found in many English crewel-work embroideries of the early 18th century. It had its origins in the Indian painted and printed cottons of the 17th–18th centuries.

UNDRESS Informal—particularly morning—dress. Characteristic male undress in the 18th century would be a loose nightgown or banyan, and a nightcap in place of a wig. (mostly 18th century)

UNIVERSITY COAT See catalogue no. 112

VENT A slit or open section, usually longitudinal, between two pieces of fabric. It is most commonly used to give extra fullness to the skirts of a coat or jacket.

WATERED TABBY See MOIRÉ

WHITEWORK (of embroidery) Any embroidery worked with white linen or cotton thread on a white linen or cotton ground. Often combined with openwork techniques or quilting.